The Questions of Tenure

The Questions of Tenure

EDITED BY
RICHARD P. CHAIT

HARVARD UNIVERSITY PRESS

Cambridge, Massachusetts
London, England 2002

Copyright © 2002 by the President and Fellows of Harvard College
All rights reserved
Printed in the United States of America

Library of Congress Cataloging-in-Publication Data

The questions of tenure / edited by Richard P. Chait.
    p.   cm.
  Includes bibliographical references and index.
  ISBN 0-674-00771-9 (alk. paper)
    1. College teachers—Tenure—United States. 2. Universities and
  colleges—Faculty—Employment—United States. I. Chait, Richard.
  LB2335.7 .Q84 2002
378.1′21—dc21   2001039892

To my son, Adam,
and my daughter, Rachel

Contents

Tables and Figures

Figures

Acknowledgments

The policy-oriented research presented here was one part of a larger Harvard Project on Faculty Appointments funded by the Pew Charitable Trusts and conducted in affiliation with the New Pathways Project of the American Association for Higher Education (AAHE). I am deeply indebted to Russell Edgerton, then Director of the Education Program at Pew, and to Ellen Wert, a program officer. At AAHE, Eugene Rice and Christine Licata have been both gifted and steadfast colleagues. At Harvard, we have been blessed with a talented administrative team of KerryAnn O'Meara and Jordan Bach. In addition, we benefited immensely from the consistently superior work of four extraordinary doctoral students: Jared Bleak, Heidi Neiman, William Mallon, and Frances Shavers. Cheryl Sternman Rule was a splendid research assistant, a tireless trouper, and a superb editor. James Honan was as supportive and collaborative a colleague as one could be. On all fronts, Cathy A. Trower provided intellectual leadership, endless energy, and boundless goodwill; we simply would not have succeeded without her. Three colleagues from other universities made important contributions to particular studies: Janice Ballou from the Eagleton Institute at Rutgers University ably conducted focus groups with doctoral students and new faculty; William Connellan of Oakland University added significantly to the development of the "tenure template"; and

John Urice of Illinois State University offered important insights into the study of campus governance.

Finally, the chapter authors and I greatly appreciate the prudent counsel of Elizabeth Knoll, Senior Editor for the Behavioral Sciences, and the meticulous editing by Donna Bouvier, Senior Production Editor, both of Harvard University Press.

The Questions of Tenure

Introduction

RICHARD P. CHAIT

*T*HIS BOOK IS ABOUT the *questions* of tenure, not the question of tenure. The difference is more than an "s." In the singular, the question of tenure signifies a matter of political doctrine or moral principle. With equal fervor, interested parties either defend or attack the idea, often based on philosophical predisposition, anecdotes, and personal experiences or preferences. For the defense, we have, among others, *The Case for Tenure* (Finkin 1996), "In Defense of Tenure" (Machlup 1964), and "Tenure: A Summary, Explanation, and 'Defense'" (Van Alstyne 1971). These works of ardent advocates summon the arguments on behalf of tenure. For the prosecution, the titles are a bit more colorful, but the arguments no less impassioned: *Profscam* (Sykes 1988), *Impostors in the Temple* (Anderson 1992), and "A Conscientious Objection" (O'Toole 1979). There are ill-reasoned and factually erroneous briefs for (e.g., Wiener 1998) and against tenure (Carlin 1999). Neither side has a monopoly on diatribe. And, lest anyone be confused, the United Faculty of Central AFT/NEA (2000) has disseminated "The Truth about Tenure." Published opinions about the value and the evil of tenure are plentiful enough to comprise a genre of academic literature.

The contributors to this volume wanted to write a book different in substance and in tone from these polemics. Our goal was to write a book that would inform discussions of faculty work life through

1

research-based, data-driven answers to important, practical, and frequently posed questions about tenure policy and practice. Despite the academy's standards for scholarly research and discourse in the disciplines, questions about tenure are typically answered by impressions, convictions, and stories, or not at all. We approached these questions as scholars, not as proponents or critics of tenure—more in the manner of professors in a department of religion than faculty members in a school of theology. Academic orthodoxy and heresy are not at issue here; more than enough trees have been felled for that purpose. Instead, we attempt to furnish fresh data and balanced analyses.

We could not, of course, address every significant policy question. Some—for instance, the effects of post-tenure review on faculty performance and turnover—still lack sufficient data for us to draw conclusions. We bypassed others, like collectively bargained exceptions to standard tenure policies, as too limited in scope. For the questions that we did ask, definitive and universal answers were not always at the ready. We were, however, able to gather relevant data, offer analytical insights, and reach defensible conclusions, all with an aim of expanding knowledge and understanding—objectives no different from those of scholars of physics or French.

Tenure is a topic better illuminated by multiple spotlights than a single floodlight. Few questions about tenure—never mind the answers— apply uniformly across the vast and varied terrain of higher education. In each chapter, however, a single question dictated the focus. To be sure, certain questions have a broader reach than others. Therefore, some chapters have a wider angle than others. Taken together, the eleven chapters provide not so much a single, integrated picture as a collage.

Chapters 1 and 2 offer an overview of the larger academic context and the current state of tenure policy. "Why Tenure? Why Now?" by Richard Chait discusses the forces that rekindled the tenure debate in the 1990s after some twenty years of relative calm. Chapter 2, Cathy A. Trower's "What Is Current Policy?" presents the results of a broad-scale analysis of current academic personnel policies at 217 four-year institutions of higher education selected to constitute a stratified random sample by Carnegie classification. In summarizing both normative and unconventional policies, this chapter reveals the range and patterns of policy provisions by institutional type.

Chapters 3 through 10 focus on actual and potential changes in tenure policy and practice. Chapter 3 examines the assumption that tenure empowers faculty. Richard Chait explores the relationships among tenure, power, and campus governance at eight comparatively small, unselective, and undercapitalized colleges, four with tenure systems and four without.

Chapter 4 offers a critical analysis of the criteria, standards, and procedures by which faculty are considered for tenure. Through interviews with new faculty members and graduate students on the pathway to the professoriat, R. Eugene Rice and Mary Deane Sorcinelli examine the disconnect between faculty preferences and institutional priorities and the pressures induced by the heightened and broadened expectations institutions have for faculty.

Arguably, the most widespread transformation in faculty employment arrangements has been the increased reliance on part-time and non–tenure track faculty. In Chapter 5 Roger Baldwin and Jay Chronister document and explain the shift from tenured and tenure track appointments to part-time and tenure-ineligible positions. In analyzing this trend across the spectrum of four-year colleges and universities, the authors trace the evolution of the shift, discuss related policy implications, and offer suggestions for how to preserve institutional vitality and educational quality in the face of these changes.

Philip Altbach offers an international perspective in Chapter 6, "How Are Faculty Faring in Other Countries?" With particular emphasis on the practice of tenure, the changing nature of academic appointments, increased attention to faculty evaluation, and deteriorating conditions of academic work around the globe, Altbach draws on recent changes in the United States both as context and as a comparative touchstone and extends his analysis from Western Europe to Asia, and from Africa to Latin America.

Based on focus groups and an extensive, web-based survey of first- and second-year faculty and doctoral students about to enter the academic labor market from top-ranked departments in the natural sciences, the social sciences, the humanities, and select professions, Cathy A. Trower in Chapter 7 answers the question "Can Colleges Competitively Recruit Faculty without the Prospect of Tenure?" Tenure track positions were clearly the "gold standard." Nonetheless, new and prospective faculty could be lured to non–tenure track positions if the institution's location and the balance of work between teaching and research proved to be very attractive to the candidate. Based on these results, Trower discusses some practical implications for faculty recruitment.

Charles Clotfelter's Chapter 8 takes the debate over tenure one step further. Drawing on four focus groups of tenured faculty members from premier research universities and liberal arts colleges, Clotfelter considers whether any incentives might persuade professors to waive tenure. Treating tenure as a condition of employment with a potentially quantifiable market value, he asked what, if any, alternative employment arrangements would constitute an acceptable and voluntary trade-off for individual faculty members.

William T. Mallon in Chapter 9 asks "Why Is Tenure One College's Problem and Another's Solution?" Mallon examined six largely undergraduate colleges of modest means and reputations: three that replaced contracts with tenure systems and three that abolished tenure in favor of contracts. All six colleges believed that the policy shift would produce increased performance accountability for faculty and more rigorous personnel decisions.

Anecdote and rhetoric seem to drive tenure debates and policy changes, so Cathy A. Trower and James P. Honan asked "How Might Data Be Used?" They explain why data play a relatively limited role in the decision-making about faculty employment policies, and what both data providers and data users might do differently in order to increase the import of information to the process. The authors report on their experience with two data-driven initiatives: a CD-ROM policy archive of 250 college and university faculty handbooks; and a pilot project—where ten institutions, from small, liberal arts colleges to flagship, land-grant universities, used a "tenure template" that tracks faculty employment from appointment to retirement.

In the final chapter Richard Chait summarizes the findings and identifies several themes that emerged clearly, yet indirectly, from the earlier chapters.

References

Anderson, Martin. 1992. *Impostors in the Temple: American Intellectuals Are Destroying Our Universities and Cheating Our Students of Their Future*. New York: Simon & Schuster.

Carlin, James F. 1999. "Restoring Sanity to an Academic World Gone Mad." *Chronicle of Higher Education*, November 5, p. A76.

Finkin, Matthew W. 1996. *The Case for Tenure*. Ithaca, N.Y.: ILR Press.

Machlup, Fritz. 1964. "In Defense of Academic Tenure." *AAUP Bulletin*, 50 (Summer): 112–124.

O'Toole, James. 1979. "A Conscientious Objection." In George Bonham, ed., *Tenure: Three Views*. Washington, D.C.: Change Magazine Press.

Sykes, Charles J. 1988. *Profscam: Professors and the Demise of Higher Education*. Washington, D.C.: Regnery Gateway.

United Faculty of Central AFT/NEA. 2000. *The Truth about Tenure*. Available online: *www.unitedfaculty.org/truth.htm*.

Van Alstyne, William. 1971. "Tenure: A Summary, Explanation, and 'Defense.'" *AAUP Bulletin*, 57 (Autumn): 331–333.

Wiener, Jon. 1998. "Tenure Trouble." *Dissent*, 45 (1): 60–64.

1

Why Tenure? Why Now?

RICHARD P. CHAIT

*B*ETWEEN THE LATE 1970s and the mid-1990s, all was relatively quiet on the tenure front. There was a steady and low level of noise, but no great clamor for reform. In the late 1990s, however, the uneasy calm was broken; and by 1998 the *New York Times* reported, somewhat sensationally, that "open season on faculty is . . . generating pressure to modify or eliminate tenure" (Honan 1998). This chapter addresses why the controversy over academic tenure reignited and returned to center stage at that point.[1]

The relative tranquillity that began in the late 1970s followed a period of intense controversy over academic tenure. In the mid-1960s, student unrest erupted on many college campuses in the United States. There were sit-ins, marches, and protests, sometimes violent, about free speech, civil rights, and the Vietnam War. While issues external to the campus were the initial flash points, student activism expanded in many instances to matters internal to the campus; questions were raised about such issues as the relevance of the curriculum, students' role in shared governance, and the impersonal nature of the university bureaucracy (Reuben forthcoming). As student demonstrations became more disruptive, more prominent, and, from the viewpoint of some elected officials, more unpatriotic, questions increased about whether or not American campuses were "out of control" and, if so, who was accountable.

6

Some public officials harshly criticized professors as anti-American and as instigators of student disturbances. University administrators frequently appeared to be helpless to intervene because academics were perceived to be beyond the reach of accountability and invested with too many privileges and too much security. These complaints were shrink-wrapped into an antipathy toward academic tenure. In the decade from the mid-1960s to the mid-1970s, three national reports on student unrest recommended that tenure policies be reconsidered, and some twenty states introduced legislation to revise, curtail, or abandon tenure (Chait and Ford 1982). (The one bill to pass affected only new faculty at the community colleges of Virginia.) In short, the primary external impetus to revamp tenure codes was essentially political in nature: one part of a larger public policy initiative to restore equilibrium and a balance of power to the campus.

Within the academy, there was hardly an outcry for tenure reform. To the contrary, the attacks on tenure elicited rebuttals from several domains. In reaction to the ever more hostile atmosphere for tenure, the American Association of University Professors (AAUP) and the Association of American Colleges established in 1971 the Commission on Academic Tenure in Higher Education, which ultimately concluded, to no one's surprise, that "academic tenure . . . be recognized, because of its positive value in maintaining both academic freedom and the quality of faculty, as fundamental in the organization of faculty service in American higher education" (1973, p. 23). The commission presented a lengthy list of refinements "to correct deficiencies" and "to strengthen academic tenure for the future" (p. 23). However, the commission neither broached any radical reforms nor displayed any enthusiasm for contract systems as an option, let alone an alternative, to tenure. Many college presidents also publicly defended tenure, none more eloquently than Kingman Brewster at Yale in his *Report of the President* (1972).

When administrators did express doubts about tenure, their main concern was the prospect of a faculty with few newcomers and little turnover due to the onset of a "steady state" (Furniss 1973) or, worse, a "depression" (Cheit 1971) in higher education—a fear that seems ironic as the academy now confronts a potential shortfall of faculty to meet student demand.[2] Under conditions of no growth and faculty immobility, administrators worried that the pursuit of new degree programs, curricular reform, and interdisciplinary studies could prove problematic. Furthermore, meager turnover of faculty could jeopardize the diversity and vitality of the professoriat. In the minds of some (e.g., O'Toole 1979; Cottle 1973), tenure was a major impediment to Affirmative Action and revitalization of the faculty.

As the turbulence on campuses abated, the tenure controversy receded as well. Too contentious a topic to vanish entirely, tenure remained a prime target of a new wave of strident, conservative critics of American higher education (e.g., Sykes 1988; Anderson 1992; Huber 1992). While featured in the popular press, these polemics had little practical effect. For the most part, academic tenure as a matter of public policy lay dormant, overtaken by more urgent imperatives such as access, affordability, student outcomes, the quality of instruction, affirmative action, and political correctness. The AAUP (1995) did promulgate policy statements critical of "periodic evaluation of tenured faculty" (1983) and the increased reliance on "full-time non–tenure track appointments" (1986); however, neither the larger question of tenure nor the particulars of derivative policies was a "front-burner" issue nationally.

By the early 1990s, several barometers could attest to a renewed focus on tenure reform. In a 1994 survey by the Carnegie Foundation for the Advancement of Teaching, 39% of all institutions had, within the five years prior to the study, implemented changes in the criteria for tenure, and another 22% had the matter under consideration. On other elements of the tenure process, 26% of the institutions had implemented and 9% had under consideration shifts in the length of probationary periods, and 34% had implemented and 17% had under consideration contractual arrangements without tenure. In a 1999 poll, 32% of 1,511 faculty members reported that there had been "efforts in the past two years to eliminate, weaken or modify tenure at their institutions" (Sanderson, Phua, and Herda 2000, p. 35). Data on the incidence of post-tenure review indicated even greater activity. In 1989, only 3 of 46 members of the Association of American Universities practiced post-tenure review. Seven years later, 61% of 680 colleges and universities and twenty-eight states had instituted such a policy (Licata and Morreale 1997), and by 1999 the number of states had risen to thirty-seven (Licata 1999).

The new ferment was epitomized by a few celebrated attempts by boards of trustees in the mid- to late 1990s to revise tenure policies. The headline stories marked the end to "presumptive tenure" at Bennington College followed by faculty dismissals and the AAUP's first on-campus "protest and teach-in" (Leatherman 2000), the introduction of a non–tenure track with a sizable pay premium at the University of Central Arkansas, a short-lived reexamination of tenure by the Arizona State Board of Regents, and most spectacularly, an extended and ultimately unsuccessful effort by the Board of Regents of the University of Minnesota to reform aspects of the institution's tenure code.[3] Widely construed as an initiative to eliminate tenure, the Minnesota regents' proposals to amend certain policy provisions sparked intense opposition among faculty locally and nationwide (see Engstrom 1998; Farber 1997). A vote to create a faculty union, which would have been the first one at a top-drawer research university, narrowly failed.

While Minnesota was the most notorious battlefront for the "tenure wars," the controversy was in fact far more widespread. There are, as we shall see, echoes of the 1960s and 1970s in the contemporary debate, but the foremost concerns of that era, namely, political turmoil and "steady state staffing," no longer reverberate. Instead, the new debate can be attributed to a confluence of five factors, none alone sufficient to rekindle a national debate. The first three concern perceptions of tenure among key constituencies (Chait 1995a); the last two pertain to changes in the larger context of education.

Public Concerns

From the perspective of citizens at large, the notion of guaranteed lifetime employment (absent select conditions, which rarely materialize) seems outdated, even preposterous. Why should professors be insulated from the economic vicissitudes that routinely place lay citizens at economic risk? "Lifetime job guarantees border on being immoral," claimed the former chairman of the Massachusetts Board of Higher Education (Carlin 1999, p. A76).

This argument, while hardly novel, gained added weight in the late 1990s, when large-scale layoffs became commonplace. Within a span of seven months in 1998, for example, newspapers reported massive terminations at Gillette (4,700), Raytheon (14,000), Hewlett-Packard (2,500), Merrill Lynch (3,400), Ameritech (5,000), and Intel (3,000). Despite a robust economy, the trend continued during the next two years, with layoffs by Eastman Kodak (2,500), Levi-Strauss (6,000), BellSouth (2,100), Compaq Computer (8,000), and Honeywell (8,000), among others. Then, on the eve of an economic downturn in 2000–2001, the numbers swelled dramatically: 26,000 at Daimler Chrysler, 16,000 at Lucent, and 10,000 each at Nortel, Verizon, and Motorola. White-collar, as well as blue-collar, workers were dismissed from blue-chip corporations. These were layoffs above and beyond the cutbacks at dot-com start-ups. Similar stories emanated from Japan, where life-time employment with a single company was once the norm (French 1999, p. A1). Even as the economy generated new jobs, lay citizens learned, sometimes firsthand, the new reality: no one was safe, no one was exempt (Blair and Kochan 2000)—except perhaps professors and schoolteachers. (Federal judges, also endowed with tenure, were probably too far removed from the daily lives of lay citizens to be noticed.)

When juxtaposed against sizable layoffs in the corporate sector, the source of about 40% of all college trustees (Madsen 1997a, p. 8; 1997b, p. 8), the virtually impregnable security faculty enjoyed puzzled and rankled both trustees and the public at large. A summary of interviews with forty-three corporate, civic, professional, and political leaders (Harvey and Immerwahr 1995) concluded that they "are not convinced that higher education is so different from their own enterprise that a completely counter-intuitive system—ostensibly designed to provide academic freedom, but in their view largely designed to provide job se-curity—is needed to encourage high performance" (p. 13). Moreover, the tempests that erupted when even a comparatively small number of faculty were occasionally targeted for termination (for example, at San Diego State University in 1992) engendered further resentment among the citizenry. From a public viewpoint, academic tenure fre-quently symbolized an arrogant conceit and an undue, anachronistic privilege. To counteract that image, Mary Burgan, the General Secre-tary of the AAUP, suggested in a dialogue with journalists at Harvard University in 1998 that the solution was to "enhance corporate em-ployment security" rather than dismantle tenure.

Despite this and other gestures and occasional efforts by faculty to "educate" the public, tenure remains "the object of particularly caustic comments" and "symbolic of much that [community leaders] consider to be wrong with higher education" (Harvey and Immerwahr 1995, p. 12). In a 1999 survey, 83% of business executives, versus 23% of the faculty, believed that "phasing out tenure would improve higher education" (Immerwahr 1999, p. 22). While the vast majority of corporate leaders supported academic tenure in principle, only 22% thought tenure was an "essential" means to that end. The protection afforded by state and federal statutes and by access to the courts was generally deemed to be sufficient by the public and, not incidentally, by the president of the National Association of State Universities and Land-Grant Colleges (Magrath 1997).[4]

The other central public concern about tenure is a practical, day-to-day issue. Students as consumers and parents as "underwriters" want and expect talented, current, and attentive teachers. As the public's representatives, regents and legislators want and expect professors to teach, and to do so effectively and with an emphasis on introductory and intermediate undergraduate courses, not on "boutique" seminars and graduate classes.

A public perception "that tenure protects 'deadwood'" is prevalent and "alas, correct," confessed Stanford's former president (Kennedy 1997, p. 131). As a result, customers and taxpayers feel shortchanged, a concern exacerbated by the end to mandatory retirement in 1994. In the aforementioned 1999 survey (Immerwahr), 95% of corporate executives agreed that "tenure sometimes protects incompetent faculty," an opinion seconded by 74% of the tenured professors polled (p. 22). Even a few feckless faculty members can create an exaggerated effect due to the power of anecdote. To paraphrase a lawmaker's history of post-tenure review legislation in Texas: "I get a complaint, I write a bill, the bill passes, I get reelected." Post-tenure reviews are particularly popular among elected officials because the legislation, whether in Texas, California, Florida, or anywhere else, seems to respond directly to constituents' concerns about "deadwood."

The popularity of post-tenure reviews energized the debate about tenure and prompted the AAUP to reassess the practice. In 1983, the association stated that such reviews "would bring scant benefit, would incur unacceptable costs . . . and would threaten academic freedom" (1997, p. 44). Fifteen years later, the AAUP's stance was notably more tolerant as long as the reviews were predominantly, if not exclusively, focused on faculty development. The association warned, however, that post-tenure review "ought not be aimed at accountability" and should not emphasize "disciplinary sanctions," precisely the policy objectives of many lawmakers and boards of trustees. Thus the argument was joined and, in all likelihood, the argument will be sustained because "pink slips" for chronically inadequate performance have been extremely rare—not one at the University of Hawaii over ten years; and at another large state system, only 0.4% of 2,740 faculty reviewed were judged "unsatisfactory" and none were dismissed (Licata and Morreale 1997; Licata 1999).

In Arizona, the regents' motivation to reevaluate tenure policy was based principally on an apprehension that too many full-time faculty members taught too few undergraduate students, in large part because the tenure process grossly discounted the value of such assignments. In response to the regents' disquiet, faculty and administrative leaders across the university system furnished relevant data and initiated reforms that mitigated the board's concerns (National Association of State Universities and Land-Grant Colleges 1996). All parties were pleased by the results. However, without steps to loosen the ironclad guarantee of lifetime employment, to remediate or remove ineffectual faculty members, or to redress a perceived neglect of undergraduate teaching, academics should not anticipate that public skepticism toward tenure will slacken.

Managerial and Fiduciary Concerns

Changes in the vocabulary of higher education over the past thirty years reflect an altered perspective on academic tenure. Presidents have become CEOs, the administration has become management, and long-range plans have become strategic plans. The once-revolutionary notion of *Academic Strategy* (Keller 1983) has become conventional wisdom. Academics nowadays talk routinely and comfortably about scorecards, benchmarks, total quality management, productivity gains, competitive niches, market share, demand curves, price points, and yield management. The worlds of the Nobel prize and the Baldridge Award have blended; colleges and universities have become, if not businesses, then surely more businesslike (Ewell 1999; Winston 1998).

Within that context, small wonder that many managers (née administrators) and fiduciaries (née trustees) now view academic tenure not so much as an immutable principle of a profession, but rather as a personnel policy of an organization, just another variable to manipulate. From that vantage point, tenure policies pose problems on several counts. As a lifetime commitment to a disciplinary specialist, tenure inhibits the strategic reallocation of resources from areas of low demand, priority, or quality to areas of greater need, urgency, or distinction. Jean Keffeler, former chair of the University of Minnesota Board of Regents, advocated tenure reform chiefly on that basis: "The University's tenure code ensures employment even if there is no longer a purposeful job for the tenured employee . . . even if their specialty is no longer needed [or] their department no longer exists." Tenured faculty were, Keffeler declared, "nonremovable expenses" that constrained management's ability to "renew the institution" (quoted in Aitkens 1996, pp. 40–41).

Academic programs seem difficult to prune and virtually impossible to eliminate. As Stanford's former president observed wryly, "sunset is an hour that almost never arrives" on university campuses (Kennedy 1994, p. 97). At a time when resources are scarce and the skills of faculty are not always well matched to the preferences of students, these limitations make little sense to large numbers of trustees and many administrators. Companies regularly shed product lines. Pepsico divested Taco Bell, KFC, and Pizza Hut; Woolworth's, now Venator, exited the "five and dime" business. Why can't colleges restructure, trustees asked? For fiduciaries and managers, more often than not, tenure was a critical obstacle. Dennis O'Brien (1998), president emeritus of the University of Rochester and Bucknell, maintained that tenure should be "attenuated" in order to change institutional mission and programs or to preserve "the *best* faculty" when a college has to downsize. "Tenure artificially constrains the choice" (p. 44) because tenured senior faculty enjoy precedence over untenured colleagues, irrespective of relative abilities or organizational priorities.

As with program discontinuation, the economic, legal, and (above all else) political costs are usually too great for institutions to seek the removal of grossly incompetent tenured faculty members, never mind chronic low performers. Thus, from the perspective of many trustees and administrators, tenure too often exempts or insulates professors from accountability and so limits management's capacity to replace

marginal performers with demonstrably or potentially better performers. "Basically," James Carlin (1999, p. A76) asserted, "professors want
to be accountable to no one." Thomas Sowell (1998), a senior fellow
at the Hoover Institution, labeled Carlin's position "an outbreak of
sanity" and asserted that "tenure produces the deadly combination of
decision-making power without accountability for the consequences"
(p. 57).

While most faculty might dismiss Carlin and Sowell as a retrograde
industrialist and an ultraconservative professor respectively, their views
in reality differ more in tone than in substance from the observations of
three preeminent academics and staunch defenders of tenure. In a book
widely read by trustees, Henry Rosovsky, former dean of the Faculty of
Arts and Sciences of Harvard University, wrote, "Another critical virtue of academic life—I am thinking of tenured professors at, say, America's top fifty to one hundred institutions—is the absence of a boss. A
boss is someone who can tell you what to do, and requires you do it—
an impairment of freedom. . . . [A]s a professor, I recognized no master save peer pressure" (1990, pp. 163–164). Arguably the two most
distinguished economists of higher education, both at the time professors at Williams College, one now president of Macalester College
(McPherson and Winston 1996), offered a similar assessment: "in the
university where the tasks are final once the employment guarantee
[tenure] is made, monitoring performance has little value, for there is
little to do with the information. . . . [T]he central use to which such information is put in the corporation, to shape the path of the worker's
career advance, is markedly less available within an academic institution. . . . [I]t is far from obvious that intensive hierarchical efforts to
evaluate and motivate senior faculty in fact make much sense" (pp. 105,
116).

Commentaries such as these dumbfound trustees ("How could that
be?"), and the circumstances confound administrators ("How can we
manage?"). With faculty presumably shielded from accountability, self-
proclaimed to be without a boss, and profoundly dubious about the
utility of performance reviews, tenure is vulnerable to attack. Again,
the arguments are not as fresh as the frame that casts tenure in a different light, one that trustees can readily grasp. Tenure is seen as a matter
of corporate strategy, not academic philosophy. Two illustrations will
suffice.

Eager to import to the academy "Object Lessons from Big Business," Richard Mahoney (1997), formerly CEO of Monsanto and a Washington University trustee, described the modus operandum of the university as "a nightmare" where due to "guaranteed lifetime employment . . . some people were paid simply for showing up a couple of times a week." The "unavoidable" question for Mahoney was not "'Can we reform tenure?' or 'Dare we?' but rather 'How can we go about it?'" This is necessary in order to "reinvent" the university, much as corporations had reinvented themselves (p. B4). Mahoney favored five- to ten-year employment contracts. In the same spirit of corporate rhetoric, the Dean of the Boston University School of Management proposed in 1994 a plan, later adopted by the faculty, to institute an optional non–tenure track with a pay premium. Dean Louis Lataif stated that the school's aims should be to emulate as much as possible "the contemporary management principles and practices we teach. In the organizational world for which we are preparing our students, there exists a nearly universal requirement that employees, managers, and senior executives prove themselves year-in and year-out. The notion of guaranteed lifetime employment, such as is inherent in the tenure system . . . is not consistent with the competitive management environment" (1998, p. 38).

Finally, trustees and managers believe that tenured status, especially at research universities and premier colleges, create an unacceptably potent buffer against centralized initiatives. Leaders cannot lead and corporate strategies cannot be effectuated because nearly inviolate employment security enhances the faculty's capacity to hinder, delay, and derail proposed changes and to resist, passively or aggressively, enacted changes. Tenure diminishes the relative authority of executives—hence the barb "The only difference between a tenured professor and a terrorist is that you can always negotiate with a terrorist." The contention that tenure weakens the relative authority of executives, when added to the perceptions that tenure constricts institutional flexibility and undercuts performance accountability, renders tenure a likely target for criticism by boards of trustees.

Trustee "intrusion" into the realm of academic tenure should be viewed within the context of a more general activism that has marked college and university boards of trustees, especially in the public sector, since the early 1990s (Chait 1995b). At the root of trustees' newfound aggressiveness were two developments: (1) heightened criticism of the academic enterprise, particularly runaway costs, pursuit of "arcane" research allegedly to the neglect of students, political correctness, and images of an overindulged faculty; and (2) the reform of corporate governance that bolstered for-profit boards of directors to be far more assertive, inquisitive, and independent. The first phenomenon pressured college trustees to be responsive; the second emboldened boards to act. Before long, all issues, even quintessentially academic issues, were on the boardroom table: remedial education at the City University of New York, curriculum at the State University of New York and George Mason University, and admissions standards at the University of California system. Tenure and post-tenure review policies seemed to be "in play" at scores of colleges and universities. Yet the more governing boards "interfered" in these realms, the more ardently faculties resisted, especially when regents entered the hallowed territory of tenure. Thus, the stage was set for debate about this basic tenet of academic life.

Faculty Concerns

As a whole, American professors support academic tenure, many fervently so. There are, however, pockets of doubt. Three extensive surveys between 1989 and 1999 consistently disclosed that more than one third of all faculty members agreed that tenure was "an outmoded concept." Specifically, the numbers were: 37% of all faculty and 46% of female faculty in 1989–90 (Astin, Korn, and Dey 1991, pp. 45, 85); 38% of all faculty and 46% of female faculty in 1995–96 (Sax, Astin, Arredondo, and Korn 1996, pp. 41, 93); and 33% of all faculty and 39% of female faculty in 1998–99 (Sax, Astin, Korn, and Gilmartin 1999, pp. 37, 85). In a 1999 survey that included only 130 faculty from a random sample (Immerwahr 1999), 52% of both tenured and untenured professors indicated that tenure should "be modified but not eliminated"; 8% and 14% respectively agreed that tenure be "phased out altogether"; and 39% and 28% respectively preferred that tenure "remain as is" (p. 22). At institutions where efforts to "eliminate, weaken, or modify" tenure had occurred within two years prior to the study, 41% of 382 faculty members favored "some modification" of the system (Sanderson, Phua, and Herda 2000, pp. 35–36).

Distilled from multiple studies (Trower 1996; Sorcinelli 1992; Gmelch, Wilke, and Lovrich 1986), the faculty's chief reservations about the tenure process included the following: ambiguous and often contradictory criteria; conflicts between institutional rhetoric and realities of reward structures; clouded and clandestine review procedures; and unmitigated stress in the face of unreasonable expectations. (These criticisms are elaborated in Chapter 4.) At the conclusion of a process one candidate vividly described as "archery in the dark" (Rice 1996, p. 31), "people stagger to the end" (Tierney and Bensimon 1996, p. 73) and, with increased frequency, some denied the brass ring subsequently march into court. A few reversals of negative tenure decisions, an occasional multimillion-dollar judgment (Leatherman 1999a), and court orders that opened the dossiers of tenure candidates and "comparables" for defendants' review have added to the perception that the tenure process is amiss and that reforms may be warranted.

While many tenure track (and non–tenure track) faculty have expressed displeasure with the tenure system, the most acutely disenchanted subsets of academics are women and faculty of color. Compared to white males, both reported higher levels of stress with respect to the promotion and tenure process and more instances of "subtle discrimination" (Sax et al. 1996, pp. 18–19). Female faculty are more likely to regard tenure as an antiquated notion; and faculty of color perceive tenure as "a biased reward system that favors majority (white) faculty" (Aguirre 2000, p. 68). This dissatisfaction may reflect, in part, the greater commitment of women and faculty of color to community and professional service, endeavors normally rather inconsequential in tenure reviews (Antonio, Astin, and Cress 2000; Bellas and Toutkoushian 1999). More importantly, the lack of enthusiasm for tenure can reasonably be attributed to the lack of progress within the profession by members of these populations.

One longitudinal study (Milem and Astin 1993) concluded that the "most striking finding about the participation of women and minorities in different types of institutions is how little things seem to have changed over 17 years" (p. 22). Despite more than a quarter century of affirmative action, the percentage of women with tenure remained constant (at 38%) between 1975 and 1995. The fraction of blacks and Hispanics with tenure increased marginally (from 36% to 40% and from 41% to 45% respectively). Although the proportion of whites with tenure did not change, the percentage (54%) was substantially higher than any other group (Roey and Rak 1998, p. 2-12). Full-time women faculty were far more likely than men (37% versus 24%) to hold non–tenure track positions (Roey and Rak 1998, p. 2-11).[5] In the face of these results, and troubled by the collision of biological clocks and tenure timetables, women faculty from Berkeley, Columbia (Matthews 1992, p. 46), Princeton, and elsewhere pressed for "stop-the-clock" provisions, an end to confidential promotion and tenure files and secret deliberations, and even for the abolition of tenure altogether (Tilghman 1993).

As more women and minorities entered academe, even though the overall percentages did not change significantly, more voices were added to the faculty chorus for tenure reform, or at least to the ranks amenable to possible modifications. While the preponderance of faculty unquestionably favored the status quo, many shared the opinion of Professor Robert O'Neil, a stalwart advocate of tenure and former president of the University of Virginia, who said, "I am sometimes tempted to draw a line in the sand on issues like post-tenure review, re-peated studies of the tenure system, and experimentation with non–tenure track alternatives. A moment of reflection brings me to a quite different view. We would . . . have done far better had we embraced such efforts at the start, and we probably could have been more effective in shaping them to our liking. . . . [W]e should maintain a completely open mind. We should welcome not only studies . . . but also the proposal and creation of basic and drastic alternatives." While O'Neil concluded "that tenure is the worst of personnel systems save for all the others" (1996, pp. 9–10), an estimated 8% of tenured faculty and 14% of untenured faculty believed that tenure should "be phased out altogether" (Immerwahr 1999, p. 22). Most important, about one third of the American professoriat staked a territory between the pres-ervation of the status quo and abolition of tenure altogether—enough of a critical mass to encourage reconsideration of tenure policies and practices.

The New Environment

The academic landscape has changed dramatically since 1970, and the transformation has shifted tenure's relative position. The greatest areas of faculty growth have occurred in three areas: at two-year colleges where tenure has historically been less prevalent; in part-time and non–tenure track positions; and in professional schools where tenure figures less prominently.

In 1970, 1,063 community colleges enrolled 2.3 million students, or 27% of total college enrollment. By 1994, 1,471 community colleges enrolled 6.5 million students, or 42% of the total. Over the same period, the proportion of students at doctorate-granting universities slipped from 31% to 26%, even as the number of institutions within that category expanded from 173 to 236 (Carnegie Foundation 1974). Predictably, changes in faculty labor markets mirrored trends in student enrollment. Community colleges accounted for 19% of full- and part-time faculty in 1970 and 30% in 1995, almost a 58% increase. Between 1987 and 1992, the fraction of faculty, full- and part-time, at research and doctoral universities slipped from 36% to 30% (National Center for Education Statistics 1999, Table 225, n.p.). Expressed another way, of the 22,675 new full-time faculty positions added between 1987 and 1992, 13,122, or 58%, were at community colleges (National Center for Education Statistics 1997, pp. 18, 65).

These numbers are pertinent because only two thirds of all public community colleges have a tenure system, compared to nearly 100% of public and private research universities and doctoral institutions (National Center for Education Statistics 1993, p. 21). The rapid expansion of community colleges, therefore, has swelled the ranks of faculty on campuses without tenure. As a result, the notion that institutions cannot effectively recruit teachers or that teachers cannot perform acceptably without tenure has been empirically challenged.

Even more momentous was a sea change in faculty employment patterns throughout the academy between the 1970s and the 1990s. As detailed in Chapter 5, the proportion of part-time faculty doubled, from 22% in 1970 to 41% in 1995; and the fraction of full-time, non–tenure track faculty soared 52%, from 18.6% in 1975 to 28.3% in 1995. In absolute numbers, part-time faculty skyrocketed from 109,000 to 381,000, and non–tenure track, full-time faculty jumped from 81,000 to almost 149,000 (Roey and Rak 1998, pp. 2-2, 2-8, 2-12). In 1995, more full-time faculty (51%) were actually appointed off than on the tenure track (see Chapter 5).

In short, institutions of higher education staffed faculties radically differently in the late 1990s than was the case two decades earlier. The shift was prompted by a need to reduce costs, increase flexibility, and staff introductory and remedial courses, which many full-time faculty eschewed. In addition, Jay Chronister, professor of higher education at the University of Virginia (Leatherman 1999b, p. A14) speculated that "some of this [change in staffing] is an attempt to do away with tenure eventually." Whatever the motives, the outcome was clear: by the late 1990s far fewer than half of the American professoriat, on a head-count basis, held tenure. Ernst Benjamin (1998) estimated that 60% of the faculty was off the tenure track, a percentage that would be far greater still if graduate assistants with instructional responsibilities were added to the calculation, because "in 1993, the nearly 200,000 graduate assistants at four-year institutions actually exceeded the 184,000 part-time faculty positions" (p. 26).

The move toward fewer tenured faculty members coincided with the growth of professional schools; the two events are not unrelated. In general, the health sciences (e.g., medicine, nursing, dentistry) draw heavily on part-time and clinical faculty, and on full-time non–tenure track researchers supported by external grants. Indeed, 28% of the full-time faculty in the health sciences, versus 12.5% in the humanities and 7.7% in the social sciences, were off the tenure track in 1992 (National Center for Education Statistics 1993). At a time when full-time faculty nationwide increased about 25%, full-time medical faculty mushroomed by 149%, from 38,851 in 1975 to 96,733 in 1998, a trend that simultaneously added thousands of faculty to the non–tenure track (Association of American Medical Colleges 1999). Medical schools, for reasons of economic necessity triggered by the revolution in managed care, have been at the forefront of experimentation with nontenure career tracks, individually tailored assignments, and differentiated reward structures (Gappa 1996).

Compared to the health sciences, other professional schools have not experienced such extraordinary growth, either absolutely or relatively. But faculties of nursing, business, and law have expanded considerably, and all three routinely employ faculty off the tenure track. Usually, these part-timers and adjuncts are fully employed elsewhere. For the full-time, non–tenure track faculty in professional schools and select disciplines (e.g., computer science), labor markets outside the academy offer a safety net, and sometimes a more lucrative alternative, which blunts the need for tenure as a matter of economic security. To the degree that faculty, for whatever reason, are less concerned about permanent academic employment, the prospects for tenure reformers brighten.

In response to these developments, in 1998 the AAUP (1998b) and eight disciplinary organizations endorsed a statement that equated the erosion of the tenured ranks with the erosion of tenure per se. Consequently, tenure's champions have pressed colleges and universities to rely less on part-time and non–tenure track positions. At the same time, tenure's critics have cited the transition toward a predominantly untenured faculty as further evidence that lifetime employment is no longer indispensable to attract or retain teachers and should no longer be a cost and constraint that colleges have to bear. The merits of these arguments are not at issue here. Rather, the point is that drastic changes in the distribution of faculty among institutions and disciplines, and the ancillary effects of these shifts on employment arrangements, were among the primary forces that have revived and intensified discussions about tenure in recent years.

Two other momentous changes in the larger environment have started to precipitate and shape conversations about tenure. However, both are so nascent that any implications for tenure must be regarded more as forecasts than conclusions. These two wild cards, closely entwined, are "virtual" education and for-profit universities, whether stand-alone private enterprises or subsidiaries of nonprofit institutions (Marchese 1998; Winston 1999).

In brief, a bevy of universities have launched online educational programs. Some lead to degrees, others do not, and still others are licensed for use by corporations or by other institutions of higher education. (What will tenure mean when a professor "teaches" at dozens of institutions asynchronously?) The players include Columbia, Cornell, Duke, Johns Hopkins, the University of Nebraska, Penn State, and New York University, to name only a few. Many universities have established these enterprises as for-profit subsidiaries. Among liberal arts colleges, Amherst and Williams are reportedly on the precipice of an alliance with Brown University and Global Education Network, a for-profit company, to offer distance education (Carr 2000). At the same time, for-profit companies, such as UNext, Sylvan Learning Systems, Caliber Learning Network, and DeVry, have entered the academic marketplace in force, either alone or as partners with nonprofit universities. The University of Phoenix, the nation's largest private university, trades as Apollo Group on NASDAQ and enrolled over 75,000 students in 2000 (a 22% increase over the previous year) at fifty-one sites and eighty learning centers in fifteen states, Puerto Rico, and Canada. The company's online enrollments were up 44%, to 13,779, between 1999 and 2000 (Noone 2000). Jones International University, which operates exclusively online, was recently accredited, against the objections of many academics, and Harcourt General opened Harcourt Higher Education in November 2000 with a goal of 20,000 students by 2005 (Ackerman 2000).

The consequences for tenure are plain. Simply stated, the word has no place in the vocabulary or personnel policies of for-profit vendors. Not one offers tenure, and all have few, if any, full-time faculty. The University of Phoenix employs more than 5,000 part-time "practitioners" and has "140 full-time faculty members who teach at least three courses a year, but whose duties are mainly administrative" (Leatherman 1998, p. A14). Harcourt Higher Education plans to begin with 4 full-time and 30 part-time faculty. To the extent that university subsidiaries or publicly traded companies succeed at for-profit higher education, the proportion of academic positions tethered to tenure will surely decline—precipitously, in fact, if these new ventures capture market share from traditional, nonprofit colleges and universities. Further, the for-profits will offer tenure's detractors a new business model and added "proof" that quality programs, regionally accredited and attractive to consumers, do not require the award of tenure.

Online and for-profit universities have the earmarks of a "disruptive technology," where innovators (e.g., HMOs, desktop computers, discount retailers) initially offer a product "worse" than what is currently available (Christensen 2000). In the end, though, the disruptive technologies prevail and unseat market leaders due to "a very different value proposition" and "features that a few fringe (and generally new) customers value. Products based on disruptive technologies are typically cheaper, simpler, smaller, and, frequently, more convenient to use" (p. xv). Success requires that organizations' economic structures and corporate values be "sufficiently aligned with the power of their customers" (p. 228). While it is too soon to determine whether online, for-profit universities or for-profit subsidiaries will "disrupt" higher education generally or the tradition of tenure more specifically, two predictions seem relatively safe: the effects of these two developments on tenure will not be positive, and success on either front will further fuel the debate about tenure and whet the appetite for reform.

Public Schools

In the world of education, colleges and universities on the one hand and public school systems on the other are structurally and culturally separate. Professors and teachers, presidents and superintendents, and college trustees and school board members typically regard each other as unrelated or, at best, distant kin. The connections to public education for faculty, staff, and trustees at private colleges are even more tenuous.

Elected officials, however, do not always make such distinctions, especially between public schools and state colleges. Both institutions drink from the fountain of public funds, and both generate criticism from constituents. The more money required and the more complaints registered, the more likely there will be legislative intervention. On this negative scoreboard, public schools seem to have the unenviable edge.

The crucial question for higher education is whether there will be any spillover. Since 70% of all full-time college and university faculty work at public two- and four-year institutions (Roey and Skinner 1999, p. 8), the crossover effects could be monumental. Specifically, there are two initiatives where seepage could have detrimental, if not disastrous, consequences for tenure.

As a result of intense discontent with public schools, thirty-six states and the District of Columbia have enacted charter school laws, which enable community members, in conjunction with local or state school boards, to establish tax-supported alternative schools that are largely unencumbered by the rules and regulations of the formal school system. (In nineteen states, charter schools are subject to state collective bargaining laws; in some states teachers remain part of the district's bargaining unit, while in others staff may form a separate unit. See Office of Educational Research and Improvement 1998.) The number of charter schools has mushroomed from 3 in 1992–93 to 712 in 1997–

98 to over 2,000 in 2000–2001 (Center for Education Reform 2001). In the fall of 2000, 2,036 charter schools in thirty-six states and the District of Columbia enrolled 518,609 students (Center for Education Reform 2000). Of particular relevance here, a sizable majority of charter schools do *not* offer tenure.

The March 24, 2000, *Chronicle of Higher Education* carried an article that opened with the pregnant question "With charter schools becoming more popular these days, could charter colleges be far behind?" (Hebel, March 24, 2000). Discussions are afoot in Virginia and in Massachusetts, where then-Governor Paul Cellucci expressly championed the idea of charter colleges without academic tenure. *If* charter schools succeed and *if* the spirit of deregulation prevails—an idea enormously attractive to many college presidents and faculty shackled to cumbersome and rigid state bureaucracies—charter colleges may materialize. And while a feasibility study by academic researchers and pronouncements by faculty union leaders have emphasized that academic freedom must not be exchanged for regulatory freedom (Hebel 2000), the trustees of each charter college would ultimately be free to determine whether or not to heed that admonition.

If charter schools represent an indirect threat to tenure, the second development constitutes a frontal assault. New York and Alabama both enacted legislation in 2000 to abolish tenure for school principals. Moreover, the Alabama Teacher Accountability Act (passed by a vote of 81–19 of the state legislature) also "makes it easier to fire bad teachers," according to a news release from the governor's press office, because the bill explicitly added "failure to perform duties in a satisfactory manner" as grounds for the "cancellation of an employment contract with a teacher on continuing service status"—that is, on tenure. In Georgia, the General Assembly passed, by a comfortable margin in both chambers, and the governor signed, a bill that eliminated tenure for teachers appointed after July 1, 2000. Teachers can demand a written explanation for dismissal, but they have no right to a formal hearing; their only recourse is litigation (Learner 2000).

These initiatives should not yet be construed as trends. But such developments are symptomatic of a broader discontent and impatience with education, teachers, and tenure. The general malaise with public schools contributes to a climate conducive to radical notions such as the creation of charter schools and the evisceration of tenure. As

schools become more vulnerable to such measures, the soldiers of reform are apt to march steadily closer to the campus gates.

Plus Ça Change

Thus far, I have emphasized the pressures to reexamine traditional tenure policies and to entertain, if not adopt, various modifications or alternatives. Such a focus can create a false impression of great flux and
systemic overhaul of tenure systems. In fact, for all that has changed
over the past quarter century with respect to faculty employment and
academic tenure, much has remained the same.

   The basic justification for tenure—academic freedom and economic
      security—endures, and so too do the tactical arguments in favor
      of it: to ensure rigorous quality control, to sustain a competitive
      position in the recruitment and retention of faculty, and to offset
      lower salaries with greater assurances of employment security.
   The percentage of full-time faculty with tenure has stayed remark-
      ably stable between 1975 and 1998 at about 52%, with very mi-
      nor fluctuations—a high of 52.3% in 1975 and a low of 50.9% in
      1991. For women, the numbers are equally steady: 38.4% in
      1975, 38.8% in 1995 (Roey and Rak 1998, p. 2-12).
   The probability of a favorable decision among candidates formally
      considered for tenure has not varied by institutional type and also
      has not changed materially. In the early 1970s the odds of gaining
      tenure were a little better than 7 in 10 (Commission on Academic
      Tenure 1973) and remained so in 1992–93, when the probability
      rate was last calculated (National Center for Education Statistics
      1993, p. 18).
   Tenure continues to be prevalent throughout the academy. No ma-
      jor four-year college or university and no state legislature has
      abolished tenure for professors. William Mallon (2000) identified
      only thirteen independent four-year colleges that have eliminated
      tenure since 1974 (and three that instituted tenure since 1997).
   The vast majority of American faculty remain committed to the
      concept of academic tenure (Sax et al. 1999), and the lion's share
      of prospective faculty prefer a tenure-track appointment (see
      Chapter 7).

The vigor of the renewed debate over tenure and the magnitude of actual change are not perfectly correlated. The interest in reform in some quarters has stiffened resistance in other quarters. Proposals considered modest adjustments from the perspective of reformers (e.g., post-tenure review, departmental rather than institutional locus for tenure, and pay premiums for non–tenure track positions) have provoked strong, frequently vociferous responses from traditionalists, who regard these "adjustments" as assaults on the very essence of tenure. The result has been neither a standoff nor a revolution. Instead, the situation resembles a baseball-game brawl that clears the benches on both sides. A lot of words are exchanged, but few punches are thrown, even fewer reach the intended target, and fewer still affect the outcome of the game. There's a lot of commotion as the antagonists push and shove and mill about, but eventually the players disperse and the game resumes. Whether the present battle over tenure yields more noteworthy changes this time around remains to be seen. But it is clear that the players have again emptied the dugouts and taken to the field.

Notes

Thanks to Cheryl Sternman Rule and Frances L. Shavers, extraordinary research assistants.

1. For a comprehensive history of academic tenure, see Metzger 1973.
2. The University of California system alone, for example, "will need more ladder-rank faculty in the next 12 years than it currently employs on its general campuses (University of California Academic Senate 2000, p. 1).
3. The author served as an adviser to Minnesota's Board of Regents on this matter.
4. For a thoughtful treatment of academic freedom without tenure, see Byrne (1997), a well-reasoned rebuttal by Chermerinsky (1998), and a codification of a contractual guarantee of academic freedom by Michaelson in Chait (1998).
5. The numbers for women and minorities with respect to rank, salary, and representation within the overall faculty were equally gloomy. See National Center for Education Statistics reports *Fall Staff in Postsecondary Institutions, 1997* (1999a) and *1998*.

References

Ackerman, Jerry. 2000. "Cyberspace U." *Boston Globe*, August 25, p. F1.
Aguirre, Adalberto, Jr. 2000. *Women and Minority Faculty in the Academic Workplace:*

Recruitment, Retention, and Academic Culture. ASHE-ERIC Higher Education Report, 27 (6). San Francisco: Jossey-Bass.

Aitkens, Maggi. 1996. "The Trials and Tribulations of Tenure." *Minnesota,* July–August, pp. 38–45.

American Association of University Professors. 1995. *Policy Documents and Reports.* Washington, D.C.: American Association of University Professors.

—— 1997. "Report: On Post-Tenure Review." *Academe,* 83 (5): 44–51.

—— 1998a. "Post-Tenure Review: An AAUP Response." *Academe,* 84 (5): 61–67. Online: *http://www.aaup.org/postten.htm.*

—— 1998b. "Statement from the Conference on the Growing Use of Part-time and Adjunct Faculty." *Academe,* 84 (1): 54–55.

Anderson, Martin. 1992. *Impostors in the Temple: American Intellectuals Are Destroying Our Universities and Cheating Our Students of Their Future.* New York: Simon & Schuster.

Antonio, Anthony Lising, Helen S. Astin, and Christine M. Cress. 2000. "Community Service in Higher Education: A Look at the Nation's Faculty." *Review of Higher Education,* 23 (4): 373–398.

Association of American Medical Colleges. 1999. *The Association of American Medical Colleges Data Book: Statistical Information Related to Medical Schools and Teaching Hospitals, 1999.* Washington, D.C.: Association of American Medical Colleges.

Astin, Alexander W., William S. Korn, and Eric L. Dey. 1991. *The American College Teacher: National Norms for the 1989–90 HERI Faculty Survey.* Los Angeles: Higher Education Research Institute, University of California.

Bellas, Marcia L., and Robert K. Toutkoushian. 1999. "Faculty Time Allocations and Research Productivity: Gender, Race, and Family Effects." *Review of Higher Education,* 22 (4): 367–390.

Benjamin, Ernst. 1998. "On the Excessive Reliance on Part-time Faculty Appointments." *Academe,* 84 (1): 26–28.

Blair, Margaret M., and Thomas A. Kochan. 2000. *The New Relationship: Human Capital in the American Corporation.* Washington, D.C.: Brookings Institution Press.

Brewster, Kingman. 1972. *Report of the President.* New Haven, Conn.: Yale University.

Byrne, Peter J. 1997. *Academic Freedom without Tenure?* Washington, D.C.: American Association for Higher Education.

Carlin, James F. 1999. "Restoring Sanity to an Academic World Gone Mad." *Chronicle of Higher Education,* November 5, p. A76.

Carnegie Foundation for the Advancement of Teaching. 1994. *National Survey on the Reexamination of Faculty Roles and Rewards.* Princeton, N.J.: Carnegie Foundation.

Carr, Sarah. 2000. "Distance Education Company Woos Bastions of the Liberal Arts." *Chronicle of Higher Education,* January 28, p. A43.

Center for Education Reform. 2000. *National Charter School Directory.* Washington, D.C.: Center for Education Reform.

Chait, Richard P. 1995a. *The Future of Academic Tenure.* AGB Priorities, no. 3. Washington, D.C.: Association of Governing Boards.

———— 1995b. *The New Activism of Corporate Boards and the Implications for Campus Governance*. Occasional Paper no. 26. Washington, D.C.: Association of Governing Boards.

———— 1998. *Ideas in Incubation: Three Possible Modifications to Traditional Tenure Policies*. Washington, D.C.: American Association for Higher Education.

Chait, Richard P., and Andrew T. Ford. 1982. *Beyond Traditional Tenure*. San Francisco: Jossey-Bass.

Cheit, Earl F. 1971. *The New Depression in Higher Education*. New York: McGraw-Hill.

Chemerinsky, Erwin. 1998. "Is Tenure Necessary to Protect Academic Freedom?" *American Behavioral Scientist*, 41 (5): 638–651.

Christensen, Clayton M. 2000. *The Innovator's Dilemma*. New York: HarperBusiness.

Commission on Academic Tenure in Higher Education. 1973. *Faculty Tenure*. San Francisco: Jossey-Bass.

Cottle, Thomas. 1973. "The Pains of Permanence." In Bardwell L. Smith et al., eds., *The Tenure Debate*. San Francisco: Jossey-Bass Publishers.

Engstrom, Gary. 1998. "Tenure Wars: The Battles and the Lessons." *American Behavioral Scientist*, 41 (5): 607–626.

Ewell, Peter T. 1999. "Imitation as Art: Borrowed Management Techniques in Higher Education." *Change*, 31 (6): 10–15.

Farber, Daniel A. 1997. "The Miasma in Minnesota." *Trusteeship*, 5 (3): 6–10.

French, Howard F. 1999. "Economy's Ebb in Japan Spurs Temporary Jobs." *New York Times*, August 12, pp. A1, A4.

Furniss, W. Todd. 1973. *Steady-State Staffing in Tenure-Granting Institutions and Related Papers*. Washington, D.C.: American Council on Education.

Gappa, Judith M. 1996. *Off the Tenure Track: Six Models for Full-Time, Nontenurable Appointments*. Washington, D.C.: American Association for Higher Education.

Gmelch, Walter, P. Wilke, and N. Lovrich. 1986. "Dimensions of Stress among University Faculty: Factor Analytic Results from a National Survey." *Research in Higher Education*, 24 (3): 266–286.

Harvey, James, and John Immerwahr. 1995. *The Fragile Coalition: Public Support for Higher Education in the 1990s*. Washington, D.C.: American Council on Education.

Hebel, Sara. 2000. "States Start to Consider the Idea of Charter Colleges." *Chronicle of Higher Education*, March 24, p. A36.

Honan, William. 1998. "The Ivory Tower under Siege." *New York Times*, January 4, p. 46.

Huber, Richard M. 1992. *How Professors Play the Cat Guarding the Cream: Why We're Paying More and Getting Less in Higher Education*. Fairfax, Va.: George Mason University Press.

Immerwahr, John. 1999. *Taking Responsibility: Leaders' Expectations of Higher Education*. New York: National Center for Public Policy and Higher Education.

Keller, George. 1983. *Academic Strategy: The Management Revolution in American Higher Education*. Baltimore: Johns Hopkins University Press.

Kennedy, Donald. 1994. "Making Choices in the Research University." In J. Cole,

E. Barber, and S. Graubard, eds., *The Research University in a Time of Discontent*. Baltimore: Johns Hopkins University Press.

———— 1997. *Academic Duty*. Cambridge, Mass.: Harvard University Press.

Lataif, Louis E. 1998. "Lifetime Tenure and a Working Alternative." *The Manager*, Spring, 38–40.

Learner, Neal. 2000. "Georgia Reform Bill Would Revoke Tenure." *Education Daily*, February 28, pp. 1–3.

Leatherman, Courtney. 1998. "U. of Phoenix's Faculty Members Insist They Offer High-Quality Education." *Chronicle of Higher Education*, October 16, pp. A14–16.

———— 1999a. "$12.7-Million Judgment in Tenure Case Leaves Many Academic Experts Stunned." *Chronicle of Higher Education*, February 5, p. A14.

———— 1999b. "Growth in Positions off the Tenure Track Is a Trend That's Here to Stay, Study Finds." *Chronicle of Higher Education*, April 9, p. A14.

———— 2000. "AAUP Reaches Out and Takes Sides." *Chronicle of Higher Education*, June 23, p. A16.

Licata, Christine. 1999. "Precepts for Post-Tenure Review." *Trusteeship*, 7 (6): 6–13.

Licata, Christine, and Joseph Morreale. 1997. *Post-Tenure Review: Policies, Precepts, and Provisions*. Washington, D.C.: American Association for Higher Education.

Madsen, Holly. 1997a. "Composition of Governing Boards at Independent Colleges and Universities, 1997." AGB Occasional Paper, no. 36. Washington, D.C.: Association of Governing Boards.

———— 1997b. "Composition of Governing Boards at Public Colleges and Universities, 1997." AGB Occasional Paper, no. 37. Washington, D.C.: Association of Governing Boards.

Magrath, C. Peter. 1997. "Eliminating Tenure without Destroying Academic Freedom." *Chronicle of Higher Education*, February 28, p. A60.

Mahoney, Richard. 1997. "'Reinventing' the University: Object Lessons from Big Business." *Chronicle of Higher Education*, October 17, p. B4.

Mallon, William. 2000. "Abolishing and Instituting Tenure: Four Case Studies of Change in Faculty Employment Policies." Ph.D. diss., Harvard Graduate School of Education.

Marchese, Ted. 1998. "Not-So-Distant Competitors: How New Providers Are Remaking the Postsecondary Marketplace." *Bulletin*, 50 (8): 3–7. Washington, D.C.: American Association for Higher Education.

Matthews, Anne. 1992. "The Rage of a Tenured Position." *New York Times Magazine*, pp. 46–47, 72–73, 75, 83.

McPherson, Michael S., and Gordon C. Winston. 1993. "The Economics of Tenure." In Matthew W. Finkin, *The Case for Tenure*. Ithaca, N.Y.: ILR Press. (Reprinted from Michael S. McPherson, Morton Owen Schapiro, and Gordon C. Winston, eds., *Paying the Piper: Productivity, Incentives and Financing in U.S. Higher Education*. Ann Arbor: University of Michigan Press, 1993.)

Metzger, Walter P. 1973. "Academic Tenure in America: A Historical Essay." In Commission on Academic Tenure in Higher Education, *Faculty Tenure*. San Francisco: Jossey-Bass.

Michaelson, Martin. 1998 "Academic Freedom Policy and Procedures." In Richard P. Chait, *Ideas in Incubation: Three Possible Modifications to Traditional Tenure Policies.* Washington, D.C.: American Association for Higher Education.

Milem, Jeffrey F., and Helen S. Astin. 1993. "The Changing Composition of the Faculty: What Does It Really Mean for Diversity?" *Change Magazine,* 25 (2): 21–27.

National Association of State Universities and Land-Grant Colleges. 1996. "Changes in Tenure Emerging Nationwide." NASULGC Newsline, 5 (9): 1, 4–6.

National Center for Education Statistics. 1993. *National Study of Postsecondary Faculty.* Washington, D.C.: U.S. Department of Education.

——— 1997. *1993 National Study of Postsecondary Faculty, Instructional Faculty, and Staff in Higher Education Institutions: Fall 1987 and Fall 1992.* Washington, D.C.: U.S. Department of Education.

——— 1999. *Postsecondary Education Digest of Education Statistics.* Washington, D.C.: U.S. Department of Education.

Noone, Laura Palmer. 2000. "The University of Phoenix." Presentation at the Institute for Educational Management, Harvard University, July 17.

O'Brien, George Dennis. 1998. *All the Essential Half-Truths about Higher Education.* Chicago: University of Chicago Press.

Office of Educational Research and Improvement. 1998. *A National Study of Charter Schools.* Washington, D.C.: U.S. Department of Education.

O'Neil, Robert. 1996. "Tenure Today: What's Happening and Why?" Remarks at the American Association for the Advancement of Science meeting on Scientific Freedom, Responsibility, and Tenure, September 24.

O'Toole, James. 1979. "A Conscientious Objection." In George Bonham, ed., *Tenure: Three Views.* Washington, D.C.: Change Magazine Press.

Reuben, Julie. Forthcoming. *Campus Revolts: Politics and the American University in the 1960s.*

Rice, R. Eugene. 1996. *Making a Place for the New American Scholar.* Washington, D.C.: American Association for Higher Education.

Roey, Stephen, and Rebecca Rak. 1998. *Fall Staff in Postsecondary Institutions, 1995.* Washington, D.C.: U.S. Department of Education, Office of Educational Research and Improvement.

Roey, Stephen, and Rebecca Rak Skinner. 1999. *Fall Staff in Postsecondary Institutions, 1997.* Washington, D.C.: U.S. Department of Education, Office of Educational Research and Improvement.

Rosovsky, Henry. 1990. *The University: An Owner's Manual.* New York: W. W. Norton & Co.

Sanderson, Allen, Voon Chin Phua, and David Herda. 2000. *The American Faculty Poll.* New York: TIAA-CREF.

Sax, Linda J., Alexander W. Astin, Marisol Arredondo, and William S. Korn. 1996. *The American College Teacher: National Norms for the 1995–96 HERI Faculty Survey.* Los Angeles: Higher Education Research Institute, University of California.

Sax, Linda J., Alexander W. Astin, William S. Korn, and Shannon Gilmartin. 1999. *The American College Teacher: National Norms for the 1998–99 HERI Faculty*

Survey. Los Angeles: Higher Education Research Institute, University of California.

Sorcinelli, Mary Deane. 1992. "New and Junior Faculty Stress: Research and Responses." In Mary Deane Sorcinelli and Ann E. Austin, eds., *Developing New and Junior Faculty*. New Directions for Teaching and Learning, no. 50, pp. 27–37. San Francisco: Jossey-Bass.

Sowell, Thomas. 1998. "An Outbreak of Sanity." *Forbes Magazine*, September 7, p. 57.

Sykes, Charles J. 1988. *Profscam: Professors and the Demise of Higher Education*. Washington, D.C.: Regnery Gateway.

Tierney, William, and Estela Bensimon. 1996. *Promotion and Tenure: Community and Socialization in Academe*. Albany: State University of New York Press.

Tilghman, Shirley M. 1993. "Science v. Women—A Radical Solution." *New York Times*, January 26, p. A23.

Trower, Cathy A. 1996. "Junior Faculty Behavior and Experiences: Work Life on the Tenure-Track, off the Tenure-Track, and at Institutions without Tenure." Ph.D. diss., University of Maryland.

University of California Academic Senate. 2000. "With Wave of Faculty Hiring, UC Stands to Remake Itself During the Next Twelve Years." *Notice*, 24 (2): 1, 4.

Winston, Gordon. 1998. "Why Can't a College Be More Like a Firm?" *Change Magazine*, 29 (5): 32–39.

———— 1999. "For-Profit Higher Education: Godzilla or Chicken Little." *Change Magazine*, 31 (1): 12–19.

2

What Is Current Policy?

CATHY A. TROWER

$\mathscr{A}$T THE START of the twenty-first century, American higher education confronted intense pressure to change due to widespread public disenchantment, marked shifts in revenue sources, and unprecedented competition via technology from nonprofit and for-profit institutions alike. Faced with "discontinuous," or radical, change, colleges and universities were compelled to consider new ways to do business, even regarding the delicate arena of faculty roles and rewards, once considered largely off-limits for reform. A 1994 study by the Carnegie Foundation for the Advancement of Teaching (Glassick, Huber, and Maeroff 1997) revealed that more than 80% of all institutions of higher learning recently conducted policy reviews related to faculty work life.

Typically, individual institutions lacked reliable and comprehensive information about policies and practices elsewhere. Often, anecdotes and impressions substituted for analysis. Among the unanswered questions were these: What is normative? What is unconventional? What changes would be outside of the mainstream? Who else does . . . ? and Would any other respectable institution . . . ?

In an effort to infuse policy reviews with relevant and accurate data, The Project on Faculty Appointments at the Harvard Graduate School of Education decided to inventory academic personnel policies at U.S.

32

four-year colleges and universities. We hope that this information—summarized and analyzed in this chapter—will assist all constituencies engaged in a reconsideration of faculty employment policies.

From a random sample of 1,380 U.S. four-year institutions, stratified by Carnegie classification,[1] we requested policy statements in the following areas: academic freedom, probationary periods, definition and locus of tenure, faculty ranks and titles, promotion, post-tenure review, dismissal for cause, financial exigency, and program discontinuance. We also requested employment provisions for faculty at institutions without tenure. We received the employment policies of 217 institutions, which were placed on a keyword-searchable CD-ROM and published as the Faculty Appointment Policy Archive (FAPA 1999). The sample of institutions matches the overall population quite closely in all respects—by Carnegie classification and by institutional control. Of the 217 institutions[2] in the sample, 43% are public and 57% are private, almost 10% do not offer tenure, and 19% have faculty unions. All fifty states and the District of Columbia are represented.

We compared institutional policy statements to the Recommended Institutional Regulations of the American Association of University Professors (AAUP 1995), widely recognized as the definitive compendium of standard practice. We examined how many policy statements use AAUP language in whole or in part and how many use other language (referred to as nonstandard or outside of the norm). The policy analyses differentiate by Carnegie classification, affiliation, or control, and by whether the institution has a collective bargaining agreement.

Academic Freedom

The Standard

Setting the standard in perhaps the most fundamental area of faculty employment, the *1940 Statement of Principles on Academic Freedom and Tenure* defines academic freedom as follows:

(a) Teachers are entitled to full freedom in research and in the publication of the results, subject to the adequate performance of their other academic duties; but research for pecuniary return should be based upon an understanding with the authorities of the institution.

(b) Teachers are entitled to freedom in the classroom in discussing their subject, but they should be careful not to introduce into their teaching controversial matter which has no relation to their subject. Limitations of academic freedom because of religious or other aims of the institution should be clearly stated in writing at the time of the appointment.

(c) College and university teachers are citizens, members of a learned profession, and officers of an educational institution. When they speak or write as citizens, they should be free from institutional censorship or discipline, but their special position in the community imposes special obligations. As scholars and educational officers, they should remember that the public may judge their profession and their institution by their utterances. Hence they should at all times be accurate, should exercise appropriate restraint, should show respect for the opinions of others, and should make every effort to indicate that they are not speaking for the institution. (AAUP 1995, pp. 3–4)

Of the 200 FAPA institutions that provided an academic freedom statement (92% of the total respondents), almost half (48% of tenure-granting and 30% of contract institutions) explicitly cite or quote verbatim the *1940 Statement*. An additional 23% of tenure-granting institutions and 40% of contract institutions use, without attribution, some or all of the AAUP's statement. In total, 77% of the FAPA institutions use standard language for academic freedom.

Statements of the other 51 (29%) tenure-granting institutions were locally drafted; six (30%) contract institutions omit one or more of the three traditional areas of protection or have completely original academic freedom statements. Of all institutions with locally drafted language, half are public and half private.

Nonstandard Provisions

Differences from the AAUP standard include either additional protections or the extension of academic freedom beyond faculty members. For example, Brown University expands the protection afforded to faculty *and* students to encompass "the freedom of religious belief, of speech, of press, of association and assembly, of political activity inside and outside the University, the right to petition authorities, public and University, to invite speakers of their choice to the campus."[3] Academic freedom at San Francisco State University "includes the right of both faculty and students to seek censure of faculty members by complaint, petition, or seeking discipline for incompetence or unprofessional behavior." The University of Detroit Mercy extends academic freedom to artists to "freely create and exhibit their works of art."

The AAUP has noted that academic freedom applies "not only to the fulltime probationary as well as to the tenured teacher, but also to others, such as part-time and teaching assistants, who exercise teaching responsibilities" (AAUP 1995, p. 6). While many statements of academic freedom cover "all faculty" without further definition, only 10 (5%) explicitly include adjunct and/or part-time faculty, and 34 (17%) extend the protections of academic freedom to probationary/tenure track and/ or non–tenure track faculty.

Fifty-five (25%) of the academic freedom statements by FAPA institutions specifically mention students. At the University of Louisville, students have the "right to their own views on matters of opinion, rather than fact, and a right to express those views in an appropriate way without fear of arbitrary reaction." Haverford College protects students' rights to "engage in discussion, to exchange thought and opinion . . . to speak or write freely on any subject . . . [and] to found new, or to join existing organizations on or off campus."

Nine (5%) institutions explicitly extend the protections of academic freedom to librarians; many other institutions consider librarians to be faculty. The University of Toledo policy mentions library materials as well as librarians.

A small number of institutions extend academic freedom to guest speakers (e.g., North Carolina State University, Smith College). Academic freedom includes "guest speakers, movies, and programs" at North Dakota public institutions and "prospective faculty to whom Auburn has extended an offer of appointment" (at Auburn University).

Some institutions, all religiously affiliated, limit the academic freedom of faculty members. For example, the Walsh University policy states: "Although faculty members are entitled to freedom in the classroom in discussing their subject and exposing students to diverse points of view, they are expected to refrain from promoting doctrines opposed to the essentials of the Catholic faith or which are inimical to the aims and purposes of the University as a Catholic institution committed to the upholding of Christian faith and morality." Similarly, the policy at Aquinas College reads: "Aquinas College declares its sole limitation to the academic freedom of its faculty shall be the prohibition of any intentional espousal of positions contrary to the defined de fide teaching of the Catholic Church." At Northwest Christian College, an institution without tenure, faculty may pursue and publish research and write and speak as citizens "provided that such activities do not . . . conflict with the purpose and objectives of the College."

The AAUP has stated that "most church-related institutions no longer need or desire the departure from the principle of academic freedom implied in the *1940 Statement*, and we do not now endorse such a departure" (AAUP 1995, p. 6). However, "a spectrum of religious institutions emerges: some institutions explicitly prohibit faculty members from advocating particular viewpoints, others require a demonstrated respect for a doctrinal position, and still others ask that faculty members exercise caution in their speech while nonetheless permitting outsiders to speak on a variety of controversial subjects" (Sternman Rule 2000b, p. 10).

The Probationary Period

Provisions vary greatly for the pre-tenure period, a time for junior faculty members "to prove themselves and [give] their colleagues time to observe and evaluate them on the basis of their performance in the position" (AAUP 1995, p. 16). While less specific about probationary periods than about academic freedom, the AAUP does provide guidelines.

Length

The AAUP calls for "the precise terms and conditions of every appointment" (AAUP 1995, p. 16) to be clearly stated before the appointment begins; the period itself "should not exceed seven years" to guard against "excessive probation" (p. 90). Most (171, 87%) of the 196 tenure-granting FAPA institutions follow the AAUP's recommendation, with maximum probationary periods of seven years at 105 (54%), six years at 54 (28%), and five years at 12 (6%) institutions. Only 7 (4%) FAPA institutions have probationary periods that exceed seven years (e.g., Columbia University, Massachusetts Institute of Technology, Asbury College, Wiley College). Among research and doctoral institutions, 77% have probationary periods of either seven or eight years. Campuses with a five-year period fall exclusively within the master's and baccalaureate Carnegie classifications.

Three (2%) institutions allow multiple tenure reviews. For example, Dana College allows junior faculty three chances at tenure by conducting the first review in year four, and then conducts reviews again in year five and year six if tenure has not been previously granted. After year six, unsuccessful candidates are given a one-year terminal contract. Similarly, probationary faculty at Langston University and Central State University are reviewed first in year five, with the opportunity to have a negative decision reconsidered in year six.

Columbia University allows junior faculty, with permission from the provost, to postpone the tenure review until year nine, if the tenure clock has not been stopped for some other reason.

> The exception is made during year six if: (1) there is substantial evidence of excellence; (2) there are specific, compelling reasons for deferring tenure (generally, the only acceptable grounds are that scholarly publications or accomplishments are expected during the forthcoming year that will have a material effect on the outcome of the ad hoc review); and (3) the department or school includes a statement that a positive recommendation is expected from an internal review of the candidate. (Bleak 2000, p. 27)

Credit for Prior Teaching Experience

The AAUP recommends that institutions may grant up to three years of credit for prior teaching experience (p. 90). Most (81%) institutions follow this guideline. For 18 (14%) of 126 tenure-granting institutions that supplied this information, the number of years of credit for prior experience is negotiable; the remainder allow either two years (27, 21%), three years (75, 60%), or four years (6, 5%).

Time to Tenure

The tenure clock typically starts when a full-time faculty member begins the probationary period and stops when the candidate earns tenure or departs; however, some institutions allow pre-tenure faculty to stop the clock for scholarly, medical, or personal reasons.

The AAUP asserts that "scholarly leave of absence for one year or less will count as part of the probationary period as if it were prior service at another institution" (p. 22). Scholarly leave is available for junior faculty at 38 (19%) institutions (almost half of these are in the research classification), but such leaves do not stop the tenure clock. At Davidson College, for example, assistant professors may take a sabbatical in year five in order to facilitate "early research and writing opportunities before, rather than after, the tenure decision is made." Haverford College permits junior faculty who demonstrate "significant effort" to take a "special" leave in year four that may or may not be counted toward probation at the faculty member's discretion.

Medical or family leaves that stop the tenure clock are offered at 44 (22%) universities, of which half are research institutions. Most of these policies allow probationary faculty to stop the clock for childbirth or adoption or to care for an ill or disabled child, spouse, or parent. Most commonly, leaves that stop the tenure clock may extend two years (26, 13%); the others allow only one year.

Just as some institutions permit junior faculty to stop the tenure clock, some allow them to accelerate the process. One third (67) of FAPA institutions offer the possibility of early tenure. While most institutions designate the final year for tenure review as one year prior to the end of the probationary period, 12 institutions (6%) afford some choice about when to stand for tenure. Rice University "allows the candidate to apply for tenure at any time during the probationary period" (Bleak 2000, p. 26); at Youngstown State University, the tenure candidate decides whether to be considered in year four, five, or six. Candidates for early tenure at West Virginia State must "have records of achievement substantially beyond that normally expected for the awarding of tenure." At Lake Forest College, reviews for early tenure call for an "even more rigorous application of the [tenure] criteria than is normally the case." Nine of the institutions with early tenure provisions explicitly permit probationary faculty to reapply for tenure if the early bid was unsuccessful, although other institutions may have the same unwritten or informal policy.[4]

Performance Reviews

The AAUP recommends that probationary faculty be reviewed "periodically" throughout the pre-tenure period so that they can be "made aware of their progress" toward tenure. Such reviews should "minimize the likelihood of reasonable complaint if nontenured faculty members are given notice of nonreappointment" (AAUP 1995, p. 17). Of the institutions that submitted provisions for pre-tenure reviews, 92 (47%) conduct reviews annually, and 58 (30%) do so at the midpoint of the probationary period; some institutions conduct both annual reviews and an in-depth evaluation at the midpoint. These reviews afford opportunities to discuss the faculty member's performance, to review the needs and priorities of the department and college, and to counsel marginal candidates to leave prior to a negative tenure decision.

Tenure Quotas

The AAUP opposes any limits on the number or percentage of tenured faculty in departments or institutions. Only 8 (4%) FAPA institutions restrict the percentage of tenured faculty at the institution or in a department. At some institutions the quota policy sets a floor as well as a ceiling on tenure. Institution-wide quotas exist at Idaho State University, where no more than 75% of the faculty may be tenured; and at California Lutheran University, with a quota of 66%. The percentage of tenured faculty at Springfield College cannot fall below 55% or exceed 67%. Elon College and Colby-Sawyer College state that no department may be fully tenured, and they stipulate that the institutional tenure quota shall be between 50% and 75% of the full-time faculty at Elon and no more than 50% at Colby-Sawyer.

Tenure Criteria

Typically, tenure criteria include teaching, research, and service. Thirty-seven (19%) institutions set exceptional teaching as the top priority in the tenure decision; five (3%) place research excellence at the top. Eight institutions (4%) require that teaching and one other category be outstanding, and 11 (6%) explicitly leave the weighting of tenure criteria to the individual departments.

Some institutions state explicitly that institutional needs can affect tenure decisions. For example, Santa Clara University has no tenure quota; however, the policy states that "as the percentage of tenured faculty increases, the application of criteria inevitably becomes more rigorous." During annual reviews at Brown University, probationary faculty receive an explanation of the needs of the department, program, or division "so far as these [needs] may affect the appointee." At Columbia University, tenure is offered "only to the most able scholars and in those areas of research which are the most promising and in which the needs of the University are most pressing."

Still other institutions tie tenure to financial considerations above and beyond standard financial exigency clauses, such as "stability in academic programs, sufficiency of registration, and financial ability" (City University of New York). At the University of West Virginia, "Tenure may be granted only to people in positions funded by monies under the Board of Trustees' control." Similarly, the University of Arizona policy of the Arizona Board of Regents (ABOR) states: "It is neither the President's nor the ABOR's power to commit the State of Arizona to an obligation for which an appropriation has not been made. The use of the term 'with tenure' neither constitutes nor implies a legal obligation which the President of the Board is not empowered to undertake. In practice, renewals of appointments of tenured faculty members have been approved and funds have been allocated annually for these appointments."

Collegiality

While excellent teaching, research, and service are the primary requirements for tenure, collegiality is often a factor, sometimes unmentioned, in the decision. The AAUP, however, frowns on considering collegiality in tenure and promotion. In a 1999 report titled "On Collegiality as a Criterion for Faculty Evaluation" the AAUP asserts that the use of collegiality as a fourth criterion is "highly unfortunate" and "should be discouraged": "At some institutions, the term 'collegiality' or 'citizenship' exists in regulations or understood institutional practice as a synonym for 'service.' Our objection is to the use of the term 'collegiality' in its description of a separate and additional area of performance in which the faculty member is to be evaluated. . . . Certainly an absence of collegiality ought never, by itself, constitute a basis for nonrenewal, denial of tenure, or dismissal for cause" (AAUP 1999, pp. 69–70). The AAUP does grant that while collegiality should not be a fourth criterion for tenure, "the virtues of collegiality" can be reflected in definitions of scholarship, teaching, and service.

Eighteen (8%) FAPA institutions discuss collegiality in clauses that define faculty responsibilities and faculty ethics; such statements borrow heavily or quote entirely from the AAUP's "Statement of Ethical Conduct":

> As colleagues, professors have obligations that derive from common membership in the community of scholars. Professors do not discriminate against or harass colleagues. They respect and defend the free inquiry of associates. In the exchange of criticism and ideas professors show due respect for the opinions of others. Professors acknowledge academic debt and strive to be objective in their professional judgement of colleagues. Professors accept their share of faculty responsibilities for the governance of their institution. (AAUP 1995, pp. 105–106)

Twelve (6%) of the FAPA institutions discuss collegiality in unique ways: seven as a criterion for promotion and tenure (discussed later in this chapter), three in the context of service (Hamilton College, Northern Kentucky University, Western Baptist College), one as a criterion for merit (Shepherd College), and one as a general expectation of the faculty (Hiram College).

The following are the briefest policy statements submitted about the role of collegiality in tenure or contract renewal decisions:

"General desirability as a faculty member or colleague (for peer review)" (North Carolina State University).

"Evidence of recognition by colleagues . . . as possessing qualities of collegiality, such as the ability to work cooperatively and professionally with others" (Saint Louis University).

"'Community Building' functions are those which advance the role of the College and make it a better institution. This could be development of new programs. It could take the form of leadership, collegiality, or positive support" (College of the Atlantic).

At the other end of the spectrum are lengthy descriptions of the definition and role of collegiality in tenure decisions. At Valparaiso University, for example, faculty are evaluated on "acceptability as a colleague": "the University also assumes of its faculty a congenial and collegial relationship that manifests itself in a willingness to 'carry one's share of the load' in teaching, advising, research, committee work, and other forms of University service." Saint Norbert College's "collegial activities" include "active and productive participation in the functioning of one's discipline [and] . . . those which improve the intellectual, cultural, and religious climate of the College." At Auburn University, candidates for tenure must "demonstrate professional collegiality" because "the successful candidate for tenure will assume what may be an appointment of 30 years or more":

> Collegiality should not be confused with sociability or likability. Collegiality is a professional, not personal, criterion relating to the performance of a faculty member's duties within a department . . . Concerns relevant to collegiality include the following: Are the candidate's professional abilities and relationships with colleagues compatible with the departmental mission and with its long-term goals? Has the candidate exhibited the ability and willingness to engage in shared academic and administrative tasks that a departmental group must often perform and to participate with some measure of reason and knowledge in discussions germane to departmental policies and programs? Does the candidate maintain high standards of professional integrity?

The Santa Clara University policy devotes several pages to the importance of collegiality in promotion and tenure decisions. Relevant excerpts follow:

> To improve the overall quality and academic culture of learning of the department, the College, and the University, the College places great value on collegiality, the mutually respectful sharing of intellectual authority and professional responsibility for the

quality of our curriculum, our instruction, our scholarly/creative work, and our campus culture of learning.

Evaluators at all stages are reminded that collegiality is not the same as popularity and that the thoughtful and professional articulation of divergent views and the considered expression of constructive criticism, even if unwelcome to many, can be evaluated as positive collegial contributions.

Collegiality means that a faculty member can be counted on to discharge his or her professional responsibilities in a reliable, conscientious, energetic, civil, and effective manner. Collegiality is not the same as conformity.

Collegiality thus combines the essential components of academic inquiry and democratic participation, mutual respect, freedom of speech, open-minded consideration of ideas, and the principles of good citizenship, helping us work together more effectively to advance the cause of learning.

Collegiality will be explicitly named in Faculty Handbook criteria for promotion and tenure and carefully defined and weighted so that it does not become a pretext for denying tenure or promotion to people who are merely eccentric or personally disliked.

The Definition of Tenure

Of the 190 FAPA institutions that define tenure, 87% (165) refer to it as "permanent" or "continuous" employment until retirement, barring dismissal for cause; 14% (27) as an expectation of annual contracts until retirement; and 5% (10) as a "contractual right to continuing appointment." (Percentages sum to more than 100 because some institutions use multiple definitions.)

Academic Freedom and Economic Security

Tenure has traditionally been linked to academic freedom and employment security. According to the AAUP, "Tenure is a means to certain ends; specifically, (1) freedom of teaching and research and of extramural activities, and (2) a sufficient degree of economic security to make the profession attractive to men and women of ability" (AAUP 1995,

p. 3). In addition, academic freedom and security, "hence, tenure, are indispensable to the success of an institution in fulfilling its obligation to its students and to society" (p. 3). Just over one quarter of FAPA institutions (52, 27%) use AAUP language to link tenure to both academic freedom and economic security. Of these 52 institutions, 17 have a collective bargaining agreement with the AAUP.

More than two thirds of the FAPA institutions link tenure to academic freedom—52% in the tenure clause itself, and 17% in the sections on academic freedom that explicitly endorse the AAUP guidelines. Thus, a total of 131 (69%) institutions expressly tie tenure to academic freedom. Only one third of the policies explicitly connect tenure and economic security. One third (61) of the FAPA institutions either enhance or limit the standard meaning and protection of tenure.

Enhancements to Tenure

At 14 institutions, tenure provides additional guarantees beyond lifetime employment. Tenure guarantees full-time employment at some institutions (Lake Forest College, Georgia College and State University), and full-time employment at a certain salary at others (Ohio Wesleyan University, Pacific University, Richard Stockton College of New Jersey). Others provide tenured faculty with a guarantee against demotion or reduction in rank (Northern Kentucky University, University of Louisville, North Carolina State University).

Other interesting tenure provisions include:

> A "reduction in the required number of student evaluations" and "an increase in maximum faculty development funds" (Shawnee State University).
> A "voice in the formulation of the academic policies of the college" (Asbury College).
> "Equitable compensation and benefits, continued institutional support for teaching and scholarship, and continued involvement in the academic mission of the university" (Rice University).

Limitations on Tenure

Several institutions qualify or delimit the rights and privileges of tenure (Trower 2000). The following are some examples:

"Permanent status relates to Faculty status and not to specific assignment of duties" (Coe College).

"Tenure does not preclude the possibility of legitimate redeployment . . . tenured faculty are expected to respond to the needs of
the University to maintain educational flexibility" (Drew University 1969, p. 23).

"Tenure is not a guarantee that the terms and conditions of employment will not change from year to year" (Hiram College).

"A tenure contract is for a contract year and gives the faculty member the contractual right to be reemployed for succeeding years
. . . but subject to the terms and conditions of employment which
exist from contract year to contract year" (Cedarville College).

Tenure for Part-Time Faculty

Only three (2%) institutions (University of Iowa, University of Alaska,
University of Wisconsin at Superior) grant tenure to part-time faculty.
At the University of Iowa, part-time faculty may be awarded tenure if
they are "found to meet University standards for granting tenure, with
the performance expectations to be identical with those required of
full-time faculty members." Length of service is calculated by adding
together all part-time service; therefore, "12 years of 50 percent service
will be deemed the equivalent of six years of full-time service." The
maximum probationary period for part-time faculty at the University
of Wisconsin, Superior, is 14 years; however, the policy is not explicit
about requirements for part-time faculty to achieve tenure. The University of Alaska policy states: "For exceptional cases, and when in the
judgement of the Chancellor the best interests of the university will be
served, a faculty member may be appointed to a tenure-track position
at less than 100% but more than 50% of a full-time appointment."
Again, the policy is not explicit about whether requirements for tenure
for part-time faculty differ from the expectations for full-time faculty.

Non–Tenure Track Faculty: Ranks, Titles, Roles

In the 1970s, about 19% of all full-time faculty nationwide were appointed to non–tenure track positions; by 1995, that percentage had
risen to 28% (Roey and Rak 1998, pp. 2-8 and 2-12). Most (175, 89%)
tenure-granting FAPA institutions have tenure-ineligible faculty.

These appointments include positions that are full-time or part-time, have indefinite or limited renewal, and are internally or externally funded.

The AAUP prefers that all full-time faculty appointments be either probationary or tenured, with the exception of "special appointments clearly limited to a brief association with the institution"; it contends that "non–tenure track appointments do considerable damage both to principles of academic freedom and tenure and to the quality of our academic institutions—not to mention the adverse consequences for the individuals serving in such appointments" (AAUP 1995, p. 64).

Despite these sentiments, 101 of the 175 tenure-granting institutions with tenure-ineligible faculty have full-time, long-term, non–tenure track faculty positions variously labeled as term, extended term, fixed length, rolling, special, and at-will appointments. Such appointments are most common at research and least common at baccalaureate institutions. Typically, tenure-ineligible faculty hold the titles of instructor / senior instructor (30 institutions, 17%) or lecturer (31 institutions, 18%). However, 15 institutions use conventional tenure-track and tenured ranks (e.g., assistant, associate, and full professors) for non–tenure track faculty.

Often the responsibilities of non–tenure track and tenure track faculty differ. Several policies explicitly note that full-time non–tenure track faculty are not expected to maintain a balance among teaching, research, and service; instead, they normally concentrate on one area— for example:

> "Appointment or promotion to the level of nontenure eligible associate professor will require . . . [the] capacity to undertake high quality teaching, research, *or* service" (University of Arizona; emphasis added).
>
> "Lecturers are untenured members of the faculty whose primary roles are instructional with no obligations of research or service" (Rice University).
>
> "A person appointed to the special faculty rank of instructor . . . ordinarily assumes full responsibility for teaching undergraduate courses and generally has limited responsibility for other aspects of the standard faculty role" (Virginia Polytechnic Institute).

Nineteen (11%) FAPA institutions use "in-residence" appointments that are long-term and tenure-ineligible for poets, artists, and writers.

These faculty members perform supplementary roles with different expectations for scholarship and teaching. For example, at Santa Clara University, "distinguished artists, scholars, scientists, engineers, executives, statesmen and others may be granted appointments in-residence . . . to enrich the life of the University community."

Research and clinical tracks, also tenure-ineligible, are frequently used at Research 1 and 2 and Doctoral 1 institutions. These positions are quite common in schools of medicine, journalism, business, law, and dentistry. Titles usually include the standard tenured and tenure-track ranks (e.g., assistant, associate, and full) with the appropriate qualifier, such as clinical assistant professor or research professor. These faculty may teach clinical courses, conduct research, or oversee clinical work in hospitals or at other field sites. Contract lengths for such faculty range from nine months to five years.

Some institutions place a limit on the percentage of non–tenure track faculty that may be hired:

"No more than twenty percent of the total salaried faculty in any college (FTE)" (University of Iowa).

"No more than 15% of all full-time teaching faculty" (Asbury College).

"No more than ten appointments as lecturer may be extant in the university at one time" (Lehigh University).

The role of non–tenure track faculty in campus governance is an important issue. Only 13 (7%) FAPA institutions (6 research, 3 doctoral, 1 master's, and 3 baccalaureate) extend voting privileges to non–tenure track faculty. Nationally, according to Courtney Leatherman, "doctoral institutions gave non–tenure track faculty the least opportunity to participate—50 percent allowed it at the departmental level, only 10 percent at the level of the faculty senate. By comparison, at baccalaureate institutions surveyed, 94 percent allowed full-timers on contract to participate in departmental governance, and 58 percent allowed these employees to take part at the faculty-senate level" (Leatherman 1999, p. A15).

Promotion in Rank

A significant reward for faculty members, promotions in rank are usually based on research, teaching, and service, with an emphasis on cither teaching or research depending on institutional mission. A very small number of FAPA institutions also base promotion on factors such as enrollment, financial condition, departmental goals, and diversity.

Mission and Priorities

Over half (111, 57%) of FAPA institutions link institutional mission and priorities to promotion decisions, as recommended by the AAUP. Rather than "demanding all things of all people," institutions "should define their missions clearly and articulate appropriate and reasonable expectations against which faculty will be judged" (AAUP 1995, p. 132). Thirty institutions require that faculty advance the precepts of the institutional mission in order to be promoted, either by exemplifying the religious values of the institution or through personal religious commitment and personal conduct.

Ninety (46%) of FAPA tenure-granting institutions couple priorities and promotion by emphasizing either teaching (75, 83%) or research (7, 8%) as the principal criterion for promotion; the remaining 8 (9%) state that teaching and research figure equally in promotion decisions. Baccalaureate and master's institutions are much more likely than doctoral and research institutions to prioritize faculty work in promotion policies, and they are more likely to emphasize teaching over research. Still, 12 research and doctoral institutions stress the importance of teaching. At the University of Iowa, for instance, the "first step in promotion and tenure decision-making is an evaluation of teaching effectiveness. Only after affirmative judgement as to [teaching] effectiveness has been made can serious consideration be given to scholarship and professional service." Likewise, the University of Rochester states that the first threshold is teaching, adding, "No matter how good the scholarly or artistic work, nobody belongs in the university unless he or she is a good teacher."

Ten institutions explicitly require that promotion committees consider financial and strategic planning issues (e.g., enrollment, percentage of tenured faculty, fiscal constraints, departmental goals, program needs). Colby-Sawyer College, for example, states that promotion decisions are affected by the number of faculty a department has at various ranks, documented program viability, institutional financial viability, and potential changes in the program. The Michigan State University policy declares that deans must take into account "unit, college, and University criteria and other factors such as quality, progress, resources, program needs, percent of tenured faculty in the unit, and any other relevant University policies and goals" when making promotion decisions. At Georgia Institute of Technology, instructional units must have "clearly defined and prioritized objective[s] defined in accordance with the mission of the unit" that are "not static." Promotion decisions must consider such factors as "changing enrollment patterns, and changes in the unit's and Georgia Tech's mission within the University System of Georgia."

Defining and Documenting Faculty Work for Promotion

The AAUP's "Statement on Teaching Evaluation" (1995, pp. 133–136) asserts that, "as a first order of business," institutions should "declare their values and communicate them with sufficient clarity to enable colleges and departments to set forth specific expectations as to *teaching, research, and service,* and to make clear any other faculty obligations" (p. 133). Forty-four percent (86) of FAPA tenure-granting institutions with ranks outline specific criteria in the faculty handbook[5] for how teaching, research, and service should be assessed. Of the 86 institutions, almost all (90%) include teaching criteria, 85% detail research criteria, and 61% list what will be counted in the category of service.

In addition to defining and assessing classroom instruction as "teaching," standard policy includes advising as part of teaching; 174 (89%) institutions do so. Activities less frequently evaluated as "teaching" include:

curriculum development and the establishment of new, interdisciplinary, integrative, and team-taught courses (53% of institutions);

the development of new pedagogical techniques (28%);

the supervision of student research (23%);

attendance at workshops designed to improve teaching (16%);

writing about teaching and preparing instructional materials and learning aids (16%); and

the supervision of field trips, internships, and clinical and field activities (9%).

The AAUP recommends that a "judicious" evaluation of teaching include "(1) an accurate factual description of what an individual does as a teacher, (2) various measures of the effectiveness of these efforts and (3) fair consideration of the relation between these efforts and the institution's and the department's expectations and support" (p. 134). In addition, "Student learning, teaching performance, student perceptions, classroom visitation, self-evaluation, and outside opinions should be a part of assessing the effectiveness of instruction" (pp. 134–135).

For promotion in rank, almost all institutions (90%) have criteria to assess the quality of teaching that focus on the teacher, the students, and the curriculum. Common *teacher-focused* criteria include:

> the faculty member's knowledge of and expertise in his or her subject matter (at 61% of institutions);
> presentation, communication, and organization skills (57%);
> conscientious preparation for all classes and the use of effective teaching methods (40%);
> willingness to evaluate and improve one's own teaching (17%);
> ability to communicate enthusiasm for the discipline (15%);
> innovation, experimentation, and creativity in teaching (14%);
> ability to establish and communicate course goals and requirements (10%); and
> demonstration of personal and professional growth in teaching (8%).

The most often cited *student-focused* criteria are the ability to:

> relate to students in and outside of the classroom (69%);
> motivate, inspire curiosity, and stimulate the intellectual interest of students (51%); and
> improve student skills, including oral and written communication, problem solving, critical thinking, capability to reason, and analytical thinking (14%).

Finally, some institutions appraise *curriculum-focused* criteria, such as:

> leadership in the development of new programs and courses (66%);
> preparation, scope, and currency of course materials (42%); and
> whether course syllabi are well organized, well conceived, and well written (30%).

Standard means to document teaching include student evaluations, course syllabi, peer evaluations, enrollment levels, number of student advisees, supervision of independent study courses, teaching awards and other forms of recognition, and curriculum development materials. Less conventional documentation of teaching includes:

evidence of student learning through samples of student papers, tests, and class projects (Santa Clara University);

feedback from randomly selected recent graduates whom the faculty member taught (College of Charleston);

student exit interviews and alumni surveys (North Carolina State University); and

opinions of graduates who have achieved noteworthy professional success since leaving the institution (University of California at Irvine).

The AAUP recommends clear definitions of research responsibilities in order to avoid "excessive demands on the faculty" (1995, p. 127) and an expanded definition of scholarship in line with Boyer's (1990) work: "Though discovery and publication are the core of scholarly endeavor, scholarship seen in its many forms offers a wider context within which to weigh individual contributions" (AAUP 1995, p. 131).[6] For most FAPA institutions (98%), documentation of research activities involves publications in scholarly journals, books, technical reports, grant applications, inventions, patents, original artwork, and presentations of papers at national conferences. In addition, institutions have broadened definitions of research to include:

creative work, recitals, artistic creation, public performances (at 73% of institutions);

grant writing, reviewing, directing (31%);

postdoctoral fellowships, academic awards, and honors (21%);

textbook and pedagogical publications (17%);

publication of research in nonacademic outlets (16%);

incorporation of new disciplinary developments into courses or the development of experimental programs such as distance education (14%);

inventions, designs, innovations, and patents (13%);

innovative use of computers and the development of computer software (10%);
applied, theoretical or basic, and clinical research (7%); and
initiation of new pedagogical methods (7%).

When assessing scholarship, institutions apply a wide variety of standards to gauge whether the faculty member's scholarship

is recognized and respected by peers (51% of institutions);
makes a substantial, high-quality contribution to the field (36%);
is original and innovative (12%);
is widely disseminated (9%);
is part of an ongoing program of study rather than an isolated project (4%);
is communicated effectively (4%); and
brings credit to the university (3%).

Some institutions also measure whether the faculty member plays an
active leadership role in professional activities (44%) and has a broad,
scholarly knowledge of the field (20%).

FAPA policies define service as contributions to the general welfare
of the university; public service, extension, or outreach; and professional and administrative activities. At some institutions, service essentially means within the university, while others embrace community-
based activities.

Forty-four percent of FAPA institutions subdivide service into two
or more components; the majority do not. Specific service categories
include:

University service (e.g., chairing committees, chairing a department, developing programs, fund-raising)—100% of FAPA institutions that have multiple categories of service.
Service to the community requiring expertise (e.g., consulting and
technical assistance, extension teaching, extension publications
and grants, clinical activities, public policy and strategic studies,
economic and community development, field services)—49% of
institutions.
Service to students (e.g., nonacademic advising and counseling,
sponsorship of student organizations, and participation in student
events)—44% of institutions.

Service to the community as volunteer rather than expert (e.g., leadership on nonprofit boards, civic associations, and churches)—44% of institutions.

Service to disciplinary associations (e.g., holding a leadership position, reviewing conference proposals)—30% of institutions.

Service activities are assessed primarily by the level of faculty involvement and some measurement of leadership, time, and effort. Two other less often applied criteria are (1) whether the service adds to the effective operation of the institution and (2) whether the service brings favorable attention to the faculty member, department or institution, and discipline.

The documentation of service for purposes of promotion includes little more than a listing of membership on committees, professional organizations, community groups, boards, and involvement with student organizations. Only six FAPA institutions require more detailed evidence of service, such as letters from peers and colleagues that evaluate performance.

Post-Tenure Review

During the 1980s, post-tenure review became increasingly common as the public, especially state legislators and trustees, demanded greater accountability (Licata and Morreale 1997).[7] The AAUP initially denounced post-tenure review in 1983 as a threat to academic freedom and tenure; however, during the 1990s, its position changed. In its report "Post-Tenure Review: An AAUP Response" (1998) the association set "minimum standards for good practice if a formal system of post-tenure review is established." Paraphrased, these ten standards are:

- Academic freedom must be protected at all costs.

- Post-tenure review must not be a pretense for revisiting the tenure decision, nor should the burden of proving "just cause" for dismissal shift from the administration to the faculty member under review.

- Faculty should play the primary role in developing and conducting post-tenure reviews, and the standard for appraisal should be the competent and conscientious discharge of one's duties.

- Post-tenure review should be developmental in nature, and institutional funds should be made available to encourage faculty development and reward meritorious performance.

- Post-tenure review should be flexible based on discipline and career stage.

- Post-tenure review processes and outcomes should be kept confidential.

- A faculty development plan, if part of the review process, should be jointly designed by both the faculty member and the administration.

- Faculty members should be permitted to comment on and challenge the findings of their evaluations.

- In cases of severe and persistent underperformance, remedies should be mutually constructed and agreed upon; if they fail, faculty peers should be involved in any discussions of sanctions.

- The standard for dismissal should remain just cause, and the process must ensure ample procedural safeguards. (Sternman Rule 2000a, pp. 183–184)

Almost half of the tenure-granting institutions in the Faculty Appointment Policy Archive have post-tenure review policies. Of these, 55% are public and 45% are private, and at least one third of the institutions in each Carnegie category have a formal post-tenure review system.

How Often?

Of the 88 FAPA institutions with post-tenure reviews in addition to annual reviews for salary and merit adjustments, 78 (89%) conduct cyclical, or blanket (AAUP 1998), reviews. These procedures do not single out individuals based on performance; rather, all tenured faculty are assessed at regular intervals. With the time frame ranging from two (1%) to seven years (4%), cyclical reviews are most commonly conducted every five years (35% of institutions conducting cyclical reviews). Of FAPA institutions with cyclical reviews, 15% evaluate faculty at different ranks at different intervals, with full professors reviewed the least often.

Triggered post-tenure reviews, by contrast, occur not on a fixed cycle but according to demonstrable need. Targeted reviews arise as a result of poor performance or at the request of administrators or the faculty member him- or herself. Of the 88 FAPA institutions with post-tenure review, 37 (42%) have triggered reviews. Poor performance is signaled by "two consecutive annual evaluations of Unsatisfactory performance" at Virginia Polytechnic Institute and State University, by "a determination of unsatisfactory performance" on annual evaluations at Valparaiso University, and by an unsatisfactory rating during the standard review cycle at Claremont Graduate University. At another group of institutions, post-tenure reviews may be triggered at the request of an academic administrator (at Greensboro College and Clarkson University) or by a member of the faculty (University of Rhode Island).

Nature of the Review

Post-tenure reviews may be further classified as either formative or summative. The former are developmental in nature and do not result in any formal administrative action. While the latter may have a developmental purpose, they may also result in personnel action (e.g., reward, sanction, a faculty development plan, a letter to the file). One quarter of the FAPA institutions with post-tenure reviews conduct formative reviews and 69% have summative reviews; the remaining 6% have review processes that are both "formative and summative." In the summative review process at Georgia Institute of Technology, financial rewards and extra development funds may accrue to high-performing faculty; poor performers must adhere to development plans designed to monitor and correct deficiencies.

Faculty Development Plans

Of the institutions with post-tenure review, 43% (38) utilize development plans as part of the post-tenure review process. At 13 institutions, development plans serve as a goal-setting mechanism for all faculty members regardless of performance. At the remaining 25 institutions,

development plans are written in response to unsatisfactory performance. Typically these plans, the result of negotiations between faculty
members and administrators, include goals for the coming year, remedies for poor performance, and a time line for compliance. Most development plans allow faculty members one to two years to improve. In
addition, 36% of the institutions explicitly earmark funds or other resources to help faculty members carry out their plans.

Post-Tenure Review Sanctions and Rewards

Sanctions, usually prompted by prolonged, unremedied, unsatisfactory
performance, may be levied at 33 of the 88 (38%) institutions with
post-tenure reviews. The sanction cited most often for sustained poor
performance is dismissal, specifically mentioned in the post-tenure review policies of 25 institutions (and discussed in the next section on
dismissal for cause).[8] Only 9 other institutions cite the remaining 11
possible sanctions (i.e., demotion, ineligibility for promotion or travel
funds, salary reduction or freeze, loss of sabbatical, career redirection
program, reassignment of duties, revocation of tenure, placement on
probation, suspension) in place at FAPA institutions (see Table 2.1).

Rewards, including letters of commendation, development funds,
merit pay increases, salary increases, extra sabbaticals, or other, unspecified rewards and recognition for outstanding post-tenure reviews,
are available at 12 (14%) of the FAPA institutions with post-tenure
review (California Lutheran University, Georgia Institute of Technology, Montana State University, North Carolina State University,
North Park College, Northern Arizona University, Santa Clara University, University of Arizona, University of Louisville, University of
Wisconsin at Superior, Valdosta State University, and Valparaiso University).

Dismissal for Cause and Other Sanctions

Dismissal

The AAUP (1995) maintains that "adequate cause" may lead to termination of tenured appointments and that "adequate cause for a dismissal will be related, directly and substantially, to the fitness of faculty

Table 2.1 Institutions and possible sanctions for sustained poor performance

Institution	Sanctions
California Lutheran University	Reassignment of duties Revocation of tenure Salary freeze
Claremont Graduate University	Denial of sabbatical Salary freeze
Colby-Sawyer College	Career redirection program Revocation of tenure Suspension
James Madison University	Salary reduction
Taylor University	Probation
Texas Woman's University	Revocation of tenure
University of Colorado	Demotion in rank Denial of sabbatical No travel funds Reassignment of duties
Virginia Polytechnic and State University	Demotion in rank Revocation of tenure Suspension
Wiley College	Ineligibility for promotion Salary freeze

members in their professional capacities as teachers or researchers." Furthermore, such procedures should not be "used to restrain faculty members in their exercise of academic freedom" (p. 26). While the AAUP does not elaborate on what constitutes "adequate cause," FAPA institutions list a variety of behaviors that could lead to dismissal-for-cause proceedings: incompetence (63% of FAPA institutions), neglect of duty (55%), moral turpitude (33%), criminal behavior (30%), poor performance (23%), misrepresentation and falsification of documents (19%), other forms of dishonesty (18%), ethical violations (14%), violations of policy (13%) and others' rights (7%), and personal conduct impairing duties (11%). Sexual harassment, drug abuse, and mental and/or physical impairment were also cited as grounds for dismissal at some institutions.

Less common grounds for dismissal include insubordination (15 institutions), disruption of university operations (10), disregard for the institution's religious mission (8), inefficiency (6), irresponsibility (6), causing public scandal (6), using one's position as a faculty member to exploit others (5), conduct unbecoming a faculty member (3), contumacious conduct (2), indifference (2), lack of scholarly objectivity (2), indolence (1), breaking guidelines regarding divorce (1), and malicious and deliberate disloyalty to the college (1). Inefficiency and indifference are nowhere defined in policy statements. Irresponsibility is defined by only one institution, Austin College; the policy of that institution states, "A pattern of inadequate professional development on the part of the individual, when after adequate warning the person still fails to make serious efforts toward continued growth and development, is interpreted as a serious irresponsibility or a professional incompetence."

Other Sanctions

The AAUP (1995) prescribes that reprimand (a "minor sanction") or suspension from service (a "severe sanction") may occur when conduct is not so egregious as to justify dismissal for cause. Other sanctions and penalties at FAPA institutions were: suspension with or without pay (at 27% of institutions); oral or written reprimand (21%); adverse salary adjustments (13%); reassignment of duties (9%); demotion in rank (8%); removal of privileges, benefits, or perquisites (7%); or warnings (7%). Sanctions mentioned less frequently included revocation of tenure (4%), probation (4%), and restitution (3%).

Financial Exigency and Program Discontinuance

Apart from dismissal for cause, tenured faculty may be released only under extreme conditions. All FAPA institutions allow for the termination of tenured faculty in the event of financial exigency, in general accordance with AAUP (1995) policy. AAUP regulations also permit termination "as a result of *bona fide* formal discontinuance of a program or department of instruction" (p. 25). Almost all (98%) of FAPA institutions with policy language on the termination of tenured faculty have such provisions. In both cases, however, the AAUP considers academic freedom and the education of students, and not economics, to be paramount concerns.

Financial Exigency

Only 15 (8%) of FAPA institutions explicitly adopted the AAUP definition of a bona fide financial exigency[9] as "an imminent financial crisis that threatens the survival of the institution as a whole and which cannot be alleviated by less drastic means" than the termination of tenured faculty (1995, p. 23). Most institutional policy statements (69%) do not include a formal definition of exigency. Among the institutions (23%) with their own definition, the degree of financial distress required to terminate tenured faculty varies from "extraordinary financial emergency" (Coker College) to a need to "preserve the financial soundness of the College" (Wofford College).

The collective bargaining agreement at the University of Central Florida uses broad language, allowing "layoff . . . as a result of adverse financial circumstances." At the other end of the spectrum, Bloomfield College, an institution that declared financial exigency in the mid-1970s, specifies that

> the following set of circumstances, in any combination, may be indicative of [financial exigency]: (a) When total liabilities exceed total assets; (b) When current liabilities exceed current assets and the College is unable to secure additional funding; (c) When the College is unable to meet its financial obligations on long-term liabilities or covenants required of those obligations; (d) When there has been a substantial drop in day enrollment for two consecutive years; (e) When the College has operated at an actual deficit of $200,000 or more for three or more consecutive fiscal years; (f) When the College has operated at an actual deficit of $500,000 or more during the previous fiscal year. (Bloomfield College 1997, p. 26)

One third of FAPA institutions explicitly adopted the AAUP's guideline that alternatives short of faculty layoffs be explored. For example, the University of Toledo's (1998) policy lists several alternatives:

Income generation.

Reduction of support staff and administrative personnel and services.

Encouragement of voluntary early faculty retirement, leaves of absence, and resignations through financial inducements, including "buy-out" plans.

Reduction in internal funds allocated to research and equipment.

Reduction in the number of graduate assistants.

Replacement of part-time, visiting, retiring, superannuate, resigning, and untenured faculty with existing tenured faculty members where qualified to teach.

The AAUP (1995, pp. 24–25) recommends that faculty play a substantial "participatory role" in: (1) declaring that a financial exigency exists, (2) identifying alternatives to termination for tenured faculty, (3) defining academic programs where terminations will occur, (4) choosing the criteria for termination, and (5) determining which appointments should be terminated. Just over half (52%) of FAPA institutions stipulate a participatory role for faculty. In addition, the AAUP recommends that

untenured faculty be terminated first (a provision of 40% of FAPA institutions);

the institution "make every effort to place" faculty in other positions prior to termination (57%);

a terminated faculty member receive appropriate notice or severance pay (74%);

a terminated faculty member have the right of first refusal on his or her old position if it is to be filled within three years (65%).

While the AAUP recommends that institutions offer to retrain faculty displaced by program closure, only 32 (18%) FAPA institutions make similar provisions for faculty terminated due to financial exigency.

Program Discontinuance

Institutions use a variety of terms to describe program discontinuance, such as curtailment, modification, consolidation, reorganization, reduction, abandonment, and curricular exigency. Two thirds of FAPA policies refer to possible termination of tenured faculty because of "changes in educational programs."

Thirty-five percent of FAPA institutions conform to the AAUP's program discontinuance guidelines by basing layoffs of tenured faculty for program closure on purely educational—that is, nonfinancial—reasons. But 28% authorize program discontinuance for some combination of educational and financial reasons because they find that the two are often difficult to separate.

Consistent with their recommendations on financial exigency, the AAUP (1995) prescribes that program discontinuance be *"bona fide"* and based on "educational considerations" (p. 25); that faculty should determine the need to excise programs; and that the institution "make every effort" to retrain and reassign displaced tenured faculty. Further, terminated faculty should receive notice and severance pay, and should have the right to appeal to a faculty committee.

Only three FAPA institutions state categorically that tenured faculty members will be terminated in the event of program discontinuance. All three are Research 1 universities: Indiana University at Bloomington, University of Iowa, and Massachusetts Institute of Technology. Faculty are assured a role in determining the need for program discontinuance at only 54% of FAPA institutions, but three fourths explicitly pledge to assist displaced faculty members to find another position. Just over one quarter of FAPA institutions provide retraining, but most (81%) provide severance pay in the event of termination.

Institutions without Tenure

Ten percent (21) of the FAPA institutions do not offer tenure. Instead, faculty are hired on contracts. Seventy-one percent offer multiple-year contracts, ranging from three to ten years; 3 colleges offer only one-year contracts. However, the employment policies at these contract sites, with a couple of important exceptions, mirror provisions at institutions with tenure.

Of the contract institutions, 95% include statements about academic freedom and 29% quote verbatim the AAUP's *1940 Statement of Principles on Academic Freedom and Tenure*. Most (81%) contract sites provide notice of nonrenewal to faculty, and 24% conform to AAUP guidelines for nonrenewal. Likewise, 81% offer rank and promotion, and 95% include statements for dismissal for cause.

The most conspicuous deviation (aside from the absence of tenure) from the policies of tenure-granting institutions lies in the area of shared governance. Of the contract sites, 62% have no stated provisions for faculty involvement in peer evaluations, and only 38% explicitly mention the faculty's role in declaring financial exigency or discontinuing programs.

This chapter highlighted the degree of adherence to AAUP Recommended Institutional Regulations on faculty employment (see Table 2.2). In general, AAUP policy constitutes a national standard; however, the diversity of American colleges and universities has produced numerous deviations from standard practice.

What's Standard?

All tenure-granting institutions:

> have probationary periods for junior faculty;
> define tenure similarly—as permanence of employment;
> offer promotion in rank; and
> allow the dismissal of tenured faculty for "adequate cause" and
>   financial exigency.

Almost all tenure-granting institutions:

> allow the dismissal of tenured faculty in the event of program discontinuance; and
> eschew tenure quotas.

Most tenure-granting institutions:

> have a maximum probationary period of seven years;
> follow AAUP guidelines for allowing credit toward tenure for prior
>   teaching experience;
> periodically review probationary faculty;
> have fairly standard academic freedom clauses; and
> link academic freedom and academic tenure in policy statements.

Table 2.2 Adherence to AAUP standards among FAPA institutions

Policy type	Number of policies analyzed	Adherence to AAUP standard	
		Number	Percent
Academic freedom	200	142	71
Probationary period	196	196	100
Length[a]	196	171	87
Credit for prior experience[b]	126	102	81
Periodic performance review	196	150	77
No tenure quota	196	188	96
Definition of tenure[c]	190	190	100
Link tenure and academic freedom	190	131	69
Link tenure and employment security	190	62	33
Full-time, long-term, non–tenure track faculty[d]	175	74[e]	42
Promotion in rank	196	196	100
Link to mission	196	111	57
Specific criteria to assess faculty	196	86	44
Post-tenure review[f]	192	88[g]	46
Dismissal for cause/sanctions[h]	196	192[i]	98
Dismissal for financial exigency	178	178	100
Refer to or use AAUP language	178	85	48
Dismissal for program discontinuance	159	156	98
Refer to or use AAUP language	159	71	45

a. The AAUP recommends a maximum seven-year probationary period.

b. The AAUP recommends that no more than three years of prior credit be awarded to probationary faculty.

c. The AAUP defines tenure as permanency of appointment until death, barring "adequate cause" for dismissal, financial exigency, program closure, or retirement.

d. The AAUP recommends that institutions have zero long-term, non–tenure track faculty; instead, the AAUP believes that all full-time appointments should be with tenure, on the tenure track, or short-term/visiting, if absolutely necessary.

e. This number represents those FAPA institutions that do *not* make use of full-time, long-term, non–tenure track appointments and thus follow the AAUP recommendations against their use.

f. The AAUP does not expressly recommend post-tenure review but does provide guidelines for its use.

g. This number represents the number of FAPA institutions that have post-tenure review policies.

h. The AAUP has stated that "adequate cause" may lead to the dismissal of tenured faculty but is not specific about what constitutes such cause.

i. This number represents those FAPA institutions that included a section on dismissal for cause in the materials sent. It is safe to assume that all institutions may dismiss faculty for adequate cause.

What's Nonstandard?

The protections of academic freedom less often:

> are explicitly extended beyond the full-time faculty to students,
> guest speakers, librarians, part-time faculty, non–tenure track fac-
> ulty, and prospective faculty; and
> are explicitly extended beyond teaching, research, and extramural
> speaking to works of art, performances, and library material.

Probationary periods:

> May be extended beyond seven years.
> Allow early tenure.
> Allow probationary faculty flexibility in deciding when to stand for
> tenure.
> Allow probationary faculty the opportunity to stop the tenure clock
> for a variety of reasons, including childbirth or adoption of a
> child, illness, assisting aging parents, or (less often) unforeseen
> problems with research activities.
> Involve the solicitation of letters from current students, recent
> graduates and/or alumni, or from faculty outside of the institu-
> tion as part of the tenure review process.
> Allow student participation on departmental tenure review commit-
> tees.
> Allow faculty to choose a tenure or a non–tenure track.

The following are some less common features of tenure:

> It is made available for part-time faculty.
> Tenure decisions consider financial conditions, market demand, or
> departmental needs.
> As the percentage of tenured faculty at an institution rises, more
> stringent standards for tenure are applied.
> Collegiality is a criterion for tenure.
> Tenured positions involve a reduction in the required number of
> course evaluations, an increase in faculty development funds, and
> guarantees of full-time employment or a certain salary level.
> Achieving tenure does not mean that the contract, the terms, and
> the conditions of employment will never change (e.g., the possi-

bility of redeployment may occur; terms and conditions may vary from one year to the next).

Non–tenure track faculty:

May be in full-time positions.
May enjoy departmental and university voting privileges.

Promotion in rank:

Is tied to financial or market conditions, or to departmental needs.
Takes service to the community, students, and disciplinary associations into account.
Is concerned with finding new ways to document service.

Post-tenure review:

Is usually in the nature of targeted/triggered, instead of cyclical, reviews.
Provides rewards or recognition for outstanding performance documented by post-tenure review.
Evaluates faculty of different ranks on different schedules (higher-ranked faculty have less frequent reviews).

It is remarkable how little variation there is in faculty employment policy language across institutional type; that is, one might read very similar statements for academic freedom at Columbia University and at Colby-Sawyer College, or policies concerning post-tenure reviews at North Carolina State and at Valdosta State. For the most part, the norms and variations summarized here are no more likely to be found in private than in public institutions, at large research universities than at small colleges, and at selective than at nonselective institutions.

However, some broad distinctions between research universities on one end of the spectrum and baccalaureate institutions on the other may be made. Research institutions, when compared to master's and baccalaureate institutions, are more likely to:

use locally crafted academic freedom language;
extend the probationary period beyond six years;
allow two years of (stop-the-clock) leave during the probationary period;
allow early tenure; and

hire full-time, non–tenure track faculty and extend voting privileges to those faculty.

Baccalaureate institutions, when compared to research institutions, are more likely to:

explicitly consider financial conditions, market demand, or departmental needs when making tenure decisions;

explicitly apply more stringent standards for tenure as the percentage of tenured faculty at the institution rises; and

consider service in making promotion decisions.

The fact that there are so few policy distinctions by institutional type seems extraordinary given the very different missions across Carnegie classifications, but speaks at least in part to the influence of the AAUP's guidelines in shaping academic policy. It should also be noted that what cannot be gleaned from perusal of policies are institutional cultural variations and the context within which faculty work occurs. Whether and how policies are enacted and any subsequent effect on faculty behavior cannot be derived from simple analysis of policy statements. Faculty work life and behavior under various conditions is the subject of other chapters in this book.

Notes

1. The Carnegie classification system used in this chapter is the one in place in 1999. This system may change by the time this book is printed; in addition, institutions may be reclassified.

2. The CD-ROM contains policies from the following types of institutions: 21 Research I, 16 Research II, 10 Doctoral I, 17 Doctoral II, 59 Master's I, 13 Master's II, 26 Baccalaureate I, and 55 Baccalaureate II.

3. Throughout the chapter, specific policy language is quoted. In all cases, unless noted, policies quoted are examples and do not represent a definitive list of all institutions with a particular provision. In addition, we present policy language without judgment, endorsement, or opposition. Any specific policies highlighted here are intended as illustrations and not necessarily as model practices.

4. The nine are Auburn University, Central Connecticut State University, Creighton University, Kent State University, Northern Kentucky University, Saginaw Valley State University, the University of Detroit Mercy, the University of Nebraska, and Virginia Polytechnic Institute and State University.

5. One should not assume that the remaining 110 institutions do not detail specific criteria for the assessment of teaching, research, and service; it is likely that they do, but those criteria are located in department-specific documents.

6. Boyer's (1990) expanded definition of scholarship includes discovery, integration, application, and teaching.

7. For additional information about the extent and types of post-tenure review nationally see Licata and Morreale (1997).

8. Termination of employment after sustained poor performance is a possible outcome of post-tenure review at numerous institutions, including Albertson College of Idaho, California Lutheran University, Claremont Graduate University, Dickinson State University, Emporia State University, Georgia Institute of Technology, Idaho State University, James Madison University, Maryville State University, North Carolina State University, North Dakota State University and University of North Dakota, Northern Arizona University, Russell Sage College, Southern Oklahoma State University, Texas Woman's University, University of Arizona, University of Colorado at Colorado Springs, University of Idaho, University of Texas at El Paso, University of Texas Pan American, Valdosta State University, Valparaiso University, Virginia Polytechnic and State University, and Wiley College.

9. For a discussion of measures of financial distress short of financial exigency see Chabotar and Honan (1996).

References

American Association of University Professors. 1995. *Policy Documents and Reports.* Washington, D.C.: American Association of University Professors.

——— 1998. "Post-Tenure Review: An AAUP Response." *Academe,* 84 (5): 61–67. On-line: *http://www.aaup.org/postten.htm.*

——— 1999. "On Collegiality as a Criterion for Faculty Evaluation." *Academe,* 85 (5): 69–70.

Bleak, Jared. 2000. "On Probation: The Pre-Tenure Period." In Cathy A. Trower, ed., *Policies on Faculty Appointment: Standard Practices and Unusual Arrangements.* Bolton, Mass.: Anker Publishing Co.

Bloomfield College. 1997. *Agreement between Bloomfield College and Bloomfield College Chapter of the American Association of University Professors.* Bloomfield, N.J.: Bloomfield College.

Boyer, Ernest L. 1990. *Scholarship Reconsidered: Priorities of the Professoriate.* Princeton, N.J.: Carnegie Foundation for the Advancement of Teaching.

Chabotar, Kent J., and James Honan. 1996. "New Yardsticks to Measure Financial Distress." Working Paper Series, no. 4. Washington, D.C.: American Association for Higher Education.

Faculty Appointment Policy Archive. 1999. CD-ROM, Version 2.1. Developed by the Project on Faculty Appointments at the Harvard Graduate School of Education. Dist. Bolton, Mass.: Anker Publishing Co.

Glassick, Charles E., Mary Taylor Huber, and Gene I. Maeroff. 1997. *Scholarship Assessed: Evaluation of the Professoriate.* San Francisco: Jossey-Bass.

Leatherman, Courtney. 1999. "Growth in Positions Off the Tenure Track Is a Trend That's Here to Stay, Study Finds." *Chronicle of Higher Education,* April 9, pp. A14–A16.

Licata, Christine, and Joseph C. Morreale. 1997. "Post-Tenure Review: Policies,

Practices, Precautions." Working Paper Series, no. 12. Washington, D.C.: American Association for Higher Education.

Roey, Stephen, and Rebecca Rak. 1998. *Fall Staff in Postsecondary Institutions, 1995.* Washington, D.C.: U.S. Department of Education, Office of Educational Research and Improvement.

Sternman Rule, Cheryl. 2000a. "After the Big Decision: Post-Tenure Review Analyzed." In Cathy A. Trower, ed., *Policies on Faculty Appointment: Standard Practices and Unusual Arrangements.* Bolton, Mass.: Anker Publishing Co.

———— 2000b. "Freedom in the Academy: Academic Freedom Explored." In *Policies on Faculty Appointment: Standard Practices and Unusual Arrangements.* Bolton, Mass.: Anker Publishing Co.

Trower, Cathy A., ed. 2000. *Policies on Faculty Employment: Standard Practices and Unusual Arrangements.* Bolton, Mass.: Anker Publishing Co.

University of Toledo. 1998. UT-AAUP Contract. Available on line: *www.toledo .edu/policies-procedures-and-contracts/ut-aaup-contract.*

3

Does Faculty Governance Differ at Colleges with Tenure and Colleges without Tenure?

RICHARD P. CHAIT

$\mathcal{I}$F ACADEMIC TENURE were just a matter of faculty performance and employment security, the debate over tenure would still be heated and opinions still divided, but the fundamental issues would be relatively uncomplicated. Tenure, however, extends well beyond the terms and conditions of faculty employment to encompass, for instance, faculty status and institutional self-image. (See Chapter 9.)

Even more germane, tenure concerns power—who has the authority to decide and direct, and who has the prerogative to refuse and resist. A common yet elusive term, power has been variously defined as the "capability of one social actor to overcome resistance in achieving a desired objective or result" (Pfeffer 1981, p. 2), "an institutionalized pattern of influence behavior" (Greiner 1986, p. 168), and "the capacity to effect (or affect) organizational outcomes" (Mintzberg 1983, p. 4). When people within a particular social structure expect and accept the exercise of power as legitimate, then power "is denoted as authority" (Pfeffer, p. 4). In the academy, the term "governance" signifies the distribution of authority, or legitimate power, for the purposes of making decisions and taking actions.

The conventional view contends that tenure is the linchpin of legitimate power for faculty:

It is useful to think of academic tenure as a set of constraints on the discretion of managers (the "administration") over various as-

pects of the academic enterprise. The effect of these constraints is
to influence the distribution of authority between administration
and faculty. . . .

Faculty members with tenure will have more independence.
Administrators will need to rely more on persuasion and less on
negative sanctions in influencing the behavior of individual faculty. . . . [T]enure will also influence the structure of decision-
making in universities. Tenure increases the ability of faculty collectively to shape institutional decisions through their actions in
departments, colleges, or the institution as a whole. (McPherson
and Schapiro 1999, pp. 92–93)

Academics generally presume that tenure empowers the faculty. Dis-
agreements center on whether the balance of power should be adjusted
and, if so, whether tenure should be the fulcrum. Representative of one
side of the argument, Cary Nelson, a professor of English at the University of Illinois, contended (1999) that attacks on tenure and the introduction of post-tenure reviews constituted a "war against the faculty," which would render faculty "less able to resist pressures from
administrators and governing boards" (p. B4). On the other side, Dennis O'Brien, former president of the University of Rochester, recommended (1998) that tenure policies be reformed in order to precipitate
a "subtly changed view of faculty" and to redefine "the role of the faculty and other constituencies in university management and governance" (p. 14). Toward the middle, Donald Kennedy (1994), former
president of Stanford, accepted the reality that "tenure, disciplinary
loyalty, the structure of academic politics, monumental patterns that
create huge regret functions . . . make it difficult for the university to
take new directions nimbly. It enhances a distribution of decision-making power in which the periphery has a clear advantage over the center"
(p. 98).

Rather than enter the fray about the distribution of power on campus, this chapter reports the results of a study designed to address the
initial assumption that tenure empowers the faculty. What difference
does the presence or absence of tenure make to the faculty's role in
campus governance? I first present data suggesting that the degree of
faculty authority does differ as a function of the presence or absence of
a tenure system. I then consider whether factors other than tenure con-

tribute to these differences. Next, I examine the apathy toward campus governance prevalent among all the faculties in the study. Finally, I explore whether the faculty's role in governance affects faculty work satisfaction.

The Study

No single research project can comprehensively answer a question as multifaceted as the relationship between tenure and governance. However, as a place to start, we conducted a comparative study of the faculty's role in governance at four colleges with tenure and four colleges without tenure.

We identified 88 four-year colleges without tenure, exclusive of specialized institutions (e.g., seminaries and conservatories). Of the 88 schools, 15 responded affirmatively to an inquiry about participating in a study of campus governance. After reviewing governance documents and conducting telephone interviews with the college presidents, we selected four sites where major institutional decisions had recently been made. We then paired each of these four colleges without tenure with a peer institution with a tenure system. The match was made through a commercial, computer-based program that compared institutions along various dimensions of mission, finances, and demography. The eight sites in the study were: Bluffton (Ohio), Brenau (Georgia), Columbia (Missouri), D'Youville (New York), Flagler (Florida), Lourdes (Ohio), University of Charleston (West Virginia), and Virginia Wesleyan.

In reality, the sample population was predetermined because there are no major universities, very few public colleges, and less than a handful of highly competitive independent colleges without tenure. In order to study the effects on governance of the absence of a tenure system one must perforce target a certain genre of institutions. While we cannot generalize broadly from the present study, there are well over 300 colleges in the United States that share a similar overall profile. These institutions are typically categorized as Baccalaureate General or, less often, as Master's I institutions under the Carnegie classification system.

Although the study highlights differences among the sites, the institutions were actually far more alike than dissimilar. All are small,

tuition-dependent, private four-year colleges with an average enrollment of 1,700 students and about 75 full-time faculty. None boasts
a large endowment or highly selective admissions standards. For the
seven sites that reported median SAT scores in 1997, the averages
(nonrecentered) were 440 verbal and 480 math. Five of the institutions,
three with contracts (Brenau, Flagler, and Lourdes), and two with
tenure (Columbia and D'Youville), formerly educated only women.
One campus with contracts (Lourdes) and one with tenure (Columbia)
started as two-year colleges, and two (Brenau and Charleston) abolished tenure in the 1970s. Only D'Youville has a faculty union (AAUP).

Project researchers visited all eight sites and interviewed more than a
dozen formal and informal faculty leaders, senior administrators, and
trustees. We asked them to characterize campus governance, to identify the most powerful people on campus, and to recount in detail how
important decisions had been made. We also reviewed documents that
described the faculty's governance structure and scope of responsibility.

Five project researchers independently reviewed all of the interview
transcripts and institutional data and then ranked the sites both or-
dinally and on a scale that measured the relative differences between
and among the sites with respect to the degree of faculty power. Scores
were assigned based on whether the faculty inaugurated or responded
to important initiatives, on the degree of consultation, on the division
of responsibility, and on the informants' perceptions of campus governance. In order to assess the degree of consistency among the raters,
Kendall's coefficient[1] of concordance was applied to the scores (Siegel
1956). Interrater reliability was 0.79, indicating a fairly high level of
agreement among the raters.

Tenure and Power

Among the sites studied, faculty at institutions without tenure generally exercised less power and influence than faculty on campuses with
tenure.

The Data

Project researchers rated sites with tenure first, second, third, and fifth
with respect to faculty power; campuses without tenure ranked fourth,

sixth, seventh, and eighth.[2] The average score of the lowest-ranked college with tenure (5T) and the highest-ranked institution with contracts (4C) was nearly the same: 4.83 versus 5.0. (The next smallest interval was 0.4 and the average interval was 0.9.)

Because small differences can affect rank order, we also scored the relative degrees of faculty power among and between the sites (1 = most powerful, 8 = least powerful). There were four tiers. One site with tenure had a faculty rated 1.0, far more powerful than any other. Two other sites, also with tenure, formed a second tier, with scores of 3.9 and 4.4. Three colleges, one with tenure and two without, clustered with scores of 6.0, 6.1, and 6.2; and the other two, both without tenure, were grouped at 7.0 and 7.7. In no matched pair was the faculty at the institution without tenure rated more powerful than the faculty at the institution with tenure. By all measures, the pattern, though not perfect, was clear: faculty on campuses without tenure were less powerful than colleagues at comparable colleges with tenure.

The same conclusion can be drawn from an analysis of the adjectives and phrases faculty used to describe the nature of shared governance at their institutions. On the campuses with tenure, 73% of the responses were consistent with the concept of shared governance. The words most often cited included collegial, collaborative, communal, open, participative, and consensual. By contrast, at colleges with contract systems, 63% of the descriptors can be construed as antithetical to shared governance: autocratic, centralized, hierarchical, top-down, nonexistent.

Pronouncements by senior officers about shared governance generally mirrored the faculty members' characterizations. The president of College 8C was most outspoken. "I don't govern. I administer. . . . We don't govern by committee. We use a hierarchical approach. . . . In areas where the faculty have no expertise, we don't ask for their advice." The academic vice president at College 7C declared, "I'm opposed to establishing a faculty senate here. Faculty senates generally serve the best interests of the faculty and not the institution. That's not in the best interest of a small, tuition-driven place like this." And the chairman of the board of trustees at College 6C stated, "I grew up in a small business where you called all the shots. It's not that different here; it's a business."

On campuses where the faculty was more influential, leaders expressed a different point of view. For instance, the dean at College 1T, who had been a faculty member at the institution for nearly thirty years, emphasized "that everyone can make a constructive contribution to the policy-making process. . . . It's important to keep faculty in the loop. . . . We wouldn't want to get away from this model." With a definition of good governance as "civility, respect, and understanding between faculty and administration," the president of College 2T, formerly the provost of a research university, deliberately appointed a new academic dean committed to shared governance. "There has to be faculty involvement in governance," the dean stressed. Upon arrival on campus, "I immediately made the decision that all general education course approvals would go through governance because that's an important purview of the faculty." And the board chair at College 3T, while a businessman, remarked, "I can't overstate the importance of having good relations with people on campus, including the board. We are like distant cousins, but we are family. This is one community. Having this sense of oneness is a real luxury."

From the data—assessments by outside researchers, characterizations of governance by local faculty, and statements by senior officers—an unmistakable pattern starts to emerge. The picture becomes even clearer from comparisons of how major decisions were actually made.

At College 7C, the president instructed the academic vice president to study a reorganization from departments to schools in conjunction with a possible move from college to university status. The vice president discussed the matter with department chairs; but then, as recounted by one professor and corroborated by others, "The administration had a retreat and came back with four schools and the players in place. The faculty was not involved; it was simply announced by the president that we would have schools." In fact, the faculty was informed of the decision, another professor reported, "when an organization chart was left in our mailboxes!"

Prompted by a concern from regional accreditors about the low proportion of full-time faculty, the president of College 8C decided to add four new faculty members and determined which departments would be expanded. As recounted by a department chair, "The president did not follow a formal process. He did not assemble a search committee, and he did not advertise in the *Chronicle*. . . . Instead, he proceeded on his own." Even more notably, the president, without any search, selected a long-time associate, who did not have a doctorate, to be the executive vice president and academic dean. Similarly, at College 6C, the creation of a school of education and the institution of a salary freeze were accomplished respectively with little and no faculty involvement.

Academic decisions on campuses with tenure were handled quite differently. At College 2T, the president, after consultation with the provost and key trustees, broached the possibility of eliminating a one-time "signature" department. The proposal was first discussed extensively by the Curriculum and Academic Programs Committee, which endorsed the move, and then by the whole faculty, which defeated the measure. In the end, the president decided to proceed nonetheless. "It was a painful, contentious, maybe even hurtful decision all along the way. . . . It was handled in a very civil way. . . . We were not heavy-handed. This was not punitive." Because the president was attentive to process, and because other momentous decisions—the addition of graduate programs and the creation of a non-tenure track line for up to 15% of the full-time faculty—were vetted and approved by faculty committees and the faculty as a whole, the aftermath of the program closure was neither bitter nor protracted. Would the president have imposed the non–tenure track had the faculty rejected the idea? "No, but I would have come back to it. But because of my respect for the governance process . . . I wouldn't have fallen on my sword over this issue."

Whereas the president of College 8C single-handedly appointed faculty, the academic dean at College 1T would not implement a new policy of centralized position control unless and until the idea had been entertained by the All Faculty Assembly. "There was a process of persuading the faculty that it was in the best interest of the college to make faculty positions belong to the college," as opposed to individual departments. After reservations were expressed, the model "was approved with minimal dissent." Respect for shared governance also explains a multiyear effort to revise the college's mission statement. "The president," a professor remarked, "spent a great deal of time consensus building with the faculty." "Academic decisions are left to the faculty," another said. "Promotion and tenure is almost entirely a faculty matter," added a third.

In order to achieve consensus, College 3T endured a nearly eight-year process to change the academic calendar from quarters to semesters. Along the way, there were polls of faculty attitudes, a delay to allow the science faculty more time to adjust, appointment of a calendar conversion task force, and a slowdown to permit further consultation. Eventually the measure was adopted, and while some faculty would have preferred a swifter process or a different outcome, the marathon demonstrated to the faculty, a professor stated, that the college "is not really a top-down institution."

These are only a few representative cases from the academic realm. A similar pattern of decision-making occurred in other domains—for instance, facilities. At College 8C, the board chair effectively decided that a new library would be constructed. Faculty had no say in the decision and little input into the design. The faculty at College 1T, by contrast, were sufficiently displeased with an architect's approach to a new academic center that the board agreed to retain a different firm, and "numerous faculty were involved in the process along the way."

The contrast with respect to the faculty's role in campus governance was sharpest between Colleges 1T, 2T, and 3T as a group, and Colleges 6C, 7C, and 8C. Between these two groups the relationship between academic tenure and faculty power was clear. The differences blurred at Colleges 4C and 5T, even though one had contracts and the other had tenure. At both colleges, the faculty were consulted on some issues and ignored on others, invited to provide feedback but then short-circuited as "urgencies" dictated.

Faculty at College 4C participated in an elaborate, nineteen-committee effort to overhaul the curriculum, with every faculty member assigned by the administration to some committee. The faculty perceived their participation as illusory. "We were told, 'This is our goal; you, the faculty, come up with the means to achieve it.' But then the administration created a lot of committees, the topics each would discuss, and the faculty committee assignments. . . . The faculty were basically out of the process . . . and while faculty have some degree of control, administration will always get their way." Because the process bypassed the faculty assembly, the curriculum committee never voted on the extensive reforms now in place. In the words of the provost, "We kept talking to them all along, but we had a pretty clear idea of where we wanted to go."

At College 5T, new programs in the health sciences were "forced" on the faculty by the then dean and never approved by the curriculum committee. The proposal officially lies "tabled." The faculty was consulted on a new library much as administrators conferred with faculty at College 4C: a cumbersome process yielded a sheaf of recommendations five years later; then, the administration decided to move rapidly with no further dialogue. Eighteen months later, a new library opened. Along the way and without faculty input, the president appointed an associate of the board chair to the newly created vice presidency for operations. As for the professors' role in campus governance, a faculty leader commented, "Now you see it, now you don't."

Interpretation

The weight of evidence decidedly supports the proposition that the presence of a tenure system provides a reliable indicator of greater faculty voice in governance. On balance, colleges with tenure exhibited more properties of shared governance, and the faculties there had more sway than colleagues at institutions with contracts. This conclusion echoes the opinion issued by the landmark report by the Commission on Academic Tenure in Higher Education (1973): "The substantive role of administrative officers will increase and that of the faculty will decrease" on campuses with contracts (p. 16).

None of the tenured faculties in this study, however, enjoyed the degree of power or influence associated with the faculty of a research university or a prestigious private college. Any number of organizational analyses of these institutions (e.g., Cohen and March 1974; Birnbaum 1991; Kerr 1991) highlighted the formidable and ingrained tradition of faculty authority and self-regulation. This power often precluded, thwarted, or at the very least confounded centralized initiatives. David Damrosch (1995) observed, "It is remarkable how little influence the administration exerts on the intellectual direction of the typical university . . . basic policy is rarely set from the top" (pp. 58–59). Similarly, Donald Kennedy (1997) allowed that "presidents and governing boards, however influential they may appear, have sharply limited powers. . . . Without faculty support, leadership from the administration building simply does not work. Proper respect for the faculty's prerogatives in the academic domain restricts the zone of possible intervention" (p. 271).

Faculty leaders at research universities frequently make the same point, usually with greater enthusiasm. A university professor, for example, informed a trustee committee, "It's important to understand that I, and each of my tenured colleagues, *is* a strategic plan." When replicated across the faculty, this notion leads to a highly desirable state, from a professorial perspective, where "boards end up approving, after the fact, the continuing and developing mission that lurches up from below" (Nelson 1999, p. B4).

This model, so widespread among research universities and preeminent colleges, does not accurately capture the dynamics at the eight project sites. Faculty at the tenure sites did have more power than colleagues under contracts, but neither approached the level of authority or the degree of self-direction professors have at more distinguished institutions. That faculty power varies, even among institutions with tenure, begs the question whether tenure systems *create* a powerful faculty. Despite the connection established here between academic tenure and faculty authority, we should not assume a causal relationship.

Even within the scope of research limited to just eight institutions, there are contradictory indications. For instance, tenure at College 2T was instituted by a president universally described as a "dictator" with a "kiss-my-ring" style. The advent of tenure did not change that situation. "Everything still came down from on high," recalled a longtime faculty member. Conversely, College 4C abolished tenure in the late 1970s. All four faculty members whom we interviewed did not believe campus governance had changed much as a result. "Tenure makes no difference. People are still outspoken and raise questions." An advocate of tenure acknowledged that its absence was not an impediment to robust debate. "I do not think there would have been any real difference in the outcome, but the process might have been different if we had tenure." And if academic tenure generated faculty power, professors at College 5T would probably not have been so toothless when dramatic changes, such as the incorporation of a high school onto the campus or the introduction of new degree programs, were imposed by management. Finally, based on a previous study (Chait and Trower 1997) of Hampshire and Evergreen, institutions without tenure, we would maintain that faculty on those two campuses enjoy greater autonomy than peers at any of the four sites with tenure in the current study.

Other considerations, less mutually exclusive choices than multiple explanations, lead to more complex and subtler interpretations of the roots of faculty power. First, prior research has related the degree of faculty authority to certain institutional traits. J. Victor Baldridge (1971) determined that faculty autonomy was linked to size. "The faculty in large institutions are much more likely to develop a strong faculty government. Those in smaller institutions . . . are more often subject to decrees of administrative officials. In the latter, it is likely that the 'role' of the faculty government would be restricted to that of a body within which information is disseminated" (p. 65). At larger institutions, faculty are more apt to have specialized functions and expertise, and decisions are more likely to occur within departments than centrally. "Results suggest that while the independence of the faculty in larger universities is never complete, it is considerable indeed. . . . This is in contrast to the corporate structures characteristic of small colleges" (p. 69).

Burton Clark (1993) tied faculty power to institutional prestige. "To sum the story on authority: at the top of the institutional hierarchy, faculty influence is well and strong . . . ; departments and professional schools are strong, semi-autonomous units; and all-campus faculty bodies have dominant influence in personnel and curricular decisions. . . . As we descend the hierarchy . . . faculty authority weakens and managerialism increases" (p. 170). Congruent with Clark's thesis, of the seven project sites rated by Barron's (2000), four were classified in the fourth lowest of six tiers of prestige, two in the third tier, and one in the fifth.

Large-scale observations about the effects of size and prestige on shared governance illuminate why the presence of a tenure system, taken alone, offers few clues about the extent of faculty power. Data that compare the four colleges with tenure with the four without are more instructive because even though these institutions were selected to minimize disparities on key variables, other distinctions surfaced that partially explain the differences between the two groups with respect to faculty authority.

The contract colleges had, on average, tuition levels (a common yardstick for prestige) 25%, or about $3,000, less than the tenure sites. In three of the four matched pairs, the contract sites had lower tuition; in the fourth (and anomalous) case the differential was only 9%.

The most noteworthy differences, however, concerned faculty credentials. Among the eight sites, the three institutions having the lowest percentage of full-time faculty with doctorates were campuses with contracts: 21% at College 6C, 29% at College 8C, and 33% at College 4C. Conversely, at the four colleges with tenure, the percentage of doctorally qualified faculty ranged from 61% to 68%. In two of the four pairs, the campus with tenure had more than twice as many faculty with doctorates, and in a third case nearly double the number. (The one exception is College 7C, where 73% of the faculty hold doctoral degrees versus 65% at College 5T.) The four institutions with tenure had a far greater percentage of faculty with doctorates from members of the Association of American Universities (AAU)—from 44% to 32%, versus 18% to 5% at the contract sites. In no instance did the college with contracts have more faculty with AAU doctorates than the matched site with tenure, nor was there any case where the contract site faculty earned more money.

Why are these numbers important? First, numerous studies (e.g., Van Mannen 1976; Feldman 1981; Tierney and Bensimon 1996) have revealed the importance of socialization, the process by which newcomers learn the values and behaviors necessary to be effective participants in an organization. More particularly, graduate school entails "anticipatory socialization—all the learning that occurs before a new member joins an organization" (Trower 1997, p. 68). As doctoral candidates, prospective faculty learn, usually by acculturation, the normative values of the academy and form expectations about academic life based on that experience. The more a college hires teachers imbued with these values, the more likely faculty will manifest the associated attitudes and behaviors.

Second, faculty with doctorates (especially from AAU institutions), compared to faculty without terminal degrees, tend to be more "cosmopolitan" than "local." The former are "low on loyalty to the employing organization . . . and likely to use outer reference group orientation," whereas the latter are "high on loyalty to the employing organization . . . and likely to use an inner reference group orientation" (Gouldner 1957, p. 290). "Cosmopolitan" faculty typically attend more disciplinary conferences and interact more with colleagues at other institutions. With a better informed sense of the larger academic context, they are more attuned than "locals" to professional and disciplinary norms as a standard of reference, and so are predisposed to assume, expect, and act as though the faculty will have a pivotal role in campus governance. A faculty member's expectations and actions with respect to governance, therefore, will be affected as much or more by socialization and by reference group orientation as by the presence or absence of a tenure system.

In terms of financial solvency, the more dire a college's straits, the more probable the president will assert control. Jeffrey Pfeffer (1981) determined that tight resources intensify the use of power because interdependence and scarcity increase; this produces conflict, which in turn foments the exercise of power. Financial exigencies raise the stakes, shorten the time lines, and render consultation and consensus unaffordable luxuries in the midst of disruptive change (Kotter and Schlesinger 1977). Such circumstances are conducive to "war time powers," a greater tolerance of "high-handed administration" (Walker 1979, p. 19), and the emergence of the heroic leader. If and when the hero succeeds, values become beliefs and ultimately assumptions that have "worked well enough to be considered valid" are therefore "taught to new members as the correct way to perceive, think, and feel in relation to (organizational) problems (Schein 1985, p. 9).

College 1T has "almost always been in black ink" and has experienced "few financial difficulties." One notch down the scale, at College 2T, a seasoned faculty member reflected on the democratic style of the new president: "We had a benevolent dictator, an entrepreneurial leader who was in a struggle for survival. But his style saved the college. His dictatorship serves this place well. I'm not sure it's *not* the right model for a small college." The chairman of the board at College 3T, where the new president has embraced openness and consensus, noted that "if the college were in financial trouble, it might be a different situation."

Most significantly, four of the five colleges with the least powerful faculties (4C, 5T, 7C, and 8C) weathered severe financial crises (as did College 2T). In every case, save College 4C, the incumbent president played the role of hero, moving the institution from the brink of bankruptcy to financial equilibrium. Faculty members spoke of these presidents with unusual but genuine awe. "He has such incredible insight. He's the reason we're in such a fabulous financial position." "The college was going bankrupt twelve to thirteen years ago. . . . The president turned the whole school around." "We had a $3 million deficit, and the president erased that in three years and gave the faculty 5% bonuses."

"Whatever the president wants, the president gets. . . . He turned this institution around." And therein hangs much of the tale: "When an organization is threatened with survival . . . its influencers tend to defer to its leader to set things right. . . . The choice open to insiders is essentially one of loyalty or exit, not voice. There is room for the building of only one empire in this configuration, that of the chief executive. Insurgency games are risky—challenges to the CEO's power are quickly snuffed out" (Mintzberg 1983, p. 357).

The average tenure of the three "heroes" still on campus exceeds twenty years. Each wields enormous power. At the contract sites, the president's tenure averaged seventeen years, with none fewer than eight years—versus an average of seven and a half years at the colleges with tenure. Over time, presidents can accumulate power when they are viewed on campus as saviors and experts, when they are positioned to control rewards and sanctions, and when they are situated to screen and select new members of the community (Bensimon, Neumann, and Birnbaum 1989).

This leads to an important, indirectly related, observation. Widely cited literature on colleges and universities (Kerr 1984, 1986; Kennedy 1997; Damrosch 1995) instills the impression that campus presidents have severely limited and often insufficient power. Presidents "may not be able to make dramatic changes in their institutions most of the time" (Birnbaum 1991, p. 202). The most popular metaphor equated presidential power with the degree of control exerted by the driver of a car skidding on ice (Cohen and March 1974, p. 203).

However valid these assertions are for universities and selective colleges, they hardly applied to the eight institutions we studied. Presidents mattered a lot. They established priorities, made decisions, promulgated rules, dispensed rewards, and frequently saved the day. The longer and greater the president's success, the more likely power and authority were centralized, regardless of faculty employment arrangements. Moreover, across all eight colleges, the president also set the general tone and the specific ground rules for campus governance. A change in presidents, therefore, would probably do more than a change in employment arrangements to affect the balance of power between the faculty and the administration. At College 2T, for example, where a collaborative president followed an "imperious and capricious" leader, "most faculty seem to be marching toward feeling more empowered."

Any analysis of faculty power must take into account organizational stability as well as the president's performance record, political philosophy, and length of service.

Based on the evidence, we cannot conclude that the mere presence or absence of a tenure system entirely, or even chiefly, explains the relative degree of faculty power. Institutional size, status, and finances; faculty credentials; and presidential aura seem to have a more profound effect. The proposition becomes somewhat circular because with very few exceptions (like Hampshire and Evergreen) the lack of a tenure system invariably corresponds to limited institutional prestige, financial strength, and market draw; to a modestly credentialed faculty;[3] and to broad presidential prerogatives. Thus, without any other information except whether an institution offers tenure, one can far more accurately characterize a college without tenure than one with tenure.

We will never know definitively what difference tenure would make in terms of faculty authority on campuses with contracts. However, we did ask the question of 49 individuals at contract colleges. Nearly half (49%) replied that tenure would make no difference, 6% indicated that tenure would make a difference, 18% were ambivalent, and 26% offered no opinion. Among the 24 respondents doubtful that the adoption of tenure would change the political dynamics on campus, the most frequently cited reasons were that the faculty already have de facto tenure, that academic freedom has not been an issue, and that the administration supports open debate and usually acts in the best interests of the institution. In a comment typical of the near majority, a professor at College 1T stated, "Here tenure seems to be more cosmetic. There's nothing you can't do without tenure. Faculty tenure doesn't really affect faculty governance."

The answer to the question that animated this study can be encapsulated as follows: Tenure is systematically associated with a greater faculty voice in governance, but a causal relationship should not be inferred.

Tenure and Faculty Interest in Governance

Across the project sites, we found that the vast majority of faculty members had little interest in governance and modest expectations about participation or results. With incremental differences across the sites, faculty demonstrated little interest in or appetite for shared governance, especially the formal mechanisms for participation. Faculty members at Colleges 1T and 2T, and to a lesser extent 3T, expressed greater expectations of involvement, and more displeasure when bypassed, than colleagues at Colleges 4–8; however, overall the faculties had no discernible dedication to campus governance. What was noticeably absent? Passion.

Absent, too, was controversy. There was an almost eerie quietude on the campuses. Almost all faculty described "marker events" without intensity or rancor. No proposals—from a presidential inquiry about the adoption of a tenure system, to the addition of new programs, to preemptive faculty and staff appointments—galvanized the faculty. When asked what might constitute a 4, let alone a 10, on the Richter scale, a professor at College 6C replied, "I've often wondered about that. Things don't cause an uproar here." Even that institution's salary freeze produced barely a murmur.

Absent from campus governance were large numbers of faculty members, even on the three campuses where attendance at faculty meetings was technically mandatory. Turnout was no better at Colleges 1T and 2T. "At our last meeting," the president of the faculty association at College 2T indicated, "we had 30 of 56 faculty in attendance." Likewise, at College 1T, a professor lamented that "attendance at faculty meetings is down. Recently we failed to make an important decision because we lacked a quorum. It's not the fault of the administration." A professor at College 6C admitted, "Most faculty don't take an interest in governance." The academic vice president at College 4C offered a similar assessment. "At other campuses where I have worked, faculty have been much more proactive in governance. Here it's not a big issue for most faculty, even in the face of major change." The dean at College 2T sounded the same note. "Some faculty want a steady paycheck and want to be left alone. They think governance should be left to the administration." "Passive" was the most frequently invoked word to describe the faculty's stance toward governance.

Why were faculty on these campuses mostly unresponsive to a tradition and principle so integral to academic life elsewhere? The answer does not rest with faculty governance structures. None of the eight sites had a faculty senate, and none seemed inclined to establish one. The president of College 4C dismantled that institution's senate. The seven other institutions have a faculty organization, variously called "forum," "assembly," "council," or "association," that includes the entire faculty. Their agendas were often bland, dominated by management, and sprinkled with complaints from faculty. "I don't feel powerless at all," said the president of College 5T; "I can control the agenda at the faculty assembly." Colleges 1T and 2T, which, along with College 3T, have nonvoting representatives to the board of trustees, officially recognize the faculty organization respectively as "primarily responsible for academic governance" and as the "voice of the faculty . . . on matters related to academic life and faculty welfare." Yet professors there were only marginally less cynical about what can be accomplished by these bodies. On the other campuses, the roles of faculty organizations were either unspecified or innocuous. The Faculty Forum at College 6C, for example, "exists to identify and address issues and concerns of importance to the faculty, to develop recommendations . . . and to facilitate communication."

Faculty apathy toward shared governance can best be explained by three reasons: faculty futility, confidence in the president, and campus climate. These reasons do not pertain equally to each college or to every professor on a particular campus. When considered together, however, the faculty's posture toward campus governance becomes more understandable.

Faculty Futility

At Colleges 4 through 8, most faculty members believed that the president and, by extension, the administration had most or all of the power. That every major, and most minor, decisions would be made by the president, either preemptively or eventually, was a foregone conclusion. All agreed that power was concentrated at the top. A professor at College 4C believed, "Any and all administrators have more power than any faculty member does." A faculty member described College 8C as a "benevolent patriarchy"; another depicted College 7C as "a private little world the president runs here. . . . What he says goes." At College 5T, one faculty member described governance as "highly centralized with the president at the center," and another portrayed the president as "a person who knows what she wants . . . and gets what she wants . . . because everybody does what she says."

Most professors (College 1T excepted) ascribed little or no power to the faculty. At College 8C the faculty, one professor reckoned, "has very little real power here, the final decisions on everything are made by the president." At College 7C, "no one on the faculty has power." The chair of the faculty assembly at College 6C stated, "We have no perception of power, although our influence has increased. We're heard and we're provided feedback . . . but we still don't have any power." Even at College 2C, the president of the faculty association reported that "we're only reactionary, we don't propose anything. The strong questions, whether about resource allocation, program development, admissions, and student life, they're all reactionary."

Faculty committees were also widely regarded as "passive," "inactive," "very weak and not helpful," and "weak and no one really wants it to change." "The Budget Committee goes and listens to the administration . . . but really contributes nothing. It's an audience, not a committee." "Why bother discussing something on which we have no impact, like the budget?" (By contrast, at College 1T an AAUP chapter representative participates in budget meetings.) This assessment was hardly limited to campuses with contracts. At College 3T a tenured associate professor said, "While the faculty is supposed to be advisory on admissions, we play no real role in the process. In fact, we play no formal role even in curriculum." In more than 80 interviews, on only 9 occasions was a member of the faculty, a faculty committee or association, or the faculty generally cited as one of "the three most powerful people" on campus, and in all nine instances the nomination was from an administrator.

Under these circumstances, resignation and withdrawal are to be expected. As a newly arrived senior administrator at College 7C related, "The old-timers [on the faculty] say, 'You can try to change things, but you can't.' There's nothing we can do, so we throw our hands up and say, 'I can't influence anything here, so I'll go along.'" Pfeffer (1981) theorized that political activity increases as power and control are diffused. "When power is highly concentrated, the other participants in the system have little ability or motivation to engage in a contest for control. . . . There will be little political activity observed. Power will be used to make the choice, but it will be the power of central authorities" (pp. 87, 96). In other words, "Why fight city hall?" or, in this case, "Why fight the president's office?" Faculty decided that participation in campus governance was "useless" and that faculty meetings were "a waste of time, a fait accompli." Better "to meet as little as possible because it doesn't matter." The most colorful explanation was offered by a humanities professor at College 2T: "Why take governance seriously? I think of faculty governance in the same way they used to do Boys Town in the governor's office for a day—you know, where the governor invites the orphans to the capital. 'C'mon, Johnny, do you want to sit in the governor's chair?' Or 'Jimmy, you can be this cabinet secretary today.' . . . The faculty association is not useful at all. When the powers want something, the powers get it."

Inertia was commonplace. At College 4C, the president dissolved the faculty senate with little resistance. Efforts to establish an AAUP chapter at College 7C "went nowhere," as did an attempt to start a faculty union. "We said, 'Go ahead,'" the president recalled. "Only one person showed up for the meeting." Not until the regional accreditation association raised questions about the informal, annual appointment process at College 6C did the faculty address the issue, and even then the administration ultimately decided the outcome: three-year contracts that many professors misconstrued to be "rolling contracts." In short, the perception of autocracy fueled a sense of futility among the faculty. Nearly all assumed that the basic dynamics of campus governance would not change, and some preferred it that way.

Confidence in the President

Many faculty members remained on the sidelines because they had confidence in the president's integrity and/or competence. Their confidence was predicated primarily on trust, a conviction that the president made decisions "for the greater good" and without favoritism. At College 3T, faculty had a "very high degree of trust in the president. Without it, outcomes would be different, worse." With a relatively new president wedded to collegiality, faculty were less concerned about power and structure. In fact, the president's "willingness to share decisions" was cited as "a source of authority." "There is no real governance," one said, "just administration and collegial faculty." As an associate professor observed, "Things work well here because of collegiality and goodwill. The structures are not very effective, but goodwill and collegiality compensate for this."

Even at the more hierarchical institutions, there was trust. The president at College 7C, for example, was "not retaliatory," one professor believed, and thus "faculty here feel reasonably safe speaking out." A colleague described administrators as "decent people." At College 8C, the president was described by a professor as a "throwback to the Middle Ages. He believes in fealty. 'You work very hard for the college,' he says, 'and we'll keep up our end of the bargain.'"

Where good faith prevailed between faculty and administrators, many professors preferred personal relationships and informal networks, which could be readily established and easily sustained, to bureaucratic arrangements and formal channels. At small colleges of this ilk professors were at least as disposed to seek solutions through one-on-one conversations with trustworthy decision-makers as through campus governance or petitions and resolutions. Hallways and offices were more apt to be the venues for negotiations and conflict resolution than the faculty assembly. Prescribed procedures mattered less because individual faculty members had direct access to senior management to request resources or to resolve problems. In effect, faculty trusted more to free agency than to collective action. "You can see the president tomorrow if you have to, about anything," said a professor at College 6C. Another confirmed that some faculty will "march into the president's office or go to the academic dean. They feel very comfortable going right to them with requests." At College 4C, a chair said, "There is always a door open somewhere that you can walk into and make a point if it is important."

The "family," not the "organized anarchy" (Cohen and March 1974), was the operative metaphor. Differences among the institutions concerned the degree and benevolence of parental control, not the basic model. No matter how hierarchical the organization, the president and other senior officers were also accessible. The bureaucracy was at once entrenched and penetrable.

The faculty's confidence was also inspired by a perception that the president was a proficient administrator. As previously discussed, three presidents were heroic turnaround artists. These stories, over time, became "sagas" (Clark 1972), "a collective understanding of unique accomplishment" (p. 178) transmitted passionately from old-timers to newcomers in ways that "capture allegiance" (Clark 1970, p. 235). Consequently, the faculty accorded these presidents great deference. As Baldridge and his colleagues noted, "The hero's job is to assess problems, propose alternatives, and make rational choices. Much of the organization's power is held by the hero. Great expectations are raised because people trust the hero to solve their problems and to fend off threats from the environment" (Baldridge et al. 1977, p. 21).

Presidents did not need to take legendary action to gain esteem, admiration, and a nearly free rein. Instead, the litmus test for many faculty was whether or not the administration had a "favorable balance sheet" over time. The president and dean at College 6C "make excellent and positive decisions," a faculty member explained, "so we let them." Because the president of College 4C effectively implemented "a planning model that could bring about institutional change," the faculty accepted an administratively redesigned curriculum. And after the president of College 2T established a strong track record and overruled the faculty association on a program closure, the dispute was "quickly forgotten . . . because the administration has made so many decisions that benefit the faculty."

Whether from firsthand experience or secondhand accounts repeated by "tribal elders," faculty at financially imperiled institutions realized that, as one put it, "If we're wrong, we could lose our jobs." Faculty members recognized a direct connection between presidential performance and professorial paychecks. In addition, more than a few questioned whether the faculty *could* make difficult decisions because they "are too close" to the issue, or doubted that the faculty could make wiser decisions because "no one really had a better idea." A participatory process that involved faculty governance was no guarantee of "good decisions," nor was "everything that comes out of an autocracy bad." In one statement or another, many faculty, especially at contract institutions, indicated that the stakes were too high, the needs too vital, and markets too cruel to rely on the protracted, insular, and—for some—amateurish qualities of shared governance. These attitudes prevailed when certain circumstances existed: when prior events suggested that leaders were more than equal to the tasks at hand; when faculty were not socialized to expect meaningful participation; and when the institutional environment reinforced the notion that faculty should teach and administrators should manage.

Campus Climate

A presidential directive that all faculty and staff shall wear name tags. Monitored attendance at faculty meetings with excused and unexcused absences. A one-for-one exchange of the current faculty handbook for

previous editions, allegedly to make comparisons difficult. Recollec-
tions of days when the prior president walked the halls to see whether
any faculty members dared to smoke in class. These tales do not have
the ring of a traditional college, yet all actually occurred at the study
sites, the first three at colleges with contracts. Several professors at
Colleges 6C, 7C, and 8C explicitly stated, and others implied, that
"faculty here are treated like high school faculty, not as true professionals." As one said, "It doesn't feel like a 'real' college. We have no accou-
trements of professionalism."

Small wonder that at Colleges 4C, 5T, 6C, 7C, and 8C, and to a
lesser degree at Colleges 2T and 3T, the majority of the faculty had little expectation of participation in governance or a sense that such activity (any more than scholarly research) was a hallmark trait of a faculty
member. "Power is a strange word to me; I don't associate it with faculty members," commented one professor. A faculty member at College 2T stated matter-of-factly, "I'm not interested in power"; and a
peer at College 8C stated, "I'd just as soon not worry about institutional governance." However, both added the same contingency: as
long as I have autonomy in the classroom. This was the Maginot Line
for nearly all faculty, and the boundary that some drew to separate college faculty from high school teachers, who usually have lifetime tenure but rarely have sovereignty in the classroom.

The faculty's lack of concern for governance can be attributed in part
to self-selection. Faculty members uninterested in scholarly research
or shared governance, but eager to teach at the college level, gravitated
toward institutions where faculty power was muted. Two faculty members at College 7C, for instance, sounded a common refrain. The first
stated that "some [colleagues] are not even aware of what a faculty
could do. Many previously taught in a high school, and that's their basis
for comparison." The other observed, "We don't have a lot of Ph.D.s
. . . so the commitment is different. . . . There's a different demeanor.
We don't bring in many people from outside of our sphere. . . . They
bring a feeling of being a 'professor' that comes with being a Ph.D." At
College 8C, a new assistant professor, previously employed for ten
years at a two-year college where "the president was even more dicta-
torial," stated unabashedly that "we hire people who are barely qualified, less than a Ph.D. If you don't rock the boat here, you can be pretty
secure. Otherwise, it's back to the community college."

As the last comment implies, climate can also be shaped by institutional choices about recruitment. This was widely suspected to be the case by faculty members at College 8C, although not elsewhere. "They don't hire boat rockers," confided a longtime professor. "There is a weeding out at the hiring stage of anyone who would challenge the administration. . . . The president is careful to select the plain vanilla candidate," confirmed another. In a very few instances, faculty on other campuses alleged that outspoken critics of the administration were not reappointed occasionally in retaliation and to set an example.

With a mind-set and an operational definition of "faculty member" that departed from the national norm, several faculty members, at the extreme, rejected the concept of shared governance altogether. "In the end, it's not my responsibility," declared an associate professor at College 8C. A professor at College 7C asserted that "the faculty wants more say in governance, but it's not willing to take the responsibility, so the administration is left to do it. . . . The faculty complain, but they really don't want to do it." A colleague echoed this sentiment: "Part of the blame rests with the faculty. We think there's no reason to put ourselves in jeopardy."

At the other end of the range, faculty and administrators at Colleges 1T, 2T, and 3T had a more customary professional self-image. At College 1T, the dean commented that "most faculty consider themselves part of the policy-making process. . . . It's important to keep the faculty in the loop. . . . [W]e wouldn't want to get away from this model." The president agreed: "We have lots of consensus-making. This is important." Thus, the president of College 1T meets twice a year over lunch with the officers of the AAUP chapter, and the board of trustees now has a faculty representative. Underneath these actions was an attitude captured by a professor on campus since the late 1960s: "The faculty don't like to be left out of decisions." The president of College 2T noted that "curriculum is the right of the faculty" as are "the promotion and tenure process, faculty leaves, and matters stipulated in the handbook. All go through the governance process."

The faculty at these three institutions were often skeptical about the degree of faculty influence and about whether consultation by the administration and the board was not more often ceremonial than substantive. Here too, there were governance dropouts, although not as many. When contrasted to the other sites, professors at Colleges 1T,

2T, and 3T assumed some degree of involvement and resented exclusion from the decision-making process. The extent of involvement may not always have satisfied the preferences of the faculty, but the principle was never in doubt. On the other campuses, there was far less awareness that anything was amiss. "We're comfortable with autocracy," a faculty member at College 7C admitted. Therefore, faculty at that institution agreed to wear name tags. "The faculty attitude was mostly 'Why make a big deal out of this?' I could get away without wearing my name tag, but why bother? Why make a point of this?" Remembering the lean years, the professor sighed, "This was a headache, but it doesn't matter if you have appendicitis."

To summarize, a sense of futility, an air of informality, a mix of trust and confidence in the administration, and a degree of diffidence combined to curb interest in campus governance among most faculty members at all eight sites, and to a greater degree at Colleges 4–8. Most faculty were indifferent or oblivious to shared governance, especially the farther removed issues were from the classroom or the curriculum.

Governance and Work Satisfaction

Despite their limited role in campus governance, the vast majority of faculty members, both on campuses with tenure and campuses without tenure, reported that they were quite satisfied at work. Across all eight sites, with or without tenure, whatever the distribution of power, faculty members expressed generally high levels of work satisfaction. From College 6C: "This place is a little slice of heaven, and I'm happy to be here." From College 3T: "This place is mostly positive compared to where I have been." From College 7C: "This is a good place to work." From College 2T: "It is civil, pleasant, cooperative, more than any other place I've worked." Even a recent transplant from a tenured position at a regional university described the faculty at College 8C as "ten times happier. That was one reason I came here." No one painted a negative picture, and no one mentioned a desire to leave. In fact, one professor stayed at College 6C for "the same money now that I made at [a land-grant university] in 1980, but I've never been sorry about being here. I could go to [another land-grant university]; they've tried to steal me for twice the salary. But here there's the . . . relating to students that's worth so much more than money."

The contentment and allegiance of faculty members at colleges with contracts may baffle advocates of tenure quick to catalogue the purported drawbacks of contract systems. The Commission on Academic Tenure in Higher Education (1974) conjectured that "prolonged exposure to the uncertainties of contract renewal and all that goes with it seems likely to have damaging effects on faculty morale" (p. 17). More dramatically, Matthew Finkin, Professor of Law at the University of Illinois and a prominent AAUP advocate, equated contract systems with "indentured servitude."[4] Data from the current study challenge these assertions and confirm earlier research (Chait and Trower 1997) at five other colleges, two with contract systems and three "hybrids" with both tenure and contracts: "Across the sites, faculty reaction to the contract system was largely positive" and faculty satisfaction was quite high (p. 13). Data from both studies parallel a 1999 TIAA-CREF survey (Sanderson et al.) of 1,411 faculty members at two- and four-year colleges, which reported that the highest proportion of "very satisfied" faculty (53.9%) were on campuses without a tenure system" (p. 16).

What explains the relatively comparable levels of faculty satisfaction across the eight campuses? The vast majority of the faculty at all eight sites described work conditions that included a reasonable measure of economic security, untrammeled academic freedom in the classroom, an attractive portfolio of responsibilities, and a comfortable environment. These attributes, taken together, fostered work satisfaction.

The sense of economic security stemmed from a simple fact: few faculty, whether on tenure or contracts, have ever been dismissed at any of these institutions save the University of Charleston, where 16 professors, 8 tenured, were terminated in the late 1970s due to financial exigency. At College 6C, a department chair explained, "In a sense, the faculty here *are* tenured. In twenty years, maybe 5 have been let go. . . . If you get poor student evaluations you are given continuing opportunities to improve." The chair of the trustees' academic affairs committee confirmed that "anybody who's been here a few years is secure except for financial reasons." At College 7C, the academic vice president estimated the rate of nonrenewal to be "less than 1% annually." The president of College 8C mentioned a tacit covenant with the faculty about dismissals. "You just can't do that in a small institution. Morale would go lower than a snake's belly overnight. We had to jettison two programs. We retrained faculty instead of letting them go. We can't operate any other way." A faculty member affirmed this: "There's a lot of longevity here. . . . Once people get here, typically they don't leave." These comments were from three sites without tenure and without robust systems of shared governance; faculty on the other campuses felt every bit as secure in terms of employment.

The second element of faculty work satisfaction was academic freedom in the classroom. (Since very few faculty were engaged in research, that aspect of academic freedom did not surface.) The matter was raised everywhere, though far more often at colleges with contracts, probably because faculty there could accept the absence of tenure *if* academic freedom for teachers was otherwise assured. The compact on the contract campuses was straightforward: as long as faculty had unabridged academic freedom in the classroom, professors would tolerate administrative authority nearly everywhere else. The "bargain" was described by a professor at College 8C. "We've got a handshake deal. Part of the deal is that we're left alone in the classroom. . . . I get autonomy in my classroom in exchange for letting the administration run the college." The president corroborated the "deal": "I have to leave faculty the broadest freedom to teach what they want to teach. We have no control over what's going on in the classroom." When asked whether it was possible to work happily in a self-described "top-down autocracy," a professor at College 4C answered, "Yes, because we have control over what's going on in the classroom." The sentiment did not differ at institutions with tenure. "I'm not interested in power," declared a professor at College 2T. "All I'm worried about is that I have the freedom here in my classroom and my office. That's all that matters." Noteworthy in this context, the one major faculty rebuff to presidential resolve at any of the colleges with modestly empowered faculties concerned the refusal of the faculty at College 5T to add a religion course to the core curriculum. As one faculty member declared, "That's our domain."

Faculty at the eight colleges reported no infringements on academic freedom in the classroom. (College 8C did ban some "offensive" music from the campus radio station and frontal nudity in a student play.) However, we found a significant disparity. By a wide margin, professors on contract campuses were more apprehensive about whether faculty members were free to openly denounce the president and senior management without reprisal. There was an "element of fear" and a "fear of authority" that chastened would-be critics of the president. Academic freedom, faculty suggested, was markedly greater to teach students than to criticize the administration.

While this concern may have detracted from work satisfaction, the trade-off for most faculty was an agreeable assignment in a comfortable environment. Simply stated, faculty wanted to teach, preferably only or mostly undergraduates, and they wanted to do so insulated from any pressure to do research and publish the results. Across the sites, life on the fast track (and, for many, life on the tenure track) offered little appeal. "We have no requirement for scholarly work and publications; that's a great relief," said a faculty member at College 8C. "We don't want to do research. We're free of that," commented another. The expectations at College 7C were the same. "You don't have to worry about publish or perish. If you're a good teacher and are involved in community service, you're fine." The professors wanted to teach, the colleges wanted teachers, and the administration never interfered in the classroom. If that equilibrium was maintained at the expense of greater faculty involvement in governance, most professors resolved, "so be it."

While not as important as work content, work environment mattered deeply. Consistent with the TIAA-CREF survey (Sanderson et al. 1999), faculty in the current study valued highly time for family and personal needs (p. 28). However, the most cherished facet of the work environment was the cohesion and sense of community that epitomized all eight faculties. A chairperson characterized College 6C as a "loving, caring, warm environment." The president of the faculty association described College 2T as "civil, pleasant, cooperative, more than any other place I've worked." College 3T "is so collegial, and everyone gets along so well." Elsewhere, the "comfortable" atmosphere was distinguished by longtime friendships, volunteerism, and selflessness. There was no "cutthroat competition" or "academic one-upmanship," which faculty associated with life at research universities. "On most days, most people like each other," observed a professor at College 8C. "It's not unusual for 30 or 40 people here to go out together. How often does that happen where you work? I'll bet not too often because people are too competitive . . . trying to outpublish everyone else."

As foreshadowed in the discussion of trust, the presidents reinforced the concept of "family." All eight, however heavy-handed as managers, were typically regarded as "benevolent" individuals. There were numerous stories of kind touches, generous deeds, and "behind-the-scenes compassion."

The essential paradox was stated succinctly by a faculty leader at College 6C: "The faculty and staff here are powerless, yet this [is] the greatest place to work." Why is that the case? The chair of the curriculum committee at College 2T answered incisively, "Because the majority of the faculty don't give a damn [about governance] as long as their needs are attended to."

Three overarching conclusions, or defensible propositions, can be distilled from this study.

1. Tenure was a reliable, but not infallible, indicator of greater faculty voice and slightly greater faculty interest in campus governance. It is far more likely, however, that tenure signaled rather than created these conditions. The *absence* of tenure suggested a comparatively vulnerable college where faculty have relatively limited authority or interest in shared governance. The circumstances associated with an exclusive reliance on employment contracts—financial instability, modestly credentialed faculty, pronounced market dependency, and incomplete socialization to dominant professional norms— better explained the distribution of power and authority than did the faculty's employment arrangements. Contracts were a symptom, not a cause. The lack of faculty involvement (and the lack of tenure) was much more about economic imperatives than principles of governance.

2. The absence of shared governance was not a reliable indicator of work dissatisfaction. There were not material differences in faculty satisfaction as a function of involvement in campus governance.[5] The opportunity to educate students and to enjoy the quality of life were the coins of the realm for faculty at these institutions. Power and prestige were not. Free to teach students and interact with congenial colleagues, faculty by and large were satisfied. Because participation in governance was neither a

strong expectation nor an acute desire, limited involvement produced little discontent.

3. Contrary to numerous studies and commentaries on research universities, the presidents of these eight colleges were powerful individuals, exemplars of the personalized presidency. The president's attitudes and actions significantly shaped the contours of campus governance. Acknowledged as forceful leaders on all of the campuses and revered as heroes at some, the presidents were typically portrayed favorably as benevolent, well-intentioned, and approachable on professional or personal matters, even where faculty were loath to be openly critical of the president's decisions.

The eight colleges that comprised this study, and several hundred of the same species, constitute an important stream, if not the mainstream, of American higher education. At the very least, we are reminded that the predominant model of shared governance is not the only, or necessarily the most appropriate, model for the nearly 3,700 colleges and universities nationwide. Some colleges operate and endure with quite different assumptions about campus governance, yet still offer a work environment faculty deem attractive. For this segment of the academy, the following implications may prove relevant.

Successful efforts to strengthen an institution's financial condition and academic profile will probably increase the authority of the faculty and decrease the power of the administration. Campus executives and boards of trustees should understand the connection between these variables, and the ramifications. Administrators and fiduciaries wedded to a top-down model of management may be surprised (and disappointed) by the price of "success."

Neither the advent nor the abolition of academic tenure alone will have a profound effect on the distribution of power on campus. Policy changes with this purpose in mind are likely to be fruitless. The prudent course may be to avoid such potentially inflammatory discussions in the first place.

Administrators in search of power should seek senior positions at small, comparatively impoverished colleges. The president's authority may be inversely related to the institution's financial stability and perceived academic quality.

Collegiality and shared governance are not inextricably linked. Faculty in search of the former need not eliminate from consideration institutions that lack the latter.

Notes

Holly Madsen, William Mallon, Cheryl Sternman Rule, Cathy Trower, and John Urice participated in the site visits along with me, and offered incisive insights. Dr. Trower also contributed invaluably to the analysis of the data and to the substance of the chapter. Frances Shavers was an able research assistant.

1. Kendall's coefficient of concordance is a measure of interrater reliability especially appropriate when the sample size is small and when raters cannot apply objective criteria.

2. We pledged that no quotes would be directly attributed and no institution's ranks would be publicly revealed. Therefore, sites are referred to by the number that corresponds to the institution's rank: 1 for the college with the most powerful faculty through 8 for the college with the least powerful faculty. Each numbered ranking is followed by a T (indicating a tenure-granting site) or a C (for a site that awards contracts).

3. As described in Chapter 8, institutions sometimes adopt tenure precisely to counter the image of their being a have-not college.

4. Unpublished remarks from a panel discussion at the annual conference of the National Center for the Study of Collective Bargaining in Higher Education, City University of New York, Baruch College, April 15, 1997.

5. Austin et al. (1991) reached the opposite conclusion: "Faculty at 'high morale' colleges perceive the decision-making climate to be more participatory than do their colleagues at colleges with relatively low morale" (p. 14). Both the Austin and the present study, however, associated faculty satisfaction with "strong leadership" and an atmosphere of trust, respect, and accessibility (pp. 15–16).

References

Austin, Ann E., R. Eugene Rice, Allen P. Splete, et al. 1991. *A Good Place to Work.* Washington, D.C.: Council of Independent Colleges.

Baldridge, J. Victor. 1971. *Academic Governance: Research on Institutional Politics and Decision-Making.* Berkeley, Calif.: McCutchan.

Baldridge, J. Victor, David V. Curtis, George P. Ecker, and Gary L. Riley. 1977. "Alternative Models of Governance in Higher Education." In Gary L. Riley and J. Victor Baldridge, eds., *Governing Academic Organizations.* Berkeley, Calif.: McCutchan.

Barron's Profiles of American Colleges. 2000 ed. Hauppauge, N.Y.: Barron's Educational Series.

Bensimon, Estela, Anna Neumann, and Robert Birnbaum. 1989. *Making Sense of Administrative Leadership.* Washington, D.C.: George Washington University.

Birnbaum, Robert. 1991. *How Colleges Work: The Cybernetics of Academic Organization and Leadership.* San Francisco: Jossey-Bass.

Chait, Richard, and Cathy A. Trower. 1997. *Where Tenure Does Not Reign: Colleges with Contract Systems.* AAHE New Pathways Working Paper Series, no. 3. Washington, D.C.: American Association for Higher Education.

Clark, Burton R. 1970. *The Distinctive College.* Chicago: Aldine.

——— 1972. "The Organizational Saga in Higher Education." *Administrative Science Quarterly,* 17 (2): 178–184.

——— 1993. "Faculty Differentiation and Dispersion." In A. Levine, ed., *Higher Learning in America, 1980–2000.* Baltimore: Johns Hopkins University Press.

Cohen, Michael, and James March. 1974. *Leadership and Ambiguity: The American College President.* New York: McGraw-Hill.

Commission of Academic Tenure. 1973. *Faculty Tenure in Higher Education.* San Francisco: Jossey-Bass.

Damrosch, David. 1995. *We Scholars: Changing the Culture of the University.* Cambridge, Mass.: Harvard University Press.

Feldman, D. C. 1981. "The Multiple Socialization of Organization Members." *Academy of Management Review,* 8: 309–318.

Gouldner, Alvin W. 1957. "Cosmopolitans and Locals: Toward an Analysis of Latent Social Roles." *Administrative Science Quarterly,* 2: 281–306.

Greiner, Larry. 1986. "Top Management Politics and Organizational Change." In S. Srivasta, ed., *Executive Power.* San Francisco: Jossey-Bass.

Kennedy, Donald. 1994. "Making Choices in the Research University." In J. Cole, E. Barber, and S. Graubard, eds., *The Research University in a Time of Discontent.* Baltimore: Johns Hopkins University Press.

——— 1997. *Academic Duty.* Cambridge, Mass.: Harvard University Press.

Kerr, Clark. 1984. *Presidents Make a Difference: Strengthening Leadership in Colleges and Universities.* Washington, D.C.: Association of Governing Boards of Universities and Colleges.

——— 1991. *The Great Transformation in Higher Education, 1960–1980.* Albany: State University of New York Press.

Kerr, Clark, and Marian L. Gade. 1986. *The Many Lives of Academic Presidents: Time, Place, and Character.* Washington, D.C.: Association of Governing Boards of Universities and Colleges.

Kotter, John P., and Leonard A. Schlesinger. 1979. "Choosing Strategies for Change." *Harvard Business Review,* 57 (2): 106–114.

Magrath, C. Peter. 1997. "Eliminating Tenure without Destroying Academic Freedom." *Chronicle of Higher Education,* February 28, p. A60.

McPherson, Michael S., and Morton Owen Schapiro. 1999. "Tenure Issues in Higher Education." *Journal of Economic Perspectives,* 13 (1): 85–98.

Mintzberg, Henry. 1983. *Power in and around Organizations.* Englewood Cliffs, N.J.: Prentice-Hall.

Nelson, Cary. 1999. "The War against the Faculty." *Chronicle of Higher Education,* April 16, p. B4.

O'Brien, George Dennis. 1998. *All the Essential Half-Truths about Higher Education.* Chicago: University of Chicago Press.

Pfeffer, Jeffrey. 1981. *Power in Organizations.* Boston: Pitman.

Sanderson, Allen, Voon Chin Phua, and David Herda. 1999. *The American Faculty Poll: Final Report.* New York: TIAA-CREF.

Schein, Edgar H. 1985. *Organizational Culture and Leadership.* San Francisco: Jossey-Bass.

Siegel, Sidney. 1956. *Nonparametric Statistics for the Behavioral Sciences.* New York: McGraw-Hill.

Tierney, William, and Estela Bensimon. 1996. *Promotion and Tenure: Community and Socialization in Academe.* Albany: State University of New York Press.

Trower, Cathy A. 1997. *Junior Faculty Behavior and Experiences: Work Life on the Tenure Track, Off the Tenure Track, and at Institutions without Tenure Systems.* College Park: University of Maryland: UMI Microform, 9719841.

Van Mannen, John. 1976. "Breaking In: Socialization to Work." In Robert Dubin, ed., *Handbook of Work, Organization, and Society.* Chicago: Rand McNally College.

Walker, Donald E. 1979. *The Effective Administrator: A Practical Approach to Problem Solving, Decision Making, and Campus Leadership.* San Francisco: Jossey-Bass.

4

Can the Tenure Process
Be Improved?

R. EUGENE RICE

MARY DEANE SORCINELLI

OF ALL THE QUESTIONS surrounding the tenure debate, the most immediately pressing is this: Can the tenure process be improved? The critical nature of the question has been firmly established by a decade of research on new faculty and the early-career experiences of newcomers to the academic profession. In the eyes of many in the academy (and even more outside), the tenure process requires reexamination and possibly repair lest the system prove to be a major liability for aspiring faculty members and for the profession and institutions more generally.

Many colleges and universities are now developing and testing responses to some of the most fundamental questions about the tenure process. In this chapter, we briefly frame and describe the widely documented criticisms of the tenure process and then explore some of the proposals that have been initiated or implemented in various institutional contexts.

The Central Issue

A number of procedural concerns surround the process that leads to a tenure decision. None of these procedural matters compares, however, with the substantive question: For what is tenure awarded? For probationary faculty this issue has become increasingly perplexing.

Throughout higher education there has developed a serious mismatch between what are perceived as priorities among faculty—those tasks in which one should invest one's time and talent—and the mission of the institution. Among four-year institutions, particularly research universities and the larger, comprehensive institutions with complex missions, the tension is especially acute.

Difficulties with the tenure process are not just an individual faculty concern, solvable by minor adjustments; they are a major institutional dilemma. Universities and colleges across the country today are struggling to find or rediscover their place in the rich mosaic of American higher education. Until there is agreement on the primary purposes of the institution and its several divisions, the tenure process will remain muddled. This is seen most dramatically in large, public, urban universities like the University of Missouri–Kansas City, the University of Wisconsin–Milwaukee, and the University of Alaska–Anchorage, where the conundrum has been identified and the tenure process addressed, though not without difficulty.

We examine the dimensions and character of this problem not by reviewing surveys of academic administrators, legislators and regents, or senior faculty, but through structured conversations with new faculty and with graduate students who aspire to be professors. Three hundred fifty individuals were interviewed as part of a project called *Heeding New Voices: Academic Careers for a New Generation* (Rice, Sorcinelli, and Austin 2000). A special effort was made to interview representative groups of early-career faculty and graduate students across the various sectors of higher education and across disciplines, race, ethnicity, gender, and region.

Faculty in the early stages of a career and students preparing for academic work were asked what they hoped for, what they currently experience, what they need, and what they want in an academic career. They were pressed on what in an academic career would attract the best of a new generation into the profession. What would make the career more resilient and self-renewing for them as individuals, and at the same time would allow colleges and universities to adapt to the many changes and challenges they confront?

Heeding New Voices, more than earlier studies (Boice 1992; Sorcinelli and Austin 1992; Tierney and Bensimon 1996; Austin and Rice 1998; Menges et al. 1999), focuses on newcomers' perceptions of the tenure process. We found that interviewees' observations about the tenure system varied by institutional type, discipline, and professional field. While these differences are important, there was widespread agreement about the nature, depth, and seriousness of the problems with the tenure process.

Caught between the Times

We found that new faculty felt themselves to be caught between the times. The tenure process holds them to one set of performance criteria, supported by their academic discipline and reinforced at every turn by their recent graduate school experience. At the same time, early-career faculty are expected to respond to institutional imperatives aimed at improving the quality of undergraduate teaching, better serving the needs of the larger society, and exploiting the advantages of new technologies.

New faculty feel "under siege." In an environment in which professors are roundly criticized for not working hard enough, the greatest complaint voiced by new faculty was lack of time—"being overwhelmed" by multiple responsibilities. As the late Robert Menges and his associates gleaned from extensive interviews with new faculty, the concerns of this current generation of faculty have "shifted from anxiety about getting a job to anxiety about surviving in the job" (1999, p. 20).

Understanding the current angst of tenure track faculty, particularly at four-year institutions, requires some background on the evolution of the academic career over the past four decades. From the late 1950s through the early 1970s, American higher education experienced meteoric growth and heady affluence. For many faculty, largely white males, academic appointments were abundant. Deans and department chairs often used the award of tenure as an incentive to encourage young faculty to resist outside offers. The tenure process was seldom viewed as the tortuous gauntlet probationary faculty perceive it to be today.

New funds for research, the expansion of programs, and the rising prestige and influence of the professoriat made a college or university appointment especially attractive, enticing large numbers of graduate students to attend rapidly proliferating doctoral programs. Institutional responsibilities, such as teaching undergraduates and serving on committees, was tolerated as long as time and resources were available to do one's own work: a Faustian bargain was struck. Within a relatively short period, being an academic scholar became more narrowly focused and defined with greater specificity.

During this period of expansion and growth, a set of assumptions coalesced to redefine the prototype of a valued scholar. Central to this "assumptive world" was specialized research, published in peer-reviewed journals. Disciplines gained new importance, and knowledge was pursued for its own sake. Professional autonomy was a pivotal value, and the national or international disciplinary association became the primary reference group for faculty, not the local institution and even less the adjacent community (Rice 1996).

By the 1990s, regents, legislators, governors, and the general public regularly raised serious questions about faculty priorities and institutional incentive structures. The priorities central to the assumptive world of the academic professional began to be crowded by other urgencies. New faculty reported that, in one sense, there was a new day on campus: being good at teaching was not only expected; it was also frequently, if modestly, rewarded. At the same time, however, research and publications dominated the reward structure and the tenure system.

Peer review of research and publications remains highly valued, but now there are new demands that teaching also be peer reviewed. Simultaneously, institutional leaders encourage new faculty to engage in curriculum development and service-learning programs. Meanwhile, the priorities and preferences of colleagues and disciplinary associations remain determinative in assessments for tenure. Thus, junior faculty are uncomfortably squeezed between local and cosmopolitan pressures, and between disciplinary colleagues and institutional demands.

A number of the most impressive new faculty we interviewed were attracted to the profession by a love of teaching and a deep commitment to making a difference in society. At the same time, however, the older, established priorities remain intact. To the old, the new has been added, and early-career faculty seem pulled in all directions, with little sense of coherence in their professional lives, particularly with regard to the tenure and promotion process. Incremental change—especially when new priorities are appended to older ones—has made matters worse, not better. More has been heaped onto an already full plate, rendering the whole not only stressful and unmanageable, but also unsatisfying and even distasteful.

Caught between Cultures: The Collegial and the Managerial

Until recently, the academic career was profoundly influenced by a deeply rooted collegial culture. Today, however, a burgeoning managerial culture tugs the academy in a very different direction. There is a new and sometimes shrill call from state legislators and governing boards for performance accountability, greater productivity and efficiency, and limitations on tenure. Concurrently, campus administrators and accreditation agencies champion an assessment agenda and a culture of evidence. Faculty, particularly probationary faculty, are caught between two cultures, each with different assumptions, standards, and imperatives.

The collegial culture looks to peer review for validation and to academic peers for leadership. It assumes a community of scholars selected by merit through the tenure process. Academic freedom and shared governance are basic tenets. In contrast, the managerial culture, which has a broad base in the larger society, focuses on the "bottom line" and draws leadership from the technically competent.

Each of these cultures has its own economy, which shapes academic priorities and exerts an enormous impact on faculty and their work. The collegial culture has generated a prestige economy, with ranking systems and hierarchically arrayed categories used by fellow professors to define merit and assign classifications that control relative status. The tenure process is particularly sensitive to the influence of the prestige economy. The managerial culture, by contrast, relies on a market economy, where resource providers—that is, the market rather than faculty—determine priorities and value products and services. Newer faculty are caught between these two cultures, their competing priorities, and their influential advocates. The tension between these two cultures plays out most dramatically in the tenure process.

Caught in a Flawed Process

While early-career faculty expressed reservations about the tenure system as a whole, most identified the *process* of contending for tenure as their most urgent concern. Candidates for tenure fret about unclear and inconsistent expectations. As a new faculty member from an urban public university commented, "Everything is so vague, ambiguous, and elusive; expectations are changing all the time." The process is seen as fraught with "unwritten rules and misunderstandings." For example, an assistant professor at a large research university reported that an appointment might be represented as a mix of 45% research, 45% teaching, and 10% service when in actuality the expectation was that 90% of one's efforts should be directed to research.

To compound the problem, counsel and feedback from senior colleagues vary, and the lineup of decision-makers—department chairs, deans, and members of promotion and tenure committees—changes rapidly and unpredictably. Respondents noted that administrators emphasize the importance of service, whereas key faculty warn that involvement in "service will probably be detrimental to your career" and that new and innovative teaching strategies should be avoided, "since they take too much time." Another department chair encouraged collaboration with colleagues in research, but stressed that "you know you must publish alone to get tenure."

These concerns do not simply reflect the usual anxieties about evaluation characteristic of contemporary young professionals. Nor are they merely complaints about work pressure registered by so many early-career adults in today's fast-paced work environment (Schor 1993). Rather, what we found in the careers of pre-tenure faculty was a structural condition shaped by a very tight labor market and the practice, over time, of ratcheting up the requirements for tenure and promotion in most disciplines and across all sectors of higher education. In addition, new emphases and procedures to assess performance have been added. Because the tenure process culminates in such a high-stakes decision for both the institution and the individual, the academy must regularly rethink and, if need be, revise the system.

Addressing this issue is particularly important at this time because the faculties of the nation's colleges and universities are undergoing a generational changing of the guard. Over the next decade, the senior faculty appointed during the period of rapid expansion in the 1960s will retire in record numbers, to be replaced by a new, if perhaps smaller, core of tenured faculty. The criteria and processes used to select this new generation of faculty will set the course of American higher education for decades to come.

The Scholarly Work of Faculty Reconsidered

In 1988, the Carnegie Foundation for the Advancement of Teaching initiated a major inquiry, under the rubric *Scholarship Reconsidered*, into the changing role of faculty and the scholarly work rewarded by American colleges and universities. The project was a search for fresh conceptions of faculty work that would reunite personal and institutional endeavors, bring wholeness to scholarly lives, and, at the same time, meet the diverse and changing educational needs of society. The authors urged faculty to move beyond the tired dichotomy of "teaching versus research."

Scholarship Reconsidered: Priorities of the Professoriate (Boyer 1990) addressed directly tenure process and the reward system for scholarly work. *Scholarship Reconsidered* was intended to make a heuristic difference—to reframe the discussion and to open a lively conversation across campuses and disciplines about what faculty do as scholars on a broad range of fronts. An expanded view of scholarly work emerged as a result and included four interrelated forms of scholarship: teaching, engagement, integration, and discovery.

Scholarship Reconsidered struck a responsive chord; the monograph quickly became the Carnegie Foundation's best-selling publication. Colleges and universities across the nation began to ask the question "For what is tenure awarded?" and that, in turn, precipitated reviews of promotion and tenure guidelines.[1]

We turn now to what happened as a result. What changes, if any, were made to the substance of the tenure process and institutional reward structures? We look first at the scholarship of teaching, where large advances have been made over the last ten years.

The Scholarship of Teaching

The conceptual framework of *Scholarship Reconsidered* rests on the intellectual foundation laid by scholars William Perry, Joseph Katz, and Lee Shulman, among others, who conceptualized teaching as a scholarly enterprise. Without their contributions, the concept of "the scholarship of teaching" would not have moved forward. Their work challenged as too one-sided and insensitive to the interactive character of scholarship the traditional conceptualization of teaching as the presentation of knowledge and the way it was transmitted and disseminated. They also corrected the misperception that teaching is merely a matter of packaging and relating knowledge—that ideas are simply refined and then passed "down."

In his seminal essay "Knowledge and Teaching: Foundations of the New Reform" (1987), Shulman contended that teaching is a more dynamic endeavor, and that the knowledge base required for effective teaching is content-specific. In Shulman's words, "the capacity of a teacher" is "to transform the content knowledge he or she possesses into forms that are pedagogically powerful and yet adaptive to the variations in ability and background presented by the students" (1987, p. 5).

As with research, where scholarly work is openly shared and critiqued, institutions and disciplines now seek to make teaching a public, documented endeavor. In the past, peer review of teaching depended chiefly on the impression of a department chair, the anecdotes of a member of the tenure committee, or the report from a single classroom observation. Now leaders in specific disciplines are working collaboratively to develop an evidentiary basis to assess the intellectual quality of teaching and learning. Peer-review initiatives have enhanced the evaluation of teaching for improvement and personnel decision-making, as illustrated by several projects:

The *pedagogical colloquium* highlights teaching in the faculty appointment process. In addition to a session on one's research, candidates for faculty appointments are required to make public, scholarly presentations about their understanding of teaching and learning. Stanford's history department used this approach to introduce teaching effectiveness as an explicit expectation of new faculty and to stimulate current faculty's commitment to quality teaching.

Faculty realized that the instinct to protect professional autonomy had made teaching a highly private activity. The feedback loop had been short-circuited, and pedagogical ties to colleagues had been severed. *Teaching circles*, started at the University of Nebraska–Lincoln and patterned after Japanese quality circles, seeks to overcome this isolation through planned, purposeful conversations about good teaching and meaningful student learning. At

Rio Hondo College, faculty collaborate about teaching on-line
and assessing student learning. A teaching circle at Portland State
University encourages faculty to help one another develop portfolios for promotion and tenure decisions.

Several institutions have taken steps toward *internal and external
peer review* of teaching in the tenure and promotion process. The
University of North Carolina, Charlotte, is collecting data on
the value given to peer visits to classrooms in these review processes. The chemistry department at Indiana University–Purdue
University Indianapolis has experimented with outside review
of course syllabi and materials. Colleagues in the Computer
Writing and Research Lab at the University of Texas–Austin and
in Religious Studies at Seton Hall University are piloting a peer
review mechanism for electronic publication of the scholarship of
teaching.

In the early 1990s, campuses began to use *teaching portfolios* to capture the scholarship of teaching. As many as 1,000 colleges and
universities are now using or experimenting with portfolios
(Seldin 1993) to provide a fuller assessment of teaching for personnel decisions. The University of Massachusetts at Amherst
makes available to faculty a handbook, *Preparing a Teaching Portfolio* (Mues and Sorcinelli 2000), with step-by-step, practical information, including an extensive appendix, "Items That Might Be
Included in a Teaching Portfolio," and excerpts from portfolios
that have been prepared by faculty on campus. This approach
exemplifies Shulman's key concept: "A scholarship of teaching
will entail a public account of some or all of the full act of teaching—vision, design, enactment, outcomes, and analysis—in a
manner susceptible to critical review by the teacher's professional
peers and amenable to productive employment in future work by
members of that same community" (1998, p. 6).

In order to foster recognition and legitimacy for teaching as a scholarly enterprise, the now renamed Carnegie Academy for the Scholarship of Teaching and Learning (CASTL) established a national network of institutions with teaching academies. This program now has
over 180 diverse colleges and universities wrestling with what the
scholarship of teaching and learning means for their campuses. Schol-

arly and professional societies, such as the Academy of Management and the American Chemical Society, are also participating in these initiatives by sponsoring symposia on the scholarship of teaching at their annual meetings.

Web-based resources promise to play a significant role in the advancement of the scholarship of teaching. Randy Bass, a professor at Georgetown University (who relied on his own on-line work in a successful quest for tenure), has developed the on-line Crossroads Project of the American Studies Association. Faculty in this interdisciplinary field can make their scholarly work on teaching public and accessible for peer review and commentary. Also, George Mason University has a new on-line journal focused on the scholarship of teaching and learning.

The debate nurtured by *Scholarship Reconsidered* has blurred the division between teaching and scholarship. We now can see teaching as an intellectually challenging task that transcends the exaggerated dichotomies between content and process and between research and teaching. We can view it not only as the transfer of knowledge by faculty to students but also as an exploration of the ways in which students make meaning out of what happens in the learning environment. Teaching is emerging as a source of rich, scholarly discourse that has the potential to become the basis for intrinsically rewarding associations and cosmopolitan, public exchange. As a result, teaching now can be evaluated with increasing confidence as part of the tenure and promotion process.

The Scholarship of Engagement

While the scholarship of teaching commands more status in the faculty rewards process, another form of scholarly work is gaining strength— some would say reclaiming its place—as an essential ingredient of scholarship. Ten years ago, this form of scholarship was called "the scholarship of application," assuming that the established epistemology—that knowledge is generated by university faculty and then applied in external contexts—remained unchallenged. Over the past decade, the terminology has shifted to the "scholarship of engagement." This suggests a mutuality: the obligation of scholars to both involve and learn from members of the community as researchable problems are formulated and investigated. Theory and practice complement and enrich each other.

Ernest Lynton and Sandra Elman contended that many American universities were striving to be what they were not and "falling short of what they could be" (Lynton and Elman 1987, p. 162). Lynton and Elman were especially concerned with the disconnection between the academic knowledge generated by university faculty and society's growing needs for applied knowledge. He devoted the later part of his life and career to the subject of his 1995 book, *Making the Case for Professional Service*, which promoted the scholarship of engagement.

Lynton established a coalition of 45 metropolitan universities where regional missions are central. His work of identifying, defining, documenting, and rewarding the scholarly contributions of faculty to the university's external constituencies—business and industry, governmental and legislative agencies, public and private sector bodies, and the public at large—gave substance to the scholarship of engagement. *Making the Case for Professional Service* advanced faculty involvement in outreach and service as legitimate scholarly contributions.

Amy Driscoll has continued Lynton's work with *Making Outreach Visible: A Guide to Documenting Professional Service and Outreach* (Driscoll and Lynton 1999). This pragmatic resource provides detailed examples of faculty work at land-grant and metropolitan universities committed to rewarding the scholarship of engagement. The prototypes range from an anthropologist at the University of Memphis involved in community building to a Portland State engineer engaged in earthquake loss estimation and mitigation.

The scholarship of engagement also benefited enormously from Donald Schon's work, *The Reflective Practitioner* (1983). Schon argued that "the new scholarship requires a new epistemology" (1995, p. 28). He persuasively asserted that theory and research on the one hand and practice on the other had to be realigned, because in the modern research university theory and practice were hierarchically related, with practice secondary and derivative. These hierarchies are also embedded into the process used in granting tenure and promotion. Until this process honors and rewards participants in civic engagement, the rhetorical adulation of the engaged campus will remain just that. As Fred Ansley and John Gaventa (1997), senior professors at the University of Tennessee, noted: "A young untenured professor does not have to be a heartless or craven careerist to find herself cut off from the very social problems and people that initially drew her to her discipline. She finds in her everyday academic life no existing conduits through which to receive information about or build relationships with these people and those problems. She is functioning in an environment starved for social capital" (1997, p. 47). As faculty and institutions attempt to address this issue, can we move beyond the expert model as we envision faculty work in off-campus communities? Can we cultivate inclusion and broader participation? Or, as the University of Minnesota's Harry Boyte (1998) asked: Can we begin to think of the work of faculty as "public work"?

The assessment and evaluation of the scholarship of engagement poses perhaps the greatest challenge. How can it be sufficiently documented to assume a legitimate place alongside other forms of scholarly work that count toward tenure and promotion? As the pressure to assess learning outcomes escalates, and as we become better equipped to make informed judgments about what students learn, active, engaged learning will be more widely recognized as integral to the educational landscape.

Much has been done to reward professional service and outreach and to recognize the faculty's role in community service learning. Fruitful campus initiatives include the following:

> The 202 institutions of the National Association of State Universities and Land-Grant Colleges (NASULGC) have launched an initiative, "Returning to Our Roots: The Engaged Institution" (Kellogg Commission 1999), designed to promote deeper and more effective involvement in meeting community and national needs.
>
> Portland State University has pioneered models for engaging faculty in the scholarship of community-based learning and for helping faculty learn new ways to document this learning in promotion and tenure portfolios. Elements include identifying research approaches for assessing community-based learning and for documenting the results, a "civic responsibility" breakfast series that engages faculty in discussions on conducting scholarship of community outreach, and a team that provides ongoing support for faculty who undertake such scholarship.

At Indiana University–Purdue University Indianapolis (IUPUI) a faculty Task Force on Service researched professional service theories and initiatives at peer institutions. The task force report and the work of eleven University Faculty Service Fellows resulted in revised promotion and tenure guidelines, documentation for annual review, and criteria for service awards. IUPUI also produced a service guidebook—a resource for promotion and tenure committees, administrators, and faculty members alike.

At Oklahoma State University–Oklahoma City, a two-year branch campus, faculty, administrators, legal counsel, and regents worked together to develop a policy statement addressing the scholarship of engagement and practice and how to develop the institutional capacity to recognize and reward community outreach.

As part of the American Association for Higher Education's new series on service-learning in the disciplines, faculty in over twenty disciplines and professions have published volumes that bring together theoretical essays, pedagogical models, and bibliographical resources.

The Scholarship of Integration

While the concepts of the scholarship of teaching and the scholarship of engagement have progressed, the "scholarship of integration" suffers from inattention. Ironically, early-career faculty miss most the opportunity to work collaboratively, to find intellectual colleagueship, and to reach across disciplines—the very essence of the scholarship of integration.

Dominant interview themes included the need for "connection," "community," and "intellectual wholeness." Looking to an imagined future, one new faculty member at a research university concluded: "My view of the academy in the twenty-first century is one that breaks traditional department barriers, creates interaction among faculty across fields, conducts research around themes, and gets rid of the huge gap between research and teaching."

The most significant support for making a place for the scholarship of integration has been *We Scholars: Changing the Culture of the University* (1995) by David Damrosch, a professor of English and Comparative Literature at Columbia University. While serving as Chair of

Comparative Literature, Damrosch struggled to engage faculty across the boundaries of disciplines, language, and area studies. The tenure and promotion process proved to be a particularly troublesome obstacle. "Academic work is institutionally arranged in a patterned isolation of disciplines, and then of specialized fields within disciplines," noted Damrosch. Consequently, "a heady mix of scholarly alienation and disciplinary nationalism shapes the questions we ask and the ways in which we ask them. These scholarly values in turn foster—and reward—alienation and aggression at all levels of academic life" (p. 6).

Damrosch traced "the triumph of specialization" and conceded that "the intellectual and even ethical value of a full commitment to specialization seemed clear for a generation after World War II." However, the intellectual and ethical costs of this commitment are plainly visible today (p. 15). Interviews with early-career faculty revealed that these costs are evident in the tenure and promotion process, as review committees typically devalue or discount integrative work.

Nonetheless, ways to encourage faculty to work across disciplinary boundaries are emerging.

> Michigan State University is examining an interdisciplinary collaboration model for faculty work through a partnership of the university, a public agency, and the community. Researchers studied disciplinary distinctions, faculty roles and rewards structures, intellectual property rights, and issues relating to team-building and leadership. The study also highlighted the importance of academic units unencumbered by traditional disciplinary and departmental boundaries.

> California State University–Chico is developing ways to reward faculty for collaborative cross-disciplinary work. Organizational changes that have supported the initiative include new interdisciplinary majors and minors (e.g., leadership studies), revision of the General Education curriculum in order to link and cluster courses, and revision of retention, tenure, and promotion criteria to include the scholarship of discovery, creativity, integration, and service.

> Indiana University of Pennsylvania has created cross-disciplinary teaching circles to support discussion and research across disciplines.

The Scholarship of Discovery

As *Scholarship Reconsidered* encouraged broader definitions of the scholarly work of faculty, several serious misconceptions arose, most notably the perception that original research and publication were being denigrated and that alternative forms of scholarly work would displace traditional research. In truth, *Scholarship Reconsidered* urged a more balanced, inclusive conception of scholarship, not the substitution of one priority for another. Each form of scholarship was expected to complement and build on the others. A basic assumption was that all faculty would have a scholarly project that would be continually fueled by both the quest for and the discovery of new knowledge. No matter what the form of scholarship, learning would be at the heart of the scholarly enterprise.

This broader definition of scholarship received new impetus from a series of publications beginning in 1995. Lynton was the first to emphasize the essential similarity between the several forms of scholarship. In working on the documentation and assessment of the different categories of scholarship, it became increasingly clear that "only by seeing the whole can one arrive at a true measure of multidimensional excellence, and only in that way can institutions as well as individuals gain the flexibility to shape a profile of activities that best matches needs with capabilities" (1995, p. 61).

In 1997, *Scholarship Assessed* (Glassick, Huber, and Maeroff) emphasized not the differences, but the "commonalities" in the processes of scholarship. Six standards were identified to assess all forms of scholarly work: clear goals, adequate preparation, appropriate methods, significant results, effective presentation, and reflective critique (p. 25). Diamond (1999) offered another set of characteristics common to scholarly work. Scholarship, whatever the form, would require a high level of discipline-related expertise; break new ground, or innovate; be amenable to replication, documentation, and peer review; and carry significance and impact (p. 8).

In the search for universal criteria for evaluating scholarly work, *Scholarship Assessed* focused more on process, while Diamond concentrated on product. Both approaches have been helpful to tenure and promotion committees concerned with how the various forms of scholarship are interrelated. How do we continue to reap the benefits of specialized research without detracting from other scholarly priorities? Is undergraduate research a legitimate answer? Should original research be required of all faculty? To what extent is technology changing the research process?

Some institutions have responded resourcefully to these questions:

Virginia Tech uses an academic planning exercise to form more creative academic work groups, to stimulate imaginative action within those groups, and to demonstrate the benefits and challenges in rewarding new forms of academic scholarship.

The University of California–San Diego attempts to demonstrate how research and teaching across a variety of disciplines can close the gap between academic and community knowledge. The university has developed a process for faculty and students to think about the intellectual value of community-anchored research and teaching. Projects that integrate intellectual and substantive experiences with community engagement have emerged from the university's Supercomputer Center, its School of Medicine, and the departments of Visual Arts, Urban Studies, and History.

Rutgers University has identified alternative faculty roles, in part to integrate undergraduate research throughout the curriculum, particularly in introductory courses. Two promising approaches include a research preparation workshop for first- and second-year students and the development of introductory courses in research activities such as sample collection, measurement, and analysis.

New Promotion and Tenure Statements

Unquestionably, *Scholarship Reconsidered* spurred a vastly enlarged view of the scholarly work of faculty. In turn, numerous colleges and universities have revised various policies in an attempt to align tenure and promotion criteria with institutional priorities and to eliminate the disconnect that so many early-career faculty feel between the rhetoric and the reality of the process. For example:

Kansas State University is developing an integrated faculty evaluation and reward paradigm that builds on individualized workloads, reduces the dichotomy between research- and teaching-oriented units, provides external credibility, enhances faculty professional development, and encourages collective achievement and departmental strengths.

Clemson University has installed an electronic faculty reporting system to address concerns about faculty rewards and performance accountability issues. The system recognizes the need to redefine scholarship and links faculty evaluation to established university goals. Every college now funds public service and outreach activities, which are part of the evaluation criteria.

California State University–Long Beach has developed a new retention, tenure, and promotion policy emphasizing career-long professional development. The policy explicitly defines the responsibilities of all participants in the evaluation process, enlarges the dimensions considered in evaluating teaching, and strengthens the peer review of faculty work.

The Associated New American Colleges is developing improved policies and practices in such areas as faculty workload differentiation, unit accountability, rewards, governance, institutional service, faculty career stages, and faculty development. Faculty representatives conducted an extensive needs assessment focused on three themes: professional development throughout the career, faculty as institutional citizens, and faculty workload. Working groups are now meeting to outline both a vision and an agenda to create new relationships between faculty members and institutions.

Faculty at Florida Gulf Coast University have embarked on a new system of multiple appointment options, including multiyear and nontenure contracts, with evaluation criteria to assess performance for each type of appointment.

Addressing the "Overloaded Plate" Problem

The broader conception of scholarship and the new ways to document and assess the different forms of scholarly work, as valuable as they have been, have exacerbated another set of problems and, in some cases, made the tenure process even more difficult. Not only have research requirements escalated, but teaching, now valued more, can be assessed with greater confidence. In addition, professional service and outreach have a new currency, and scholarly engagement enjoys greater legitimacy. In short, an incremental, add-on approach to change has been put in place. The scholarly responsibilities of early-career faculty have not only expanded, but also multiplied. As the conception of scholarly excellence has become multidimensional, new faculty are being held accountable for more work in more arenas.

New faculty often described this phenomenon as an "overloaded plate." One early-career faculty member also referred to the dilemma of having to do more and do it better as an "instrument for humiliation" where tenure candidates could always be "caught off base."

The different forms of scholarship, along with other professional tasks, need to be addressed, but not by faculty members individually. Jon Wergin and Judi Swingen (2000) concluded that a major overhaul of faculty work is possible "only when institutions shift the unit of analysis from the individual to the academic department, where the work of the department is evaluated as a whole, rather than simply as the aggregate of individual accomplishments, and where faculty are evaluated according to their differential contributions to the group" (p. 3).

This means, first, negotiating with colleagues on how best to use individual talents to contribute to the overall work of the department. Faculty members would be evaluated on that basis after a designated period of time. Areas of emphasis could shift as the faculty member's career unfolds or as departmental needs shift.

Among for-profit institutions of higher education and new programs that rely heavily on technologically based distance learning, there is talk of "unbundling the faculty role." Differential staffing will likely play a much larger role in the future of the professoriat. For more traditional colleges and universities, Wergin and Swingen's (2000) warning is particularly pertinent: "As long as institutions respond to pressures for accountability with various exercises in strategic planning and creative mission building without also paying attention to changes in how the *departments* are evaluated and rewarded, they can expect only limited success" (p. 3).

The College of Liberal Arts and Sciences at Arizona State University has instituted an "integrated model of faculty responsibilities" (Krahenbuhl 1998), where individual faculty members are regarded as a variable asset, faculty responsibilities are flexible, and the climate encourages the integration of different forms of scholarly work. The campus is developing a formal system for differentiating the accomplishments of faculty as part of annual performance reviews of academic units rather than individual faculty. This approach may be a particularly attractive strategy to deal with the "full plate" problem.

Other Strategies for Improving the Tenure Process

Making the Tenure Process More Understandable

Throughout the *Heeding New Voices* interviews, early-career faculty lamented that the tenure and promotion process was unpredictable and undependable. "Everything is so vague, ambiguous, and elusive; expectations are changing all the time." In response, departments, schools, and colleges have adopted various tactics. The University of Arizona has a web site with detailed instructions for preparing tenure submissions. These instructions can be supplemented at the departmental level with checklists and other specific information. At the University of Pittsburgh, the dean of the college of arts and sciences conducts a tenure preparation workshop for first- and second-year faculty and then again for faculty in years four and five. At the University of Nebraska–Omaha, the faculty development center supplies new faculty with a set of instructions about the tenure process (e.g., how to compile material, document work, seek support) and guidelines to follow in career-oriented discussions with faculty chairs (Sorcinelli 2000).

Tenure track faculty frequently expressed concern about the lack of useful, detailed performance feedback. To remedy this deficiency, the Promotion and Tenure Committee at Indiana University–South Bend offers voluntary third-year reviews to all tenure track faculty to provide confidential, formative feedback at a time when it can be most helpful. It is fully understood that nothing from this process goes on the record. A college dean at Drake University brings together annually the probationary faculty and the college tenure review committee; committee members share information on their composition, charge, and review process. At the University of Washington, the department of Oceanography invites junior faculty to observe tenure reviews in order to demystify the process ("Future of Tenure" 1999). In a special program for minority faculty, Eastern Michigan University conducts an orientation program in which tenured faculty of color offer advice to and answer questions from the recently appointed tenure track minority faculty.

Support from Senior Faculty

The *Heeding New Voices* interviews revealed an enormous distance between senior faculty and newcomers to the profession. On many campuses, the interaction between these two groups was limited, particularly around the tenure process. Mindful of this gulf, Colorado College assigns each new tenure track faculty member to a senior or retired faculty member outside the newcomer's department, and the two meet monthly to discuss career development issues. At Kean University in New Jersey, new faculty receive a one-course reduction during the first semester to participate in a mentoring program featuring distinguished senior colleagues appointed as Presidential Teaching Scholars. At Brigham Young University, the new faculty orientation is a year-long program involving a structured mentoring relationship with a senior faculty member and an intensive two-week learning experience in which new faculty work individually, with one another, and with experienced faculty members and administrators (Sorcinelli 2000). They ultimately produce a faculty development plan, including a self-assessment, a list of professional goals, and a plan for achieving those goals that are eventually shared with their department chairs and mentors.

Leadership Development for Department Chairs

Interviews with early-career faculty returned repeatedly to the pivotal role department chairs play in the tenure and promotion process. Too often, the influence was perceived as negative and unreliable. Chairs are frequently installed reluctantly and for a relatively short period of time. The lack of consistent guidance for junior faculty is often the result of this temporary arrangement.

To meet the need for development of departmental leadership, some professional and disciplinary associations, notably the International Association for Management Education and the American Sociological Association, have initiated department chair workshops. A number of local campuses have responded to this need as well by working with department chairs to support the development of new faculty and to rethink roles and rewards issues. Michigan State University holds a Leadership Workshop Series for department chairs, and the University of Massachusetts at Amherst offers an annual Chairs and Deans Conference to explore a range of institutional challenges, including the professional development of probationary faculty.

Preparing the Faculty of the Future

Interviews with graduate students and early-career faculty disclosed a serious mismatch between the doctoral preparation they received and the needs of the colleges and universities where they work. New faculty, particularly those not at research universities, are unprepared for the demands and challenges of teaching, for responsibilities for service in the larger community, and for helping to build a department or college.

Fortunately, a major national initiative is enlisting the involvement of many of the research universities where aspiring faculty are prepared. The Preparing Future Faculty project, sponsored by the Association of American Colleges and Universities and the Council of Graduate Schools, seeks to cultivate a broader conception of scholarly work. The project has developed a number of model programs to better prepare graduate students interested in academic careers. Universities providing leadership include Arizona State, Howard, Northwestern, Minnesota, and the University of Washington.

Howard University awards a Certificate in College and University Faculty Preparation to those who satisfactorily complete a two-year, faculty-supervised preparatory program consisting of a study of higher education topics and trends, a three-credit course called "Preparing for the Professorate," a week-long training course in distance-learning techniques, and periodic lectures and symposia on issues affecting higher education.

At the University of Minnesota, four courses form the core of the Preparing the Future Professorate program. But most impressively, this program places future faculty members directly in the different settings in which the profession is practiced. Graduate students are introduced to institutions with different missions, student profiles, and faculty responsibilities. The prospective faculty experience firsthand the array of choices and challenges represented by the broad spectrum of American higher education (Gaff et al. 2000).

The *Heeding New Voices* interviews identified a key weakness in the academic career as it has evolved over the last half century: the tenure review process needs to be modified to take account of changed conditions and expectations. Because most early-career faculty face a buyer's market, most colleges and universities have been able to ignore this problem with impunity. As a new generation populates the professoriat, difficulties with the tenure process must be addressed, both the substantive question ("Tenure for what?") and the procedural issues ("Tenure, how?"). Substantively, the heuristic purpose of the Carnegie report has been largely realized. The next challenge is to institutionalize the best ideas, especially in the promotion and tenure process, and to ensure that the broader conception of scholarship takes hold. The procedural issues are made particularly pressing by the changes confronting higher education. As the context becomes more fluid, the process of evaluating faculty for tenure must become both more predictable and more legitimate. The mystery of the process must yield to clarity, and the rigidity of evaluation criteria must be offset by adaptability. Improving the tenure process is required to attract and hold the best of a new generation of faculty. The vitality of the professoriat of the future depends on it.

Notes

We gratefully acknowledge the assistance of a group of distinguished scholar-practitioners involved in the study of the graduate school experience and the life of new faculty: Thomas Angelo, Ann Austin, Roger Baldwin, Robert Froh, Zelda Gamson, Judith Gappa, Pat Hutchings, Estela Lopez, Robert Ibarra, and the late Robert Menges.

1. *The Disciplines Speak: Rewarding the Scholarly, Professional, and Creative Work of Faculty* (Diamond and Adam 1995) and *The Disciplines Speak II* (Diamond and Adam 2000) are the culmination of long and involved debates about what counts as scholarship. The volumes include statements on scholarship from twenty professional and disciplinary associations.

References

Ansley, Fran, and John Gaventa. 1997. "Researching for Democracy and Democratizing Research." *Change*, 29 (1): 46–53.

Austin, Ann E., and Eugene Rice. 1998. "Making Tenure Viable: Listening to Early Career Faculty." *American Behavioral Scientist,* 41 (5): 736–754.

Boice, Robert. 1992. *The New Faculty Member.* San Francisco: Jossey-Bass.

Boyer, Ernest L. 1990. *Scholarship Reconsidered: Priorities of the Professoriate.* Princeton, N.J.: Carnegie Foundation for the Advancement of Teaching.

Boyte, Harry. 1998. *Off the Playground of Civic Society: Freeing Democracy's Powers for the Twenty-First Century.* Minneapolis: Center for Democracy and Citizenship, University of Minnesota.

Damrosch, David. 1995. *We Scholars: Changing the Culture of the University.* Cambridge, Mass.: Harvard University Press.

Diamond, Robert M. 1999. *Aligning Faculty Rewards with Institutional Mission.* Bolton, Mass.: Anker Publishing Co.

Diamond, Robert M., and Bronwyn E. Adam. 1995. *The Disciplines Speak: Rewarding the Scholarly, Professional, and Creative Work of Faculty.* Washington, D.C.: American Association for Higher Education.

—— 2000. *The Disciplines Speak II.* Washington, D.C.: American Association for Higher Education.

Driscoll, Amy, and Ernest A. Lynton. 1999. *Making Outreach Visible: A Guide to Documenting Professional Service and Outreach.* Washington, D.C.: American Association for Higher Education.

"The Future of Tenure: Interview with Richard Chait." 1999. *Department Chair,* 10 (2): 3–5.

Gaff, Jerry, et al. 2000. *Building the Faculty We Need.* Washington, D.C.: Association of American Colleges and Universities.

Glassick, Charles E., Mary Taylor Huber, and Gene I. Maeroff. 1997. *Scholarship Assessed: Evaluation of the Professoriate.* San Francisco: Jossey-Bass.

Hutchings, Pat. 1996. *Making Teaching Community Property.* Washington, D.C.: American Association for Higher Education.

Hutchings, Pat, and Lee S. Shulman. 1999. "The Scholarship of Teaching: New Elaborations, New Developments." *Change,* 31 (5): 11–15.

Kellogg Commission on the Future of State and Land-Grant Universities. 1999. "Returning to Our Roots: The Engaged Institution." Washington, D.C.: National Association of State Universities and Land-Grant Colleges.

Krahenbuhl, Gary. 1998. "Faculty Work: Integrating Responsibilities and Institutional Needs." *Change,* 30 (6): 18–25.

Lynton, Ernest A. 1995. *Making the Case for Professional Service.* Washington, D.C.: American Association for Higher Education.

Lynton, Ernest A., and Sandra E. Elman. 1987. *New Priorities for the University.* San Francisco: Jossey-Bass.

Menges, R. J., et al. 1999. *Faculty in New Jobs.* San Francisco: Jossey-Bass.

Mues, Fran, and Mary Deane Sorcinelli. 2000. *Preparing a Teaching Portfolio.* Amherst: Center for Teaching, University of Massachusetts.

Rice, R. Eugene. 1996. *Making a Place for the New American Scholar.* Washington, D.C.: American Association for Higher Education.

Rice, R. Eugene, Mary Deane Sorcinelli, and Ann E. Austin. 2000. *Heeding New Voices: Academic Careers for a New Generation.* New Pathways Working Paper Series. Washington, D.C.: American Association for Higher Education.

Schon, Donald. 1983. *The Reflective Practitioner: How Professionals Think in Action.* New York: Basic Books.

———— 1995. "The New Scholarship Requires a New Epistemology." *Change*, 27 (6): 27–34.

Schor, Juliet B. 1993. *The Overworked American*. New York: Basic Books.

Seldin, Peter. 1993. *Successful Use of Teaching Portfolios*. Bolton, Mass.: Anker Publishing Co.

Shulman, Lee. 1987. "Knowledge and Teaching: Foundations of the New Reform." *Harvard Educational Review*, 57 (1): 1–22.

———— 1998. *The Course Portfolio: How Faculty Can Examine Their Teaching to Advance Practice and Improve Student Learning*. Washington, D.C.: American Association for Higher Education.

Simon, Lou Anna K. 1998. *University Community Collaborations for the Twenty-First Century: Outreach Scholarship for Youth and Families*. New York: Garland.

Sorcinelli, Mary Deane. 2000. *Departmental Good Practice: Helping Faculty on the Tenure Track*. Washington, D.C.: American Association for Higher Education.

Sorcinelli, Mary Deane, and Ann E. Austin. 1992. "Developing New and Junior Faculty." *New Directions for Teaching and Learning* (no. 48). San Francisco: Jossey-Bass.

Tierney, William G., and Estela M. Bensimon. 1996. *Promotion and Tenure: Community and Socialization in Academe*. Albany: State University of New York Press.

Wergin, Jon. 1994. *The Collaborative Department: How Five Campuses Are Inching toward Cultures of Collective Responsibility*. Washington, D.C.: American Association for Higher Education.

Wergin, Jon, and Judi N. Swingen. 2000. *Evaluating Academic Departments: Best Practices, Institutional Implications*. Richmond, Va.: Virginia Commonwealth University.

5

What Happened to the Tenure Track?

ROGER G. BALDWIN

JAY L. CHRONISTER

*T*HE HOST OF a lifeless cocktail party can always invigorate the conversation by raising the topic of faculty tenure. Few subjects these days stir more controversy than the idea of permanent employment of college and university professors after a relatively brief probationary period. To those outside the academy, the concept of tenure may seem a reflection of a bygone era. In today's fast-paced environment, large corporations and small businesses alike have made downsizing, outsourcing, and contingent staffing common practices in order to adjust to fluctuating economic conditions and changing market demands. In this context, the idea of guaranteed employment for professors strikes the public at large as rigid and counterproductive. Indeed, James Fairweather (1996) asserts that public mistrust of higher education in recent years is based mainly on a belief that faculty are protected from fluctuations in the marketplace by a tenure system that provides employment security not available to workers in other fields and professions.

Many critics of tenure contend that it increases the cost of higher education, stifles faculty productivity, and prevents colleges and universities from adapting to society's rapidly changing educational needs. In other words, for many, tenure is a dangerous anachronism that should be abolished so that higher education, and the society it serves, can thrive in a dynamic era.

In contrast, the most vocal advocates of tenure argue that the future vitality of higher education depends on the preservation of the tenure system. In their view, to abolish, or even to modify, established tenure customs will sacrifice academic freedom, impede recruitment of talent, and irreparably harm the American academic profession (Finkin 1996; 2000). They view the growth of faculty positions off the tenure track as, at best, an insidious trend driven primarily by financial and political considerations that ignore negative academic consequences and, at worst, a calculated strategy to eliminate the tenure system altogether.

A closer look at the tenure track today, however, reveals a much more complicated picture than advocates on either extreme of the issue generally depict. Tenure is no longer the only route through academic life or the only mode by which colleges and universities employ faculty. Although tenure track positions were the dominant form of faculty appointments for much of the twentieth century, such positions now represent only one of several types of faculty appointment options. In fact, more than half of the total instructional staff in higher education today work in part-time or full-time, but tenure-ineligible, positions (U.S. Department of Education 2000).[1] Contrary to popular notions, most faculty do not enjoy lifetime employment and probably never will.

One need only to turn to a local newsstand to see evidence of this trend. For example, the 2001 edition of *U.S. News & World Report*'s annual issue on graduate schools contains an article entitled "Is Tenure Slip-Sliding Away?" (Wildavsky 2000). The piece reveals what many in higher education already know: the tenure track is shrinking. It is gradually being supplemented by an array of alternative faculty appointments. The purpose of this chapter is to answer the question "What happened to the tenure track?" and to consider key policy implications of changes in faculty employment patterns in American colleges and universities. Initially, we consider why non–tenure track faculty appointments are multiplying and present data to document these trends. Seeking a deeper understanding of this evolving pattern, we look at non–tenure track faculty employment by discipline, type of institution, and race and ethnicity. We review significant questions that emerge from our analysis of relevant data and speculate on answers to some of the larger questions we pose. Finally, we consider what changes in tenure track employment imply for faculty personnel policy and practice. As higher education moves increasingly to a more diverse mix of faculty functions and contract arrangements, we discuss related changes that are needed to preserve institutional vitality and educational quality.

Increasing Alternatives

Initially, faculty appointments off the tenure track were almost imperceptible. For example, as recently as 1975, only 30% of the faculty was part-time and only 18.6% of full-time faculty held non–tenure track positions (Cahalan and Roey 1996, Tables 7 and 10). Furthermore, many of these appointments were temporary, and therefore raised no major concerns among academic leaders and policymakers. Institutions established formal policies to regulate and support persons in positions widely seen as peripheral, and non–tenure track academic staff (e.g., lecturers, researchers, clinical instructors) received little attention and less status or support within the academic community.

The number of these alternative types of faculty positions has now grown to the point where this development cannot be ignored without peril to the health of higher education. In 1997, more than one million people filled faculty roles in colleges and universities (U.S. Department of Education 2000). Of these, 426,151, fully 43%, worked part-time. Another 179,232, or 31% of full-time faculty, worked in positions ineligible for tenure. Like an elephant entering a circus tent, its trunk may at first be barely noticeable, but eventually the large creature to which it is attached is impossible to ignore. Similarly, non–tenure track faculty (part-time and full-time term-contract) have grown from a small appendage of the academic profession to a critical mass that demands attention from institutional leaders and government officials.

Many faculty off the tenure track are filling vital roles and serving their institutions for long periods. At many institutions, part-time and term-contract faculty teach a substantial proportion of lower-division undergraduate courses (e.g., English composition, modern languages, laboratory sciences). To cite one dramatic example, Judith Gappa and David Leslie (1993) visited a research university where part-time faculty taught 75% of the lower-division undergraduate mathematics courses. Information on the years of service of part-time and term-contract faculty also belies the notion that most are temporary staff hired to meet short-term needs. Data from the 1993 National Study of

Postsecondary Faculty indicate that more than 36% of full-time non–tenure track faculty had been employed at their institution for seven or more years (U.S. Department of Education 1993). At many schools, faculty off the tenure track have become important counterparts to faculty in standard tenure track positions. Far from being only occasional replacements for "regular" (i.e., tenure track) faculty, many part-time and full-time non–tenure track faculty play critical roles no longer served entirely by tenure track faculty.

Reasons for the Alternatives

The evolution of the tenure track has uncanny parallels to the history of America's railroads. The decline of the railroads cannot be attributed to one source, although the invention of the automobile was surely a dominant factor. Likewise, it is difficult to pinpoint why tenure track faculty appointments have declined in popularity. According to David Leslie (1998), "There is no one single, simple explanation for the increase in the number of part-time and adjunct faculty in American colleges and universities" (p. 11). Several key factors do stand out, however. Chief among these are economics, flexibility, and access to needed resources.

The automobile and trucking industry gained market share from railroads for several reasons. Automobiles and trucks could provide key services less expensively. They were more flexible as market demand shifted. They could reach raw materials and deliver consumable products in remote, even inhospitable, locations that were impossible for railroads to access.

As a fixed system, the tenure track shares some of the same limitations as the railroads. Tenure is a costly proposition for colleges and universities. As Arthur Levine (1997), president of Teachers College, Columbia University, noted, "Tenure now means, for all intents and purposes, a thirty-year appointment. In the future, it could mean fifty years" (p. 13), as people live and work longer. In contrast, part-time and term-contract faculty require no long-term commitment of institutional resources. In addition, many faculty off the tenure track receive lower salaries than tenure-eligible colleagues (U.S. Department of Education 1993). In a sector where the future is increasingly uncertain and where finances are always constrained, positions off the tenure track have become increasingly attractive to institutions as well as to some current and prospective faculty members.

Faculty positions with a limited time frame also enhance institutional flexibility. A university cannot move a tenured physics professor to the business school in order to respond to enrollment pressures. It can, however, choose not to renew a part-time or term-contract position in physics and reallocate the money to hire an adjunct professor in business. Levine sees the flexibility offered by faculty off the tenure track as an advantage. "Part-timers have been a useful vehicle for plugging holes in faculty coverage of subject areas, for teaching in specialty areas requiring less than a full-time faculty member, and for teaching introductory courses full-time faculty have not wanted to teach" (1997, p. 14). Much the same logic applies to full-time non–tenure track faculty positions as well.

Non–tenure track positions also provide higher education with access to a broader range of human resources. As colleges and universities work to bridge the gap between theory and practice, part-time and term-contract positions open the doors of the academic profession to talented experts who would not be considered for appointment under conventional tenure requirements (Chronister and Baldwin 1999). At most institutions today, appointment to the tenure track requires a terminal degree and a commitment to rigorous scholarship as well as effective teaching. These standards, however commendable, exclude many highly experienced specialists who could contribute much to the teaching-learning process. Microsoft founder Bill Gates is a perfect example. As a Harvard College dropout, he would not be eligible for a tenure track faculty position at most U.S. universities. He could, however, be hired as a part-time instructor or visiting full-time lecturer on a term contract, an attractive prospect for most business schools, university research institutes, and undergraduate colleges in America.

Many other factors also contribute to the growing popularity of alternatives to tenure track appointments. The growth of two-career families and the weight of domestic responsibilities make the demands and time line of the tenure track less attractive for some junior faculty. The growth of enrollment in "applied" majors (professional fields), which often supplement their teaching staff with practitioners or clinicians, also accounts for some of the increase in positions off the tenure track. The abundant supply, at present, of qualified candidates in most disciplines reduces the need to compete for faculty applicants with the promise of a tenure track post. Thus, like the decline of the railroads, no one cause explains the profound change in the tenure system. Several forces have converged to make alternative types of faculty appointments attractive to institutions and to some members of the academic profession.

Higher education's gradual shift in faculty staffing practices parallels recent trends in many other employment sectors. Business, government, and even the legal and medical professions have begun to supplement traditional "permanent" staff with contingent personnel hired for a limited time or to perform a specific function (Eisenberg 1999; Melchionno 1999). In an era defined by emerging technologies, global competition, and discontinuous change, higher education, like other complex systems, seeks to maintain equilibrium by balancing the forces of stability and change. Part-time and term-contract faculty appointments counterbalance the continuity provided by the tenure track.

Faculty Employment Trends

Full-Time/Part-Time Employment Changes

Clarifying tenure track trends requires that relevant data be examined over time. In the past twenty-five years a significant change has taken place in the full-time/part-time composition of the faculty. Among the approximately 628,000 faculty in 1975, 30% were part-time and 70% were full-time (Cahalan and Roey 1996, Table 7). The proportion of part-time faculty rose to 35% in 1991 and 40% in 1995 (Roey and Rak 1998, p. 2–3). By 1997, nearly 43% of all faculty worked part-time (U.S. Department of Education 2000). Although there has been a marked increase in the total faculty in higher education, a large proportion of that growth has been among part-time faculty, and as a general rule part-time faculty are not eligible for tenure.

The relative proportion of full-time and part-time faculty in 1997 varied by type of institution. At research universities 23% of faculty were part-time as compared to 32% at doctoral institutions, 37% at master's level institutions, 37% at baccalaureate colleges, and 65% at two-year colleges (U.S. Department of Education 2000). In short, teaching institutions employ a larger proportion of part-time faculty than do institutions emphasizing research.

Although many external constituents believe that part-time faculty are hired to take the place of full-time faculty who are more committed to teaching graduate students and conducting research, data from the 1993 National Study of Postsecondary Faculty (NSOPF-93) do not support such an assertion (Leslie 1998, p. 9). Data analysis by Leslie "shows that full-time faculty, on the average, taught three courses per semester, mostly undergraduates, and generated more student credit hours per course taught than part-time faculty did" (p. 9). Leslie suggests that part-time faculty may be absorbing enrollment increases or helping to develop new or evolving programs. In addition, the fact that the average years of service of part-time faculty on their campus was 6.3 years in 1992 belies the assumption that part-time faculty are principally temporary instructors meeting short-term needs (Leslie 1998, p. 5).

With the increasing use of part-time faculty two fundamental questions arise: (1) What effect does this change in the balance of full- and part-time faculty have on the workload of the full-time faculty? and (2) What effect, if any, does the increasing use of part-time faculty have on educational quality?

Tenure Status

Another significant change in the composition of the faculty in recent years has been the substantial increase in the proportion of full-time tenure-ineligible faculty. Among the 435,000 full-time faculty in 1975, 52.3% were tenured, 29.1% were untenured but tenure track, and 18.6% were non–tenure track (Cahalan and Roey 1996, Tables 9 and 10, pp. 27 and 29). By 1997, 50.1% of full-time faculty were tenured, 18.8% were tenure track, and 30.3% were non–tenure track (U.S. Department of Education 2000).

The jump in the proportion of full-time faculty in tenure-ineligible positions becomes clearer in an analysis of generational differences between senior faculty (employed more than seven years) and the new generation of faculty (employed in higher education for seven years or less). Martin Finkelstein, Robert Seal, and Jack Schuster (1998) found that 16.5% of the senior faculty cohort were in tenure-ineligible positions compared with 33.2% of the new entrants (1998, p. 56). When the authors removed from the data set faculty who were employed at institutions without tenure systems, the corresponding percentages were reduced to 9.9% for the senior cohort and 26.4% for the new entrants (p. 57). These findings disclose an even larger differentiation between the two faculty generations on the variable of tenure status.

If recent trends persist, the increase in non–tenure track faculty will continue. In 1995, approximately 51% of new full-time faculty hires were non–tenure track, 43% were tenure track, and about 5% were tenured (Roey and Rak 1998, pp. 3–7). Two years later, in the fall of 1997, 52.7% of new full-time hires were in non–tenure track positions, 39.1% tenure track, and 8.5% tenured (U.S. Department of Education 2000). It is clear that the faculty balance is shifting in higher education; both part-time and full-time non–tenure track appointments are expanding at the expense of traditional tenure track positions.

Gender

Higher education has experienced an increase in the proportion of women in the professoriat over the past quarter century. Among the total faculty of 633,210 in fall 1976, 27% were women. By 1991 the total faculty had increased to 826,252, of which 36% were women. In 1997, women accounted for 41.2% of the 1,020,786 faculty employed in higher education. This shift in the aggregate share of women faculty includes an increase from 24.7% of full-time faculty in 1976 to 36.2% in 1997, and from 32.8% of part-time faculty in 1976 to 44.7% in 1997 (Cahalan and Roey 1996, p. 14; U.S. Department of Education 2000).

Data on tenure status by gender highlight two important changes. First, both males and females lost tenure track positions as a percentage of the total and achieved gains in employment in non–tenure track positions. In 1975, nearly 57% of full-time male faculty were tenured, 26.8% were tenure track, and 16.3% were non–tenure track. For women the comparable figures were 38.5% tenured, 36.0% tenure track, and 25.5% percent non–tenure track. By 1997, 56.6% of males were tenured, 16.6% were tenure track, and 26.8% were non–tenure track. The percent of women who were tenured remained nearly the same as it was in 1975, at 38.3%, with 22.7% tenure track and 38.5% non–tenure track. Second, women experienced a significant increase in the proportion of full-time non–tenure track positions, from 33.8% in 1975 to 45.8% in 1997. By comparison, women held 36.2% of the total full-time faculty positions in 1997 (Cahalan and Roey 1996, p. 29; U.S.

Department of Education 2000). Recent data on faculty staffing suggest that women are continuing to gain in the non–tenure track employment category. In 1997, 53.7% of new women hires were non–tenure track as compared with 51.7% of men. By contrast, men achieved a slightly larger percentage of tenured hires than did women (8.8% versus 7.5%).

It is important for higher education leaders and policymakers to determine whether the continuing use of tenure-ineligible positions in the employment of women is consistent with the goal of achieving gender equity in faculty employment in the long term. Although there has been an increase in the proportion of women in the ranks of full-time faculty, this increase has not been as extensive in tenured and tenure track positions as it has been in positions off the tenure track. If gender equity in faculty positions is a major goal of higher education institutions, appointing substantial numbers of women to non–tenure track positions will not enhance efforts to balance the proportions of men and women in tenured faculty positions.

Race/Ethnicity

Institutions have made modest increases in the number and proportion of minority faculty. In the fall of 1975, 91.7% of full-time faculty were white, non-Hispanic, and 8.3% were classified as racial or ethnic minorities. By 1991, the percentage of full-time minority faculty had increased to 12.3%. In the fall of 1997, 15.9% of full-time faculty were minority, including 5.5% Asian or Pacific Islanders, 4.9% black non-Hispanics, and 2.6% Hispanics (U.S. Department of Education 2000).

Between 1975 and 1997 the employment of full-time personnel in non–tenure-eligible positions affected racial/ethnic cohorts as well as white, non-Hispanic faculty. In 1975, white full-time faculty were more likely to be tenured (53.5%) than were minority faculty (39.2%) (see Table 5.1). In contrast, minority faculty were more likely to be in tenure track or non–tenure track positions than were white faculty. In 1997, these same patterns prevailed, although the total percentages for minority faculty appear to have actually declined in tenured and tenure track positions. Part of this drop for minority tenured and tenure track faculty is attributable to the pre-1993 inclusion of nonresident alien faculty in the appropriate minority status.[2] When nonresident alien faculty who belong to minority groups were removed from the race/ethnicity categories, tenured and tenure track minority faculty categories decreased. With the exception of Hispanic faculty, all of the minority cohorts made slight increases in the proportion of tenured faculty, all experienced decreases in the tenure track category, and all had increases in non–tenure track positions. Therefore, we may assume that faculty diversity is being achieved principally through appointments of minorities to more insecure full-time non–tenure track positions.

Just as tenure status varies by racial/ethnic cohort, the proportion of part-time faculty within racial/ethnic cohorts also varies. In 1997 the cohorts with the largest proportion of part-time faculty were Hispanic (45.8%), black non-Hispanic (44.9%), and American Indian/Alaska Native (44.6%), followed by white (41.6%) and Asian/Pacific Islander (31.2%). Slightly higher than average (approximately 42%) proportions of Hispanic, black, and American Indian/Alaska Native faculty with part-time status will complicate, and probably impede, efforts to build a stable, diverse faculty (U.S. Department of Education 2000).

Table 5.1 Tenure status: percentage of full-time faculty by race/ethnicity, 1975, 1991, 1997

Tenure status	White	Total minority	Black	Hispanic	Asian	American Indian/ Alaska native	Nonresident alien[a]
Tenured							
1975	53.5	39.2	36.0	41.4	44.2	38.0	—
1991	52.5	39.3	38.4	42.3	38.9	38.6	—
1997	52.2	35.9	40.8	40.1	45.1	48.1	13.9
Tenure track							
1975	28.4	36.5	39.3	35.6	31.7	33.3	—
1991	20.9	27.7	27.5	27.5	28.1	24.2	—
1997	17.7	24.0	26.5	23.1	23.1	21.4	25.1
Non–tenure track							
1975	18.1	24.4	24.7	23.0	24.1	28.6	—
1991	26.6	33.0	34.0	30.2	33.0	37.1	—
1997	30.1	35.9	32.7	36.8	31.7	30.5	60.9

Sources: Roey and Rak 1998, Table 2-4, p. 2-12; U.S. Department of Education 2000.

a. Nonresident alien was not included as a racial/ethnic minority category until the 1993 survey. Therefore, there are no prior data in this table for the years 1975 and 1991 for comparison purposes. See note 2.

Employment Status by Institutional Type

The distribution of faculty by tenure status differs by type and control of institution. By Carnegie classification, the proportion of tenured faculty was highest for master's level institutions and lowest for institutions classified as "other"[3] in both 1995 and 1997 (Table 5.2). Baccalaureate institutions had the highest percentage of faculty on the tenure track in both years, while institutions in the "other" classification had the largest percentage of faculty off the tenure track. Among traditional institutions, two-year colleges had the largest percentage of non–tenure track faculty. Between 1995 and 1997 there was a decline for each institutional classification in tenured and tenure track faculty and increases in full-time faculty not on the tenure track.

Public institutions tended to have higher tenure rates among full-time faculty than did private institutions in 1997. For example, among research universities, public institutions reported 53.4% of faculty with tenure as opposed to 43.3% among the privates. Public master's level institutions had the highest percentage of tenured faculty, at 62.5%, versus 51.7% at private schools. Independent institutions tended to

Table 5.2   Percentage of full-time faculty by tenure status and type of institution, fall 1995 and fall 1997

Type of institution and year	Tenured	On tenure track	Not on tenure track
1995			
Research	53.0	18.9	28.0
Doctoral	57.5	22.4	20.1
Master's	59.6	24.9	15.5
Baccalaureate	50.4	26.4	23.2
Two-year	48.2	11.6	40.2
Other	31.4	18.7	49.9
1997			
Research	50.6	16.7	32.7
Doctoral	57.4	21.4	21.2
Master's	59.5	24.0	16.5
Baccalaureate	51.3	26.0	22.7
Two-year	46.2	11.9	41.9
Other	28.9	18.5	52.6

Sources: U.S. Department of Education 1998; U.S. Department of Education 2000.

have a higher percentage of full-time faculty in non–tenure track positions than did public institutions of the same classification (U.S. Department of Education 2000). If a primary reason for tenure-ineligible positions is to maintain a degree of staffing flexibility, then private institutions appear to be making the most use of this tactic.

Employment of part-time faculty also varies by control of institution, with private institutions employing a larger proportion of part-time faculty at each institutional level (research, doctoral, comprehensive, and baccalaureate) than do their public counterparts. The one exception to this pattern is the two-year institution, where public institutions (mostly community colleges) have the larger proportion of part-time faculty (Kirshstein, Matheson, and Jing 1997, p. 15).

Employment by Program Areas

The number of full-time faculty, part-time faculty, and faculty by tenure status varies significantly across program areas. Table 5.3 shows the distribution of full-time and part-time faculty by program teaching area in 1992. The disciplines with the highest percentage of part-time faculty were fine arts (50.9%), business (46.5%), education (45.3%), humanities (44.8%), and "all other fields" (49.3%), which includes areas such as architecture, industrial arts, law, and public administration. These "other" fields typically have a strong professional orientation and often draw on in-service or retired professionals as part-time faculty. It is important to note that many of the disciplinary fields with a

Table 5.3 Percentage distribution of full-time and part-time faculty by program area, fall 1992

Program area	Part-time faculty	Full-time faculty
Agriculture and home economics	19.5	80.5
Business	46.5	53.5
Education	45.3	54.7
Engineering	32.3	67.7
Fine arts	50.9	49.1
Health sciences	36.0	64.0
Humanities	44.8	55.2
Natural sciences	37.3	62.7
Social sciences	36.8	63.2
All other fields	49.3	50.7

Source: Leslie 1997, p. 4 (Table 2).

high level of part-time employment include large proportions of faculty employed at two-year colleges.

Many departments also employ part-time faculty to teach lower-division undergraduate classes that are enrollment driven, creating short-term, and sometimes unpredictable, instructional needs. The lower level of instruction provided by many part-time faculty and the fact that they are hired primarily to teach allows institutions to hire faculty without terminal degrees at lower salaries, which saves money.

The tenure status of faculty across program areas varies considerably. More than 85% of the full-time faculty in agriculture/home economics, engineering, natural sciences, and social sciences in four-year institutions had tenure or were on the tenure track in the fall of 1992 (see Table 5.4). Conversely, more than 20% of full-time faculty in education, fine arts, humanities, and "other fields" were employed in non–tenure track positions. In English and literature (24.2%), foreign languages (24.1%), and computer science (21.8%), more than 20% of the full-time faculty held non–tenure track positions (U.S. Department of Education 1993). A large proportion of English/literature and foreign language faculty off the tenure track are hired to teach lower-division courses, including elementary composition and introductory foreign language classes. The substantial percentage of computer science faculty in positions ineligible for tenure may reflect the difficulty of recruiting doctorally credentialed candidates for tenure track positions in this highly competitive field. Little research has assessed the long-term

Table 5.4 Percentage distribution of full-time faculty by tenure status and program area in four-year institutions, fall 1992

Program area	Tenured	On tenure track	Not on tenure track
Agriculture and home economics	72.4	19.3	8.3
Business	51.5	29.9	18.5
Education	54.9	23.6	21.5
Engineering	61.8	27.5	10.7
Fine arts	52.9	22.1	25.0
Health sciences	—	—	—
Humanities	59.9	18.7	21.4
Natural sciences	63.7	21.4	14.9
Social sciences	63.4	23.0	13.7
All other fields	49.1	25.7	25.2

Source: U.S. Department of Education 1993.

impact of an increasing proportion of faculty in narrower, fixed roles as opposed to the traditional, interconnected roles of teaching, research, and service. There is, however, incontrovertible evidence that a two-tiered class structure of faculty has arisen on a number of campuses and within certain disciplines that employ a large proportion of part-time (Gappa and Leslie 1993) and full-time tenure-ineligible faculty (Baldwin and Chronister 2001).

Teaching Load

"Who is doing the teaching?" is a question that often arises in discussions about faculty employment policies. Many critics of tenure systems charge that tenured faculty do not teach enough.

Teaching load provides one of the measures of the difference between full-time and part-time faculty. Analysis of data from NSOPF-93 (U.S. Department of Education 1993) showed that, on average, full-time faculty generated 9.1 classroom credit hours (hours per week in class) and 293.1 total student credit hours (credit hours multiplied by number of students enrolled) per semester. For part-time faculty the comparable figures were 5.5 classroom credit hours and 139.4 student credit hours per semester (Leslie 1998, p. 9). Leslie reported that full-time faculty, on average, generated more student credit hours per course taught (104.7) than did part-time faculty (77.4). These figures indicate that the use of full-time faculty is more productive (salary differentials set aside) for institutions when measured by teaching load per credit hour. Not considered in this evaluation is the total workload of faculty, which may include individualized instruction, independent study supervision, supervision of student theses and dissertations, academic advising, committee assignments, governance and administrative duties, and research and scholarship. Many institutions appear to be hiring part-time faculty not to reduce the teaching loads of full-time faculty, but to meet instructional needs that full-time faculty are otherwise too busy to address. To this analysis one must also add the typically lower rate of compensation per credit hour for part-timers. Both of these factors appear to underlie the policy of increasing the use of part-time faculty.

Teaching load is also a consideration in the increasing use of full-time non–tenure track faculty. Analysis of NSOPF-93 data reveals that full-time faculty differ by tenure status in the number of hours they work per week. Non–tenure track faculty work fewer hours per week than tenured or tenure-eligible colleagues. However, non–tenure track faculty reported more hours per week teaching (10.40) than tenured (8.81) and tenure track faculty (9.77). Consistent with the differences identified in teaching load between full-time and part-time faculty, tenured faculty teach fewer courses than non–tenure track faculty, but their classes are larger, on average (Baldwin and Chronister 2001). These data suggest that tenure track and full-time non–tenure track faculty fill qualitatively different roles at many institutions. Non–tenure track faculty tend to spend more time on instruction-related activities, often in small, intensive, skill-building courses, while tenure track faculty have more broad-based work lives that encompass governance and scholarship as well as teaching.

The roles of full-time non–tenure track faculty vary significantly across institutions. A number of colleges hire full-time faculty off the tenure track to fill the same range of functions as the tenured and tenure-eligible faculty, while others hire them primarily to teach. Smaller institutions, like liberal arts colleges, are more likely to employ full-time non–tenure track faculty interchangeably with tenure-class faculty. Larger institutions, by contrast, are more likely to segment tenure-ineligible faculty into specialized teaching roles or teaching roles combined with some administrative or technical responsibilities (Baldwin and Chronister 2001). It is not uncommon to find institutions at which the full-time non–tenure track faculty have teaching loads that exceed those of tenured and tenure-eligible faculty by one or two courses per semester (Baldwin and Chronister 2001).

Questions about Quality

Questions about quality are integral to discussions about the growing use of part-time and full-time term-contract faculty, yet little empirical evidence focuses directly on this question. Leslie (1998) considered the effects of increasing reliance on part-time faculty and concluded that "quality can only be addressed indirectly" (p. 13). This statement also applies to the effects on quality of the increased use of full-time faculty off the tenure track.

Some data on part-time and full-time non–tenure track faculty raise concerns about quality. For example, tenure track faculty are more likely to hold the Ph.D. than are part-time (Leslie 1998) or full-time tenure-ineligible faculty (U.S. Department of Education 1993). These data suggest that non–tenure track faculty may have a more limited knowledge and skill base than do regular tenure track faculty. The more narrowly defined professional role of many non–tenure track faculty also leads to quality concerns. The heavier teaching duties or outside job commitments of many part-time, and some term-contract, faculty limit time available for other roles such as scholarship, curriculum development, and governance. Leslie (1998) reported that part-time faculty devote far less time to research than do full-time faculty (7.1% versus 17.6% respectively). To the extent that an active research agenda stands as a proxy for keeping current in one's field, this statistic heightens concern about the effects on quality of the growing employment of faculty not eligible for tenure.

The limited professional development support available to part-time and term-contract faculty raises a related quality concern. Many institutions provide faculty off the tenure track sporadic (if any) financial support for professional travel, conference attendance, or participation in professional development workshops (Baldwin and Chronister 2001; Gappa and Leslie 1993). When this pattern persists over many years, faculty off the tenure track are undoubtedly less equipped to keep pace with their fields, advances in instructional methods, and the interests and needs of their students. This situation is not inherent to the use of faculty off the tenure track. Rather, it reflects the second-class status of many faculty who are viewed as temporary or peripheral and, thus, less deserving of support from limited institutional resources.

The positive contributions of part-time and term-contract faculty offset some of the negative evidence and perceptions. For example, Gappa and Leslie "found essentially 'no difference' in quality of teaching between part-time and full-time faculty" (Leslie 1998, p. 13). In addition, many non–tenure track faculty with current or prior career experience in areas like business, government, or medicine enrich academic programs through timely case examples, a practitioner's perspective, and knowledge of career opportunities (Chronister and Baldwin 1999). Limited-term non–tenure track positions also enable institutions to experiment with new courses and academic programs. Many colleges and universities would be reluctant to invest in such quality enhancements if a long-term financial commitment were required at the outset.

Judging the effects on quality of faculty off the traditional tenure track depends to a large extent on one's perspective. Linda Carroll, representing the viewpoint of the AAUP, asserts that employing faculty on short-term contracts "erodes educational quality by driving away talented faculty. . . . A university that views its faculty as short-term or part-time employees," she argues, "gives them little or no say in governance, and subjects them to continuous checks blunts its competitive edge by encouraging timidity and conformity among its faculty" (Carroll 2000, p. 24).

In contrast, research by Richard Chait and Cathy Trower (1998) on Florida Gulf Coast University (FGCU), an institution designed without a tenure system, suggests that the absence of tenure does not preclude highly capable faculty. Chait and Trower learned that faculty prospects at FGCU "seldom refused to consider a multi-year contract" and "the university regularly hired its first or second choice" (p. 24). Perhaps most important, "the overall faculty profile [of FGCU], as gauged by degrees, diversity, and academic experience, compares quite favorably with similar regional universities in the state and beyond" (p. 25).

The consequences of employing part-time and term-contract faculty will remain subject to debate. Like most breaks with convention in higher education, this trend provokes controversy. It leads to differing opinions based more on philosophy and value judgments than hard evidence.

Where Is the Tenure Track Going?

The bulk of the evidence on tenure track trends leads to two firm conclusions:

1. Non–tenure track appointments now constitute a significant portion of the academic workforce in higher education, and such arrangements will continue to expand.
2. The eventual outcome of this transition in faculty staffing remains unclear, but the sheer numbers cannot be ignored.

We turn now to some of the key issues with policy implications that emerge from recent tenure track trends. These issues fall into four distinct but overlapping categories:

1. Faculty roles and work life.
2. Academic careers.
3. Impact on institutions and the academic community.
4. Future of non–tenure track positions.

Following the analysis of these issues, we conclude the chapter with a set of recommendations for maintaining a vital professoriat.

Faculty Roles and Work Life

The comparative data on traditional tenure track and part-time and term-contract faculty reveal that the nature of faculty work life and the distribution of faculty workloads is gradually changing for many members of the academic profession. Tenure track and non–tenure track faculty are dividing academic work in new ways that alter the teaching, research, and service trilogy that has clearly defined professorial responsibilities over several successive generations. Researchers who study the academic profession (Baldwin and Chronister 2001; Gappa and Leslie 1993) suggest, for example, that faculty off the tenure track are providing a substantial portion of lower-division instruction, skill development teaching (e.g., English composition, foreign languages), and instruction in specialized, often career-related fields. Policymakers should consider how a redistribution of faculty labor along these lines will affect educational programs, professional evaluation standards, and faculty vitality.

The data cited earlier show that tenure track trends are not uniform across different contexts. The balance between tenure track and part-time and full-time term-contract positions differs by field and type of institution. This information raises specific questions about faculty roles and the distribution of faculty work. For instance, what are the conditions that have stimulated the increased use of non–tenure track positions in some fields but not others? Are these patterns consistent with the needs of diverse fields or do they reflect less benign developments? Does this trend suggest that resource-rich fields can afford to continue traditional faculty staffing arrangements while less affluent fields cobble together a mix of traditional academics and outside practitioners, all in temporary positions? Alternatively, are some fields and some institutions adapting readily to changing environments and new educational demands while others resist change and rigidly adhere to the status quo? Do the staffing changes apparent from national data on faculty suggest that institutions are trying to offset liabilities and gaps created by an outmoded tenure system in need of reform?

Substantial evidence shows that faculty work life in the twenty-first century will be more varied than it was in the past, when a single professional model dominated faculty roles. To date, the reshaping of faculty work has been mostly unplanned and haphazard. We believe that colleges and universities should take command of this process and redefine more systematically the nature and balance of faculty roles. Institutions should look carefully at their projected staffing needs and craft policies and positions conducive to changing circumstances and their missions. Strategic planning initiatives or institutional task forces should bring together administrators, faculty leaders, and representatives of other important constituencies to rethink and reform faculty work, positions, and policies. Periodic surveys of faculty work activity, satisfaction, and morale may help spot problems early. In any case, a systematic, broad-based effort is necessary to align faculty functions with society's educational needs and institutions' changing roles. Continuing to respond to the demand for alternatives to traditional tenure track positions with inconsistent, ad hoc solutions will prolong an awkward transitional phase in the academic profession.

Academic Careers

Important policy questions about academic careers also emerge from the data. Traditionally, academic careers have followed a well-charted path, from instructor or assistant professor to full professor. The requirements to advance in rank and achieve status in the profession were fairly well defined within the cultures of different fields and types of institutions. The rules are not so clear, however, in a more heterogeneous faculty staffing environment. Researchers who have studied part-time faculty (Gappa and Leslie 1993) and term-contract faculty (Baldwin and Chronister 2001; Gappa 1996) conclude that the route to professional advancement is not nearly so straightforward off the tenure track. Many institutions do not offer sequential ranks to non–tenure track faculty, even to those who serve for many years. Professional development support for part-time and term-contract faculty also tends to be limited and erratic on many campuses.

Many questions come to mind in this context. How does one build a stable career at an institution without a defined route for advancement? For instance, what happens to a valued term-contract instructor of English composition who sees her junior colleagues on the tenure track surpass her in rank, status, and salary? To date, only a small number of higher education institutions have acknowledged new faculty staffing patterns with well-defined and attractive alternatives to the standard tenure track career path. Some institutions have reserved resources and developed policies to support the long-term career growth of non–tenure track faculty who serve for long periods. Wherever part-time and term-contract faculty meet important and long-term institutional needs, their career development must be addressed through systematic policies and resources. Failure to do so subverts the well-being of higher education by unnaturally locking key players in the academic enterprise into place intellectually and professionally.

We recognize that taking steps to enhance the status, career stability, or professional development of faculty off the tenure track may diminish cost savings, flexibility, and other institutional benefits that often accompany non–tenure track positions. We believe it is imperative, however, that institutions differentiate between non–tenure track positions that meet short-term needs and those that serve long-term purposes. In the latter case, allocating resources and establishing policies to support effective performance and career growth are essential. Flexibility can be maintained through carefully crafted contractual arrangements. For instance, at Rhodes College, if a position is no longer needed, a faculty member on a long-term non–tenure track appointment may be terminated in two ways. One is by giving a year's notice of nonreappointment. The other is by giving the faculty member 125% of his or her annual salary to leave at the end of the current academic year. This quid pro quo recognizes a long-serving professor's need for career stability while also acknowledging the institution's need for staffing flexibility.

Impact on Institutions and the Academic Community

Alternative types of faculty appointments also raise questions about the impact of a broader range of faculty on institutions and their sense of community. Traditions of community and shared governance have been hallmarks of the academic profession for generations. In addition, a hierarchy based on discipline, seniority, and achievement has existed for a long time. Recent tenure track trends, however, suggest that the profession is being divided into even more distinct subgroups than before, based more on appointment status and working conditions than on factors over which faculty have some control. How will differing faculty employment patterns affect the balance of faculty power and the overall health of the academic community? What is the impact on collegiality and educational quality when part of the professoriat knows the steps to professional advancement and receives support for growth while colleagues who work in the same programs and serve many of the same students have few opportunities to move ahead? Ultimately, the higher education community and public policymakers must ask: Are we creating a rigid faculty class system with an advantaged class (traditional tenure track faculty) and a disadvantaged class of low-status workers (full-time non–tenure track and part-time faculty)? If a distinct class system is developing and a significant proportion of the new female and racial/ethnic minority faculty are being employed in the disadvantaged class, will institutions be able to fulfill their espoused goals of achieving gender and racial/ethnic equity in faculty employment?

Although current faculty employment practices have been defined to help institutions cope with constrained finances and rapid change, what will be the unintended consequences of these policies? Will institutions be revitalized or fragmented? Will some members of the faculty soar to great heights while others remain constrained by a system that fails to recognize their contributions and value to their community by advancing their status or nurturing their growth?

The answers to these questions are not preordained. Whether institutions benefit or suffer as a result of more non–tenure track appointments depends on how part-time and term-contract faculty are utilized and integrated into the academic community. We have visited institutions where tenure track and non–tenure track faculty seem locked into a professional caste system and where little interaction, let alone collaboration, occurs between the two groups. In such environments, collegiality is weak and the morale of "lower-class" faculty is usually low. At some institutions women, who fill a large portion of non–tenure track positions, comprise a noticeably disadvantaged (sometimes embittered) faculty subgroup. In contrast, we have also visited institutions that treat their non–tenure track faculty as full-fledged professionals, engage them in governance, and support their career advancement. At schools that work to minimize status differences between tenure track and non–tenure track faculty, the institution and individual faculty members benefit from a healthy work environment rich with professional growth opportunities. Webster University, for instance, made the non–tenure track attractive through professional development incentives, such as frequent sabbaticals, and by minimizing differences in faculty governance roles, compensation, and prestige.

Future of Non–Tenure Track Positions

Whether the employment of faculty in full-time tenure-ineligible positions will continue to increase is a function of several factors. Not the least of these are the terms and conditions under which these alternative types of faculty are employed. Can a heavy or narrowly focused teaching load be packaged as an appealing professional opportunity? How should faculty personnel policies be reformed to engage more fully this growing component of the professoriat and minimize their second-class status? If the academic labor market changes and options for employment outside the academic profession increase, will it become more difficult to recruit qualified personnel to fill positions off the tenure track?

What about the attitudes toward tenure of faculty members themselves? Recent years have seen a vocal core of faculty questioning the value of tenure. In a 1998 study of faculty attitudes by the Higher Education Research Institute (HERI) at UCLA, 67% of faculty respondents strongly or somewhat disagreed with the statement that tenure is an outmoded concept (Higher Education Research Institute, n.d.), but that still leaves one third of the faculty disenchanted with the system. More than 70% of tenured faculty responded in support of tenure, while only 45%, 51%, and 62% of untenured professors, associate professors, and assistant professors respectively responded in support of tenure. In HERI's 1995 survey, 61% agreed or strongly agreed with the statement "Tenure is essential to attract the best minds to academe"— that is, only six of ten faculty responded affirmatively to the statement. Again, fewer untenured faculty expressed support for tenure than did tenured faculty. Although the majority of faculty still value tenure, many do not. Also, different subgroups of the academic profession express various opinions regarding the merits of tenure. What do these findings suggest about faculty openness to tenure alternatives? What are the policy implications of these differing faculty attitudes toward tenure? These are questions that institutional leaders and public policymakers should consider as higher education moves further into the twenty-first century.

We have traveled throughout the United States trying to understand the growing non–tenure track faculty phenomenon. Our investigation led us to conclude that positions off the tenure track, if designed appropriately, can be attractive professional opportunities. We learned that positions with heavy teaching loads are appealing to some gifted teachers who do not want to pursue heavy research expectations. "Hybrid" faculty positions, involving teaching and administrative or technical duties, appeal to some faculty who seek a different balance of professional roles. Part-time faculty positions are attractive to some persons seeking to balance their personal and professional lives. A non–tenure track career can be fulfilling at institutions, like Carnegie-Mellon University or Webster University, that treat such faculty with respect, reward them for their contributions, and offer steps for advancement while preserving the opportunity for staffing flexibility.

The increased use of contingent (part-time and term-contract) faculty parallels the growing use of "permatemps" in business, government, and other employment sectors. This trend, coupled with the substantial segment of faculty who feel tenure is not a necessary employment condition, suggests that further growth of non–tenure track positions at colleges and universities is likely.

Questions about the Future of the Academic Profession

The data we have presented and the resulting questions they suggest lead to larger questions: What impact will changes in the tenure track have on the future of the academic profession? Will professorial careers remain attractive to a sufficient segment of society's highest-caliber talent? Will a profession containing diverse employment arrangements remain unified, healthy, and vital? The increased use of non–tenure track faculty to provide lower-division instruction, skill development teaching, and instruction in specialized or professional areas suggests that further segmentation of the academic profession is under way (Baldwin and Chronister 2001; Finkin 2000; Gappa and Leslie 1993).

Are factors such as family considerations and personal circumstances of faculty accommodated in new versions of academic appointments? Judith Gappa and Shelley MacDermid (1997) provide evidence that some "leadership" campuses have been responsive to these issues, albeit slowly and incompletely. The changes we have reported in the tenure track, especially the wider range of faculty roles and appointment options being offered, may be evidence of accommodations to an increasingly diverse professoriat. Finkelstein (1999) argues that the United States is in a process of transition to a new academic order. The changes in the tenure track that we have observed may be part of a larger realignment of the academic profession to bridge the gap between an outmoded employment system (predominantly tenure track appointments) and the new realities higher education must address.

If this country is in the midst of a major reform of academic work and careers, can—or must—consensus be achieved on alternate forms of faculty roles and a standardized range of faculty employment options across American higher education? The traditional tenure track system that dominated faculty careers for much of the twentieth century was standardized and widely adopted due in part to the endorsement of leading national organizations, including the American Association of University Professors (AAUP), the American Council on Education (ACE), and the Association of American Colleges (AAC). No similar consensus on the parameters and conditions of non–tenure track faculty employment (part-time or full-time term-contract) currently exists. Gappa and Leslie (1997) conclude that part-time "faculty staffing is ad hoc and driven by noneducational factors" (p. 4) and that "policies on the use of part-time faculty are informal and capriciously administered" (p. 4). Similarly, Chait and Trower's (1997) review of the policies of institutions that employ full-time faculty off the tenure track reveals a startling absence of consistent appointment practices across institutions. The examples Chait and Trower present have appointments varying from one year to seven years, depending on a wide range of evaluation and other employment arrangements. This crazy quilt of policies cannot be good for individual faculty working off the tenure track or for the academic profession as a whole. Some degree of standardization of roles and contract options seems essential for the preparation, development, and career advancement of faculty, whether they work on or off the tenure track.

By advocating some standardization of positions off the tenure track, we are not arguing against the flexibility and responsiveness that make non–tenure track positions so attractive in the first place. We believe it is appropriate, however, to implement some common definitions and consistent practices for differing types of faculty positions off the tenure track, similar to the common practices that characterize the tenure system. For example, we suggest that the responsibilities, rights, and access to resources of very short-term (one semester, one year) appointments be differentiated by policy from those of renewable non–tenure track positions for which there is a longer-term need. Here we are thinking of contracts that may, after a probationary period, extend from three to perhaps as long as ten years. We believe that predictability is desirable in a profession where jobs require years of preparation, staying current requires time and money, and locating another professional position often involves a national search. Likewise, locating qualified faculty who fit an institution's mission and culture is not easy. Consistent standards and expectations that candidates can rely on may help to make non–tenure track positions more attractive and also ease the transition from a term-contract faculty appointment at one institution to another faculty appointment elsewhere. Consistent definitions of non–tenure track positions would also increase understanding of these alternative types of faculty positions across institutions and help to enhance their recognition as legitimate and valued professional posts.

Within non–tenure track categories (e.g., part-time short-term; part-time renewable; short-term full-time appointment; full-time renewable contract), we are advocating common (but still flexible) definitions, expectations, standards of support, and contract arrangements. Today many persons in non–tenure track positions do not have a clear idea of their status within their institution, their rights, or their potential for a continuing appointment. Consequently, they live lives unnecessarily fraught with ambiguity and uncertainty as they perpetually search for another, more stable job. This situation is potentially harmful to the "contingent" professor, to the institution he or she serves, and especially to students. In contrast, clear definitions of distinct types of non–tenure track positions that carry differing responsibilities, provide differing levels of support, and come with differing levels of career security can better serve the interests of higher education. A range of differing types of non–tenure track faculty positions whose definitions are understood across higher education should help to fill the wide faculty staffing gap between single-course assignments or very short-term sabbatical replacement positions and potentially career-long tenure track appointments. At present, only tenure track positions are clearly defined throughout the academy. Modest standardization of other types of faculty appointments could preserve flexibility in higher education while reducing the uncertainty that accompanies many part-time and full-time term-contract positions and minimizes their appeal as a career option.

With a shrinking tenure track, will academic freedom remain secure? The answer to this question depends on whom we ask. Peter Byrne (1997) as well as Chait and Trower (1997) concluded that academic freedom can be provided under contract systems. Colleges with contract systems, Chait and Trower (1997) observed, "depend upon a mix of procedural safeguards, policy statements, *and* [their emphasis] tradition, trust, and goodwill" (p. 24) to insure academic freedom. Chait and Trower found that "the vast majority of faculty at the study sites [in their research project] were satisfied that these latter conditions prevail" (p. 24). In contrast, Matthew Finkin, in *The Case for Tenure*, asserts that "in the absence of tenure there is no prohibition against arbitrary dismissal; without tenure there is no constitutional right to a prior (and proper) hearing on the cause alleged to justify the dismissal" (1996, p. 193). Given the controversial nature of the academic freedom issue, each institution should define explicit policies and procedures to protect the academic freedom of all faculty, not just those who enjoy tenure status. As the nontenured component of the professoriat grows, it becomes increasingly important to extend overt and codified academic freedom to all faculty.

There remains a bottom-line question that the academic community and policymakers concerned with higher education must ponder: Is the declining proportion of traditional tenure track appointments a positive or negative development for faculty members, higher education, and society in general? There is no simple answer to this question. The most accurate response undoubtedly is that it is both—positive and negative. To the extent that changes in the tenure track make higher education more responsive to society's needs and accommodate the distinctive circumstances of an increasingly diverse academic profession, this is a beneficial development. To the extent that changes in the tenure track threaten educational quality and further fragment the academic profession into privileged and disadvantaged classes, it is a regrettable development. As higher education institutions work to adapt their faculty employment practices to changing circumstances, they must design policies that promote a healthy working environment for all faculty, regardless of their tenure status. To nourish one segment of the academic profession while neglecting the working conditions and long-term career needs of the other is a recipe for demoralization and perhaps decline.

We believe that colleges and universities can develop enlightened non–tenure track policies that recognize faculty needs while responding to institutions' desire for greater efficiency and flexibility. As the number of institutions developing progressive policies for faculty off the tenure track increases, it will be easier to state emphatically that increased faculty employment options in higher education are a positive development for its evolution.

The Tenure Track in Transition: Recommendations for Action

Few experts on higher education foresee, or even advocate, the abolition of traditional tenure. Many (Carroll 2000; Finkin 1996; Stimpson 2000) believe the tenure track will continue to be the cornerstone of faculty personnel systems for decades to come. The trends examined in this chapter, however, suggest that the tenure track will continue to be supplemented by substantial numbers of part-time and term-contract faculty, most likely in growing proportion to the tenure track. This tendency confronts higher education leaders and policymakers with very important challenges to craft policies that will:

1. support an increasingly diverse profession as it adapts to a changing environment and rapidly evolving educational needs;
2. increase the efficiency and improve the cost effectiveness of faculty work;
3. enable faculty to stay current in their fields and deliver cutting-edge instruction and scholarship; and

4. maintain a faculty work environment conducive to creativity and productivity.

Changes in the tenure track require decisive action throughout higher education and within individual institutions. We believe that each of the following recommendations is critical to maintaining a diverse and vital academic profession in a time of transition.

Preparing and Recruiting Future Faculty

Graduate schools traditionally socialize their students primarily for careers on the tenure track. This narrow career focus is no longer consistent with the growing numbers of part-time and term-contract faculty appointments. Graduate programs must seek new ways to prepare students for a volatile employment market that may involve multiple job changes and continuous transformation of faculty roles and functions. Institutions must move beyond the informal mentoring process where students learn about the academic career primarily by observing tenured faculty advisors or classroom instructors, as such an approach provides a very limited perspective on the range of faculty careers today. Informal mentoring needs to be supplemented by seminars or workshops on academic career options. These programs could introduce graduates to the contemporary academic labor market and the various types of faculty employment relationships that institutions are now utilizing. For example, the College of William and Mary offers a course on nonacademic employment alternatives for Ph.D. candidates. Such a course could be expanded or supplemented to examine nontraditional faculty opportunities within colleges and universities. Information on non–tenure track teaching opportunities and discussions with persons who teach in part-time and term-contract positions are useful ways to enlarge the career vision of graduate students. Part-time or temporary teaching jobs outside the research university setting, perhaps combined with administrative or technical responsibilities, are additional means to expose graduate students to a wider range of academic career alternatives.

Institutions seeking to hire faculty off the tenure track may also need to rethink their recruitment strategies. (See Chapter 7, by Cathy A. Trower, in this volume.) Are there more effective ways to identify faculty talent than the costly national searches they typically undertake to hire tenure track faculty? Developing and sharing a faculty talent pool with other nearby institutions may be one way to insure the availability of qualified candidates to fill non–tenure track appointments. Joint appointments or exchanges across two or more institutions may be another way to reduce recruiting costs and retain faculty talent when institutions cannot afford to make long-term tenure track commitments. Combining traditional teaching duties with administrative or technical roles to form a full-time position is another technique schools can use to attract qualified academic personnel when a traditional full-time tenure track appointment is not a feasible option.

Regulating and Supporting the Work of Faculty

As the dominant employment model in higher education, the tenure track has set the parameters within which most faculty policies and support systems have been designed. Faculty who fall outside the normative model, whether part-time or full-time term-contract faculty, are often overlooked when workload, evaluation criteria, or faculty development policies are defined. This oversight should not be tolerated now that more than half of all faculty do not work on the tenure track. Institutions should insure that personnel policies and faculty support systems enhance the performance of all faculty, regardless of their tenure status.

In practice, this means that policies should be developed to structure the work and professional lives of faculty off the tenure track. Instead of taking an ad hoc approach to individual non–tenure track appointments, institutions should amend their faculty handbooks to include terms and conditions, and rights and responsibilities, for part-time and term-contract faculty. All relevant dimensions of non–tenure track faculty employment should be addressed, including appointment procedures, the purposes of these types of appointments, scope of duties, evaluation criteria, professional growth support, opportunities for advancement, and timely notice of renewal or nonreappointment. Individual faculty contracts should also address each of these issues in order to eliminate as much uncertainty from non–tenure track status as possible. Carnegie-Mellon University's policy on term-contract appointments, for example, specifies the purpose of non–tenure track faculty positions, explains varied term lengths based on seniority and performance, describes evaluation procedures, and outlines a series of career steps through which renewable term-contract faculty may advance. Carefully planned policies to regulate and support faculty off the tenure track should make these positions more predictable and appealing. They will also ease the burden of department chairs and administrators who must supervise this growing contingent of the academic workforce.

Integrating Non–Tenure Track Faculty into the Academic Community

Gappa and Leslie's book title, *The Invisible Faculty* (1993), speaks volumes about the status, function, and influence of faculty outside the traditional mold. Ignoring part-time and term-contract faculty may have been tolerable in an earlier era when their numbers were smaller. Today, when the numbers of non–tenure track faculty are substantial and the roles they play at many institutions are essential, failing to engage them in the decision-making, curriculum development, and social life of an institution is potentially harmful. All types of faculty suffer from the absence of community. Likewise, educational programs can only be diminished by the failure to include a significant component of the academic workforce in the governance process. It is incumbent upon institutions that hire faculty on different types of contracts to integrate all these positions as fully as possible into the life of the institution and its decision-making processes.

Some institutions that employ non–tenure track faculty treat them as full-fledged members of the academic community and engage them formally in all aspects of decision-making and policy development. Non–tenure track faculty even fill elected leadership roles at some of these schools. At Webster University, for instance, faculty are so well integrated that colleagues often do not know and do not care who is on the tenure track and who is not. This level of integration may be difficult to achieve for part-time faculty or faculty who fill short-term or highly specialized roles. However, we do believe it is important to engage non–tenure track faculty (part-time and full-time) as much as possible in the governance and intellectual life of their institutions. At a minimum, this means orienting them to the institution and including them in departmental governance and institutional committees pertinent to their duties. Invitations to ceremonies and social events offer another way to integrate faculty in nontraditional positions into the life of their institution. Department chairs, as faculty colleagues, should take a peer leadership role in integrating tenure-ineligible faculty into the academic community. The overarching goal should be to move non–tenure track faculty from the periphery toward the center of the colleges and universities that they serve.

Supporting the Career Development of Non–Tenure Track Faculty

Historically, faculty off the tenure track have been viewed from a policy perspective as the academic equivalent of migrant workers. Institutions rarely defined steps for their advancement or invested resources in their future development. While this strategy makes sense for academic staff who truly are temporary, non–tenure track faculty often serve their institutions for many years and perform valuable core duties. As colleges and universities attempt to craft a healthy balance between tenure-eligible and non–tenure track faculty, they must consider how to support the development of those who have a future at the institution. If non–tenure track faculty are valued as institutional assets who contribute to the achievement of institutional goals rather than as consumable resources, attention must be given to their renewal and growth. Failure to recognize and reinforce the positive contributions of long-serving faculty off the tenure track can only diminish the health and vitality of the institution as a whole.

Support for professional growth and a system of sequential ranks are important ways to support the career development of faculty off the tenure track. The intellectual capital of all faculty members must be renewed periodically. Consistent with their roles and their level and longevity of service, part-time and term-contract faculty should have opportunities to attend conferences, participate in instructional development programs, and engage in other professional development activities. For example, institutions should provide conference travel support for tenure-ineligible faculty who have served the institution for more than one year or who have a contract of more than one year. A simple rule of thumb should apply to all institutions employing non–tenure track faculty: the level of professional development support should increase commensurate with years of service and value to the institution. Carried to its logical conclusion, this means that professional growth leaves should be available to long-serving (more than five years) term-contract faculty whose work is essential. Model paid leave programs at schools such as Rhodes College and Webster University could be adapted to other institutions with appropriate modifications. At present, relatively few higher education institutions have implemented a paid leave program for non–tenure track faculty. Those that have find that paid leaves help to sustain faculty vitality, reduce the status differences between tenure track and non–tenure track positions, and probably make non–tenure track positions more attractive as alternatives to tenure track appointments.

A career ladder system providing opportunities for advancement in rank and status can also promote career growth. Some institutions choose to employ the conventional faculty ranks while others define distinctive ranks such as lecturer, senior lecturer, and master lecturer for faculty not eligible for tenure. The specific titles used are probably less important than the opportunity to move forward professionally and receive recognition for valuable contributions to one's institution.

Ensuring Academic Freedom

Academic freedom is one of the core values and prerequisite conditions of a healthy and vital academic profession. If higher education chooses to continue to employ a significant proportion of faculty in positions not eligible for tenure, then the academy must determine how to safeguard the academic freedom of all faculty. Martin Michaelson, writing in Chait's (1998) report *Ideas in Incubation: Three Possible Modifications to Traditional Tenure Policies*, proposes a straightforward means to achieve this objective. He argues that an institution's policy protecting academic freedom should "apply to all personnel of the University to the extent that they function in a faculty capacity, and shall apply no less to the least experienced, no less to the most junior than the most senior, and no less to part-time than full-time faculty" (p. 29).

Although specific strategies may differ, colleges and universities should implement clear policies and procedures to protect the academic freedom of faculty off the tenure track. To employ a major segment of the professoriat without explicit guarantees of academic freedom will erode the working conditions essential to effective teaching, learning, and the advancement of knowledge. In the process, the quality of American higher education will surely be diminished.

The "one size fits all" approach to structuring and supporting faculty careers is no longer viable, if it ever was. Today our higher education system relies on multiple types of faculty roles and appointments. For this reason, it is essential that higher education develop multiple means to promote the welfare and effective performance of the diverse professionals who now work in the academy.

The tenure track, like America's railroads, is unlikely to disappear. It still has an important role to play in our educational system. But like the railroads, it will be supplemented by new systems designed to meet more effectively our society's growing demand for education, knowledge, and expert service. Non–tenure track and part-time appointments are here to stay; therefore, the academy must learn to structure these positions to serve the greatest possible benefit for such faculty and the institutions they serve.

Notes

Sincere thanks to Christopher Foley, doctoral student at the University of Virginia, for his analysis of the IPEDS data used in this chapter.

1. We use the term "non–tenure track" to refer to both part-time and full-time college and university faculty who are not eligible for tenure status. When referring to full-time non–tenure track faculty, we use the labels "contract faculty" and "full-time non–tenure track faculty" interchangeably.

2. In years prior to 1993, members of the nonresident alien category were included in their appropriate race/ethnicity category. With the addition of a separate nonresident alien category they are removed from the race/ethnicity categories and included in the nonresident alien category.

3. Those classified as "other" included professional schools and other types of specialized institutions.

References

Baldwin, Roger G., and Jay L. Chronister. 2001. *Teaching without Tenure: Policies and Practices for a New Era*. Baltimore: Johns Hopkins University Press.

Byrne, Peter J. 1997. *Academic Freedom without Tenure?* New Pathways Working Paper Series, no. 5. Washington, D.C.: American Association for Higher Education.

Cahalan, Margaret, and Stephen Roey. 1996. *Fall Staff in Postsecondary Institutions, 1993*. Washington, D.C.: U.S. Department of Education, Office of Educational Research and Improvement.

Carroll, Linda L. 2000. "Tenure and Academic Excellence." *Academe*, 86 (3): 22–25.

Chait, Richard. 1998. *Ideas in Incubation: Three Possible Modifications to Traditional Tenure Policies*. New Pathways Working Paper Series, no. 9. Washington, D.C.: American Association for Higher Education.

Chait, Richard, and Cathy A. Trower. 1997. *Where Tenure Does Not Reign: Colleges with Contract Systems*. New Pathways Working Paper Series, no. 3. Washington, D.C.: American Association for Higher Education.

——— 1998. "Build It and Who Will Come?" *Change*, 30 (5): 20–29.

Chronister, Jay L., and Roger G. Baldwin. 1999. "Marginal or Mainstream? Full-Time Faculty Off the Tenure Track." *Liberal Education*, 85 (4): 16–23.

Eisenberg, Daniel. 1999. "Rise of the Permatemp." *Time*, 154 (2): 48.

Fairweather, James S. 1996. *Faculty Work and the Public Trust: Restoring the Value of Teaching and Public Service in American Academic Life*. Boston: Allyn and Bacon.

Finkelstein, Martin. 1999. "Academic Careers in 2000 and Beyond." *AAC&U Peer Review*, 1 (3): 4–8.

Finkelstein, Martin J., Robert K. Seal, and Jack H. Schuster. 1998. *The New Academic Generation: A Profession in Transformation*. Baltimore: Johns Hopkins University Press.

Finkin, Matthew W. 2000. "The Campaign against Tenure." *Academe*, 86 (3): 20–21.

———, ed. 1996. *The Case for Tenure*. Ithaca, N.Y.: Cornell University Press.

Gappa, Judith M. 1996. *Off the Tenure Track: Six Models for Full-Time, Nontenurable Appointments*. New Pathways Working Paper Series, no. 10. Washington, D.C.: American Association for Higher Education.

Gappa, Judith M., and David W. Leslie. 1993. *The Invisible Faculty: Improving the Status of Part-Timers in Higher Education*. San Francisco: Jossey-Bass.

——— 1997. *Two Faculties or One? The Conundrum of Part-Timers in a Bifurcated Work Force*. New Pathways Working Paper Series, no. 6. Washington, D.C.: American Association for Higher Education.

Gappa, Judith M., and Shelley M. MacDermid. 1997. *Work, Family, and the Faculty Career*. New Pathways Working Paper Series, no. 8. Washington, D.C.: American Association for Higher Education.

Higher Education Research Institute. [n.d.] "An Overview of the 1998–99 Faculty Norms." Available online: *www.gseis.ucla.edu/heri/faculty.htm*.

Kirshstein, Rita J., Nancy Matheson, and Zhongren Jing. 1997. *Instructional Faculty and Staff in Higher Education Institutions: Fall 1987 and Fall 1992*. Washington, D.C.: U.S. Department of Education, Office of Educational Research and Improvement, National Center for Education Statistics.

Leslie, David W. 1997. "Part-Time, Adjunct, and Temporary Faculty: The New Majority?" Report of the Sloan Conference on Part-Time and Adjunct Faculty. Arlington, Va. December 2–3.

Levine, Arthur. 1997. "How the Academic Profession Is Changing." *Daedalus*, 126 (4): 1–20.

Melchionno, Rick. 1999. "The Changing Temporary Work Force: Managerial,

Professional, and Technical Workers in the Personnel Supply Services Industry." *Occupational Outlook Quarterly*, 43 (1): 24–32.

"Policy on Lecturer Track Appointments." 1994. *Faculty Handbook*. Pittsburgh, Pa.:
Carnegie-Mellon University.

Roey, Stephen, and Rebecca Rak. 1998. *Fall Staff in Postsecondary Institutions, 1995*.
Washington, D.C.: U.S. Department of Education, Office of Educational Research and Improvement.

Stimpson, Catharine. 2000. "A Dean Looks at Tenure." *Academe*, 86 (3): 34–37.

U.S. Department of Education, National Center for Education Statistics. 1993.
National Study of Postsecondary Faculty, data file.

——— 1998. *IPEDS Fall Staff Survey in Postsecondary Institutions*, 1995 electronic
data file, final release (April).

——— 2000. *IPEDS Fall Staff Survey in Postsecondary Institutions*, 1997 electronic
data file, final release (February).

Wildavsky, Ben. 2000. "Is Tenure Slip-Sliding Away?" in *America's Best Graduate
Schools, U.S. News and World Report, 2001*. Washington, D.C.: U.S. News and
World Report. Pages 74–76.

6

How Are Faculty Faring
in Other Countries?

PHILIP G. ALTBACH

T IS IN MANY WAYS remarkable that universities everywhere, stemming as they do from common roots in medieval Europe and having similar purposes of teaching and research, have evolved quite different patterns of organization and structure. While academics worldwide teach, and in most cases have a role in research and institutional governance, their terms of employment and working conditions vary considerably. In discussing some of these differences, this chapter will address the following questions: (1) How have increased enrollments, diversified faculties, and reduced funding affected higher education worldwide? (2) What changes are taking place internationally with respect to tenure, academic freedom, types of appointments, and faculty salaries? And, finally, (3) what do the changing, and largely deteriorating, conditions of faculty work ultimately mean for the global academic enterprise?

The professoriat has become increasingly large and complex, with at least 3.5 million professionals involved in postsecondary teaching worldwide, serving more than 80 million students (Task Force on Higher Education and Society 2000). The professoriat is at the heart of the academic enterprise. Without a committed faculty, no university can be successful nor can effective teaching and learning take place. Yet despite the great presence of higher education in the technological world of the twenty-first century, the academic profession finds itself under increasing pressure. Working conditions have deteriorated at the same time that traditional autonomy has diminished. Increased enrollments have not been accompanied by commensurate growth in faculty appointments or salaries. At present, there are unprecedented changes taking place in appointments, working conditions, and management of the academic profession. It is timely to examine how the professoriat is changing internationally.

The Context

While the professoriat necessarily works within contemporary realities and within institutional and national settings, it is tied to universal historical traditions. One reason the academic profession is conservative in its views of the university is precisely because of its sense of history. Most universities have common roots in the medieval University of Paris and other European universities of the period (Ben-David and Zloczower 1962). Centuries-old ideas about the autonomy of teaching and research, the rightful place of the professoriat in institutional governance, and the role of the academic profession in society have salience. Academics have always seen themselves as somehow standing apart from society, with special privileges and responsibilities—as reflected in the idea of the academic profession as a calling. Many of these traditions have ebbed as universities have grown and become more professionalized. But there is still a historical residue that remains relevant.

Although there are many national variations in the organization and management of academe, there is also an important international element. Not only does academe have common historical roots, but in addition contemporary forces are making higher education ever more susceptible to global trends. Perhaps more than at any time since the Middle Ages, when universities functioned in a common language (Latin) and both faculty and students were highly mobile, academe operates in a global environment. Now, English is in some ways the Latin of the new era. There is again an international labor market for the professoriat, and more than one million students are studying abroad. New regulations concerning comparability of degrees in the European

Union, the ease of communication, and the establishment of joint-degree and other collaborative programs among universities in different countries exemplify the growing globalism of higher education.

Contemporary Realities

The central event of the past half century in higher education has been expansion. In country after country, higher education, once the preserve of the elite, has been transformed into a mass, and now almost universal, phenomenon (Trow 1972). This massification has given rise to more diverse and powerful administrative structures and diminished the sense of community among the professoriat. Academics increasingly work in large organizations and are constrained by bureaucratic procedures.

Higher education institutions have diversified. No longer is academe a preserve of the elite. Most academic systems now contain institutions with a variety of missions. Universities themselves now vary more in their level of academic quality. Today, postsecondary education is comprised of a diversity of institutional types—including vocationally oriented community colleges, polytechnic schools, undergraduate colleges, research universities, and specialized schools in both the public and private sectors. The traditional ideal, and self-concept, of the professor is no longer valid for the academic profession as a whole. Diversification of institutions has meant diversification of the professoriat as well.

Patterns of institutional control vary considerably from country to country. The United States is unusual for its decentralized higher education system. In contrast, academic systems throughout Europe, and much of the rest of the world as well, are more closely tied to the central government, both in terms of control and finance; and higher education is almost exclusively public. This means that the terms and conditions of academic work, including salary scales (which are often tied to pay scales in the civil service), as well as patterns of appointment and promotion, are in many cases determined by government policy.

Professors have traditionally valued their autonomy—the ability not only to control what happens in the classroom but also to determine the substance of their work. Few occupations have enjoyed the freedom of the professoriat to control the use of their time and the focus and range of productivity. In Europe particularly the ideals of professional autonomy combined with academic freedom in the classroom and laboratory have been hallmarks of the professoriat and remain primary values of the profession.

Traditionally, very little accountability was built into academic work. To this day, in much of the world, evaluation of teaching remains rare, and tracking faculty performance in research and other academic duties is not rigorous. Moreover, most academics around the world are paid not based on any concept of merit or productivity, but rather by rank and seniority. Again, this pattern is slowly changing as accountability and assessment become more entrenched. However, the fact remains that academics have been trusted to perform at an acceptable level of competence and productivity for centuries without any serious measurement of academic work.

Accountability is now increasingly part of the vocabulary of academic life. As higher education consumes more resources because of expansion, government and private funders demand greater accountability. A culture of accountability has emerged and has affected the academic profession. Assessment of academic work is increasingly common, with evaluation of teaching, research, service, and administrative work all part of the new academic workplace in more institutions in many countries.

The fiscal constraints on higher education in many countries have had a negative impact on the professoriat. Even in the United States, Britain, and other countries with currently favorable economic climates, higher education has not generally benefited from increased support. Student enrollments have grown at a faster rate than the size of the teaching staff. Funds, usually from public sources, have not kept up with the costs of expansion. The working conditions of academe are marked by increasing class size and deteriorating facilities. Academic salaries have failed to keep pace with inflation and have lagged behind salaries in related occupations. The financial problems that universities in industrialized countries face stem more from public policies concerning higher education than from underlying economic difficulties. In Britain, for example, fiscal cutbacks have accompanied student enrollment increases. In Germany, students have protested against deteriorating conditions caused by inadequate funding.

The fiscal crisis has hit developing and middle income countries dif-

ferently, with such regions as sub-Saharan Africa especially affected because of the combination of expanding enrollments and economic and
political difficulties. India, chronically strapped for funds and expanding nonetheless, has for several decades seen declines in the quality of
higher education. The transitional economies of Central and Eastern
Europe and the former Soviet Union have experienced pressures for
expanded access while at the same time facing the challenges of economic transformation. In short, there are very few countries, rich or
poor, in which the economic circumstances for postsecondary education are good.

The employment market for academics is in most places unfavorable. Academics in most countries experience a variety of employment-
related problems. Because fewer career-track positions are available,
new entrants to the profession have more difficulty obtaining full-time
initial appointments. Promotion is also more problematic, and many
countries have imposed quotas on promotion to senior ranks. This
means that many faculty are relegated to poorly paid junior positions
characterized by unfavorable working conditions. Although many senior professors hired in the 1960s and 1970s are now retiring, they are
not necessarily being replaced by full-time junior staff, causing additional problems for the academic employment market. In many countries, a surplus of disaffected doctoral degree holders has led many
graduates to take jobs outside academe. (Some exceptions to this bleak
picture exist—for example, fields such as computer science or management studies offer bright academic employment prospects.) While
there are major variations among nations in terms of the academic employment market, there is no country that offers ample prospects for
either junior staff or promotion opportunities for senior professors.

The professoriat has also been subjected to some criticism. For example, popular magazines such as Germany's *Der Spiegel* have printed
articles highly critical of German professors. A number of books in the
United States have appeared that claim that professors do not work
hard enough and have too much autonomy (Anderson 1992; Sykes
1988). There is no groundswell of popular discontent with higher education or with the professoriat evident anywhere; and most sociological
studies of occupational prestige show that academics continue to rank
among the most highly esteemed groups in society. Still, the professoriat has lost some of its luster as a profession in recent years.

Patterns of Academic Appointments

Systems of academic appointment are presently undergoing considerable ferment and change. For purposes of analysis, it may be useful to consider systems that have the equivalent of tenure, or permanent appointment of academics, as well as those that do not. Even though permanent appointments are by no means universal, academic careers enjoy considerable stability even without formal guarantees. Traditionally, in many countries, academics hired in the lowest rank after finishing graduate studies were "confirmed" after two or three years of satisfactory performance without undergoing a major evaluation. Confirmation meant either a de jure or de facto assurance of permanent appointment. Until Margaret Thatcher's reforms in the 1980s, British universities worked this way. Confirmation as a lecturer did not guarantee promotion, but it did assure a permanent position at that rank.

Now that tenure has been abolished in the United Kingdom, the situation has changed. Current British arrangements merit examination, since other countries have looked to the United Kingdom as a model. The abolition of permanent tenure for academic staff in Britain's universities was prompted by several factors. A key objective was to end the binary system, which distinguishes between the traditional universities and the vocationally oriented polytechnics, which did not have the right to confer academic degrees and never had a formalized tenure system. The polytechnics were upgraded to university status, and the terms of academic appointments in the reformed system reflected the preexisting practices in the polytechnic.

The Thatcher administration also intended to introduce external accountability into teaching and research and to encourage competition among academic institutions and individual academics. Measures were introduced for periodic evaluation of both teaching and research. The government also began to evaluate and rank the universities. These rankings have implications for budgetary allocations as well as research emphasis (Schuller 1991). Now British academics at all ranks hold term appointments, subject to periodic evaluation and reappointment procedures. This arrangement is not unlike proposals for post-tenure review in the United States. Terms of appointment are generally around five years and evaluation seldom leads to the loss of a position—although there is no longer any guarantee of continuing appointment in British higher education. The professoriat working in the traditional British universities strongly opposed the changes, but in the end the reforms were reluctantly accepted and caused neither major unrest nor disruption of academic life (Halsey 1992; Farnham 1999). In fact, few lost their positions, and academe continued much without major structural change. Academics holding positions at the time of the changes kept their tenure so long as they were not promoted or did not take a position at another university (Evans 1999). Most observers see the abolition of tenure as more of a symbolic loss than a real one.

In the United States, tenure is awarded by specific academic institutions rather than by government authorities or university systems. At least in the upper tier of higher education, the American tenure system has one of the most rigorous processes for evaluation and consideration of junior faculty anywhere in the world. The "six years up or out" process of evaluation provides for careful review of each applicant for tenure. Tenure can be abrogated by the university because of financial exigency, program reorganization, or other institutional reasons. Holders of tenure can also be terminated for specific dereliction of their responsibilities or for violations of university policy. While revocation of tenure is unusual in the United States, it is by no means unprecedented.

In Europe, tenure has different legal and institutional roots and provides stronger guarantees. In much of Western Europe—including Germany, Italy, France, and Spain—tenure is a right granted to senior members of the civil service. University professors, as well as most civil servants, are protected (Mora 2001). Professors are also paid according to civil service scales, and there is little variation in salaries through the academic system. The German *Beamte* status, for example, provides ironclad job security regardless of financial or other problems facing the university, including program abolition or reorganization (Enders 2001). This status is guaranteed by law. In France, the faculty's civil service status protects senior academics in all universities. Faculty members can be, but seldom are, transferred from one university to another; however, they cannot be fired. Along with the guarantees of employment and other rights, civil service appointments are highly valued in societies where they have traditionally been symbolic of elite status. Not surprisingly, senior academic staff fiercely guard their civil service appointments. Countries with this system have been slow to change, due in considerable part to the opposition to any change by members of the academic profession.

Senior academics still have significant prestige as well as power in most European countries. In Italy, for example, many senior academics serve in Parliament and several have been prime ministers. French professors and secondary school teachers constitute a significant proportion of the national assembly and have traditionally enjoyed considerable influence (Chevaillier 2001).

Tenure (permanent contract) is given to senior members of the professoriat, and appointments to senior faculty positions are carefully monitored and competitively awarded. Senior academics in those European countries with a civil service system have the strongest guarantees of tenure and job security (until the age of compulsory retirement) of any faculty members in the world. Certain other academics are given permanent contracts as well. The percentage of academics with permanent contracts varies among European countries. For example, in Germany and Finland, the proportion of tenured staff stands between 40% and 50%. In Austria, the Flemish parts of Belgium, the Netherlands, Norway, and Spain, between 50% and 60% are tenured, in France and Ireland 80%, and in Italy 90% (Enders 2000). At present, several countries are discussing abolition or modification of civil service appointments for academics, but so far only the Netherlands, in the mid-1990s, has changed its system, now having the universities directly appoint professors and other academic staff, rather than having the appointments be part of the state service.

In general, appointment to senior faculty ranks in Europe takes place after considerable scrutiny of the individual. In some countries, such as Germany, appointment to a senior professorship comes only after a national search. The American pattern of promoting a junior academic up the ranks is not the pattern in much of Europe, where a wide gulf exists between junior positions and senior professorships. The American system provides more continuity. In some European countries, it is common for a junior appointee to have the security of tenure, but no guarantee of promotion.

Employment arrangements in Japan's public universities, and many of the private institutions as well, are procedurally somewhat less secure than is the case in Europe, although in practice anyone appointed to a full-time academic job in Japan immediately has a permanent job, usually from the time of initial appointment. As in Europe, promotion through the academic ranks is more difficult, in part because of the rigid "chair" system that permits just one very powerful full professor in each department. This system, criticized for its lack of accountability and assessment as well as for the difficulties that faculty members face in advancing, is gradually changing. The Japanese appointment system works in part because it is so similar to the dominant employment pattern elsewhere in the country. Faculty members, recognizing the likelihood of lifelong employment at a single university, generally perform as effectively as possible.

In China, much as in Japan, academic staff are given permanent appointments at the time they are hired to a regular faculty position, regardless of rank. They have job security until the age of retirement, and it is highly unusual for any full-time academic to be removed from his or her position for any reason—although there have been a small number of instances of firings for involvement in dissident political activity. While academic salaries are extremely low by international standards, many Chinese faculty members are given subsidized housing on campus, access to low-cost food, and other benefits. These appointment and employment patterns are typical in China generally, although the situation is slowly changing, both on campus and in the larger society, as the economy becomes more market oriented.

The Latin American pattern of academic appointments stands in sharp contrast to that of continental Europe. Tenure, as it is known in Europe and North America, does not exist in most of Latin America. The academic profession is sharply divided between part-time instructors, who are paid a modest fee to teach a course or two, and who constitute the large majority of those teaching throughout Latin America, and the minority of full-time faculty. Full-time faculty are responsible for the governance of the university. They are appointed and have their contracts renewed on the basis of periodic "contests" in public institutions. Academic posts are publicly announced, applicants are considered, and one is selected. Renewals of appointments are based on a further "contest," announced and open to anyone. The incumbent may have to compete against other applicants. This system was established as a result of the reform movements of 1918 to insure the objectivity of academic appointments and a democratic environment in the universities. With the expansion of higher education, the system no longer works well in many countries, and "contests," which are both expensive and time consuming, are often bypassed. The actual turnover in the senior academic ranks is, in fact, quite small. Patterns of appointments in the growing private sector in Latin America vary, but permanent appointments are unusual.

Many countries have de facto tenure arrangements. Even without formal tenure, most full-time academics spend their careers in a single institution. However, the sort of legal or contractual guarantees that exist in Europe and North America are not the norm elsewhere. In countries such as South Korea, India, and a number of other Asian countries, there is a presumption of lifetime employment for academics in full-time positions, but only limited procedural guarantees. Few individuals are terminated, even when academic institutions face difficult circumstances. In India, for example, many faculty members in the undergraduate colleges, who make up the large majority of the profession, express fear of possible dismissal by management, yet few are actually fired.

Academic Freedom and Academic Appointments

In much of the world, there is little legal protection of academic freedom in the form of meaningful employment guarantees. Nonetheless, in a fourteen-country study, faculty members felt fairly confident about their academic freedom (Altbach and Lewis 1996). During periods of political crisis, academic freedom is frequently violated, especially where traditions of autonomy and academic freedom are not well rooted. Recent examples include China in the aftermath of the events at Tiananmen Square, Serbia and Croatia during recent upheavals, and Indonesia (Human Rights Watch 1998). Academic freedom is more precarious at present in Asia and Africa. In much of the Middle East, academics feel constrained from freely expressing their views or engaging in research on sensitive topics. This is the case in some African countries as well. In Ethiopia recently, government pressure on professors resulted in some dismissals. In Singapore and Malaysia, among other countries, academic researchers, especially in the social sciences, feel pressured to refrain from researching and speaking out publicly on sensitive topics. Even in the United States, which has a strong tradition of protecting academic freedom and a recognition of the connection between tenure and academic freedom, there were politically motivated dismissals during the McCarthy era purge of Communists in the 1950s. A small number of faculty members were fired, and many people feared that academic freedom had been compromised (Schrecker 1986). Academic freedom disappeared in Germany during the Nazi period and was greatly restricted in the former Soviet Union and Central and Eastern Europe during the Communist era.

Despite setbacks, academic freedom in the Western industrialized countries is reasonably well observed. Faculty members are generally unrestricted in their ability to conduct research, express their views in the classroom, and participate in public debate on issues both within their areas of expertise and with regard to broader social and political issues. Academic freedom is defined more narrowly in many parts of the world than is the case in the United States. Since the end of the nineteenth century, the American ideal of academic freedom has applied to the classroom, the laboratory, and the public arena; but the European concept is more restrictive, stemming from the commitment to freedom of teaching and research within the university and limited to the areas of faculty specialization (Shils 1991). Such differences in definitions and traditions make exact comparisons difficult. Nonetheless, academic freedom is more robust now in Central and Eastern Europe, as well as in the former Soviet Union and its successor states, than it was during the Soviet period. Though occasionally violated during periods of political unrest, the idea that professors require considerable freedom of research and expression in the classroom and laboratory is gaining acceptance, even in parts of the world where the concept is not entrenched.

The terms and conditions of academic appointments are tied to the notion of academic freedom in very few countries. The United States is one of the few countries where the two concepts are inextricably linked. Elsewhere, tenure belongs strictly to the categories of employment practices, civil service issues, and other administrative procedures. Academic freedom is simply not related to the terms and conditions of professorial appointments.

Trends in Academic Appointments

In response to the pressures noted earlier—budgetary problems, accountability, and changing patterns of enrollments, among others—academic hiring is changing considerably. Without question, the most important development is the diversification of the types of appointments related to teaching and research. Among the most significant changes are the increase in the proportion of academic staff without permanent appointments, even in countries that retain tenure arrangements, and the greater use of part-time teachers.

Part-Time Faculty

In the United States, it is estimated that less than half of new hires are on the tenure track (see Baldwin and Chronister, Chapter 5 in this volume); a growing proportion of classes are taught by part-time teachers (Finkelstein 2001). In Latin America, higher education has traditionally been dominated by part-time faculty, and despite widespread agreement that greater numbers of full-time staff are needed to raise academic standards in universities and create a research culture, little has changed. Part-time teaching is less entrenched in other parts of the world, although the phenomenon is growing as institutions struggle to cope with ever-expanding enrollments and inadequate government funding.

Part-time faculty bring some advantages to higher education (Gappa and Leslie 1993). They are typically professionals already working in their specializations who bring practical knowledge and experience to their teaching. This is especially valuable in applied fields where links between theory and practice are central. Part-timers may also be able to guide students toward knowledge that will be useful in obtaining jobs after graduation. Part-time faculty cost institutions less than full-time staff, as they receive only a modest stipend for their teaching, often an hourly rate of remuneration, and no other benefits. Part-time staff seldom get offices or laboratory space, thus saving scarce university resources. Because the university's contractual commitment to them is minimal, the institution retains complete flexibility in hiring. As budgets, curricular interests, and student demand dictate, adjustments to the number and specialization of the part-time teachers can be made.

. The disadvantages, often overlooked, are also significant. Part-time faculty have minimal commitment to the institution. In many cases, they simply teach their classes and leave, which is why in Latin America they are referred to as "taxicab" professors. Part-timers do not participate in research and are not involved in campus or departmental governance. Further, they are not likely to be up to date about current intellectual trends or research in their fields. They seldom have links to the increasingly important world of international scholarship and tend not to participate in the knowledge networks in their fields. The implications are especially severe for research-oriented universities, where the need for full-time researchers is especially strong, but even postsecondary institutions devoted primarily to teaching suffer the negative effects of an overreliance on part-time staff.

Part-time faculty do not have the opportunity to be fully involved in an academic community. In most universities, existing rules do not permit this, and in any case the time commitments of part-timers preclude such engagement. It is difficult, if not impossible, to build an academic institution or culture on the basis of part-time faculty, nor is it possible to develop a research base.

In a way, academic systems that rely increasingly on part-time staff, including those in the United States, are becoming "Latin Americanized." The realities of higher education in much of Latin America provide a disconcerting look into what may lie ahead for universities, and for individual teaching staff, if part-time employment becomes the dominant model. With a few exceptions—such as Campinas University in Sao Paulo, Brazil, which has a high proportion of full-time professors—universities do not produce much research. Universities are able to offer instruction to large numbers of students at low cost. In most of Latin America, tuition in the public universities is low or free, which places great pressure on institutions to keep costs low. New private universities, which now absorb a majority of enrollments in Brazil and Chile, rely predominantly on part-time faculty in order to save money. Their budgets do not in general permit them to appoint many full-time professors. Latin American analysts have pointed out that fully effective universities can emerge only when a critical mass of full-time faculty is appointed, creating a cadre of academics who can build the disciplines, engage in the governance of the university, and attend to the development of both teaching and research (Albornoz 1991).

Alternative Patterns of Appointment

The "gold standard" of American-style tenured or tenure-track appointments is not the norm everywhere. Yet many of the pressures discussed here have forced some countries to rethink the nature of academic appointments.

One of the most dramatic systemic changes in the terms of academic appointments took place in Britain in the 1980s, when the traditional tenure system was abolished for new entrants to the profession (Shattock 2001). The Netherlands also experienced comprehensive change in the nature of academic appointments. There, professorial appointments were taken away from the government and given to the universities, annulling the civil service status of the professoriat (DeWeert 2001). This shift represented a significant change in the legal basis of appointments, and it gave more power to universities to make their own decisions. Yet the working conditions and terms of appointment for faculty members changed very little.

The more predominant trend has been the movement toward the appointment of full-time academic staff ineligible for permanent positions. In continental Europe, this category of appointment has existed for more than a century and was codified in the German Humboldtian university model of the early nineteenth century. This model, based on the Humboldtian chair system, and having undergone modifications in recent years, remains the central organizational principle of academic appointments. The chair system is rigidly based on seniority, historically elevating one senior professor within each discipline, with a variety of junior staff arranged under the chairholder. Junior scholars hold term appointments and cannot proceed up the ranks at a single university to a professorship. Rather, they must compete for any available openings at other universities or, on the completion of their term appointments, they must move on to a similar position elsewhere.

In Germany, 72% of the teaching staff are on limited-term appointments, without professorial rank and without permanent tenure. The majority hold full-time appointments. Nonprofessorial appointees cannot generally be promoted up the ranks to a tenured professorship. Most must complete a second research-based dissertation (the *habilitation*) and then compete for the scarce professorial positions that become available. They cannot, however, be appointed at the university where they earned their *habilitation*. They typically have limited term appointments, but their contracts may be extended by the university. They may not be promoted. This forced mobility creates a high degree of instability in the German academic system.

In recent years, there has been a liberalization in the structure of senior professorial ranks. Several new ranks have been added, and at least the possibility exists of having more than one senior professor in the same department or discipline. Yet the system remains hierarchical, with a great gulf between senior professors, who have completed the *habilitation* and hold civil service rank, and the rest of the teaching and research staff. While there has been some discussion of modifying or even eliminating the *habilitation*, there has been no change so far.

The German system of academic appointments had a major impact on universities in Europe and beyond. Most academic systems in Central and Eastern Europe are directly patterned on the German model. The Japanese national universities also retain the chair system, with a rigid hierarchy of academic appointments although without the necessity to move from one university to another (Arimoto 1996).

Some European countries have coped with rising enrollments and tight budgets by turning to nonprofessorial appointments. Italy recently started to reform its academic system to cope with massification (Moscati 2001). Expansion in student numbers had caused deteriorating conditions of study, higher dropout rates, and a growing time-to-degree problem. Teacher-student ratios have ballooned to 1:30, even with recent reforms permitting research appointees (who have limited-term positions) to teach. The tradition that reserved control over teaching and design of courses for senior professors has recently been modified. The ranks of full and associate professors have been expanded as well, especially at the bottom, where there are no permanent appointments.

France has tried a somewhat different approach to deal with expansion of enrollments. Rather than stock the universities with temporary staff, the Ministry of Education transferred large numbers of secondary school teachers to the universities to provide instruction in the basic courses. Since both secondary and tertiary teaching staff are civil servants and have similar academic credentials, this arrangement has been widely accepted. Secondary school teachers are accorded considerable respect in French society. Moreover, French academic secondary schools provide instruction at a level similar to the first year or two of university. It is possible to shift teachers back to secondary education if they are no longer needed in the universities, since the basic terms of appointment are comparable, and secondary school teachers and university staff have both tenure and civil service status.

Worldwide, there is a tendency to make junior staff appointments that lack the prestige, job security, and perquisites of the traditional professorship. Often these appointments are not connected to the career track of the professoriat, and the possibility of promotion in rank does not exist. There is usually a specific term of appointment that may or may not be extended. A kind of caste system has emerged, with the senior professoriat at the top and with growing numbers of proletarian part-time and term-appointed full-time staff below. The proportion of upper-caste senior academics is decreasing as institutions alter their hiring policies in response to fiscal pressures.

Patterns of Remuneration

Traditionally, the full-time professoriat could expect a salary sufficient to place its members in the middle or upper-middle class. Few people entered the academic profession to reap great financial rewards, but most expected to earn a reasonable middle-class salary. The 1994 fourteen-country Carnegie study of the academic profession found that most academics (except for respondents from Hong Kong) were dissatisfied with their salaries, with large majorities of respondents in all countries describing their compensation as only "fair" or "poor" (Altbach and Lewis 1996, p. 10). While academic salaries vary widely, the professoriat in industrialized countries still commands a middle-class salary. Academic salaries have not, however, kept up with inflation or with salaries for comparable positions in the private sector. For much of the rest of the world, remuneration has deteriorated to the extent that academic salaries no longer provide a middle-class lifestyle.

Across Europe, pay scales for the highest professorial ranks differ considerably by country. In absolute terms, without taking relative costs of living into account, I estimate that the highest salaries are paid in Belgium, Italy, and the Netherlands, followed by France, Germany, and Ireland. Finland, Portugal, and Spain offer the lowest top remuneration. Salaries in Norway, Sweden, and the United Kingdom are considered relatively low and/or declining. In these countries, there is considerable discontent among academic staff (Enders 2000). A recent

article encouraged British academics to earn extra money by moon-
lighting through accepting consultancies, manuscript evaluations, and
related income-producing activities (Sutherland 2000, p. 20). In Japan,
academic salaries at national universities seem to be on a par with
midrange salaries in European countries, with some of the well-estab-
lished private universities paying somewhat more. By comparison, the
average salary for full professors in American doctoral-level universities is considerably higher than those in almost all European countries
("More Good News, So Why the Blues?" 2000). Senior academic salaries in Hong Kong are reputed to be the highest in the world.

Salaries vary within countries according to seniority, rank, discipline,
and type of institution. In Western Europe, it is estimated that the wid-
est internal variations can be found in Austria, France, Germany, and
Ireland; in these countries the lowest starting salaries for academics are
roughly half of the highest senior salaries. In contrast, salary differentials are relatively flat in Finland, Norway, Portugal, and the United
Kingdom (Enders 2000). In the United States, when instructors and
assistant professors are included, salary differentials parallel those in
European countries with the greatest gaps.

Academic salaries in other parts of the world are in general much
lower than in Europe, North America, and Australia. Some exceptions exist, such as Hong Kong, Singapore, and a few of the Arabian
Gulf states. Yet even countries with well-developed university systems
and relatively high income levels—such as South Korea, Taiwan, Ar-
gentina, and Malaysia—have lower levels of remuneration. Throughout Latin America, the minority of full-time professors barely earn
enough from their university jobs to maintain a middle-class social
status. In most of the region, academic salaries for senior professors
are frequently only one third of average levels in Europe, and while
the cost of living may be somewhat lower, it by no means fully compensates for the difference. Typically, professors must earn additional income through consulting, additional teaching, or other remunerative
activity.

The situation in South Asia is worse, especially for the large majority
of teachers in the undergraduate colleges. While Chinese academic salaries are quite low by international standards, most teaching and research staff are provided with housing and other benefits that to a certain extent offset the low pay. Academic salaries in much of Africa,

which at one time provided a middle-class lifestyle, are no longer adequate. Indeed, the erosion of African academic salaries has contributed to an exodus of the continent's best scholars. In the transitional economies of Central and Eastern Europe and Russia, academic salaries have not kept up with the cost of living and no longer provide adequate remuneration. Many scholars have left academe, and fewer of the brightest young people are attracted to the professoriat.

Throughout the world, academic salaries have not offset inflation or matched rising incomes in other professions. Even in the United States, where remuneration has grown faster than inflation for the past seven years, academic salaries have nonetheless remained stagnant over the past three decades (Bell 1999). In Western Europe, academic salaries, which were acceptable while a small professoriat served an elite student population, are no longer considered attractive. In the developing world, salary deterioration has perhaps been less serious, but professorial remuneration was never adequate. Wherever academic salaries do not compete with those in other sectors, higher education is hard pressed to attract and retain the best minds and talent.

Increasingly, an international academic job market is emerging, which means that academic salaries and working conditions in one country have an impact on other marketplaces. Even in the absence of adequate statistics, it is clear that academics flow across national borders—a trend likely to continue. The world of science and scholarship has always been international, and the growing use of English as the primary language of academic discourse enhances this sense of an international academic community. European Union regulations requiring degree recognition have eased mobility within member nations. Variations in conditions of academic work—the availability of laboratory and research facilities, salary structures, terms and conditions of appointments, and academic freedom, among other factors—may stimulate academics to seek better positions in other countries.

Patterns of migration are evident, with a trend from the developing countries in the Third World to the industrialized countries of Europe. This has caused extreme imbalances in some cases—for example, it is estimated that as many highly trained African scholars are working in Europe as in Africa itself, representing a serious loss of academic talent. Likewise, many scientists from such countries as India, Pakistan, and Taiwan have made their careers working elsewhere. The United States,

Canada, and Australia have received an influx of academic talent from Europe, especially from the United Kingdom.

Salary levels and other issues relating to remuneration have a substantial impact on the academic profession. In China, the government has tried to make universities more self-sufficient. Professors are asked to do consulting and engage in a range of nonteaching activities. Especially at the top-ranking universities, academic culture has been affected by professors spending more time and energy on nonuniversity work. The government encourages professors to generate a portion of their own income in an effort to avoid paying them higher salaries. Latin American professors, even those with full-time appointments, must also find additional income elsewhere. Academic salaries have deteriorated worldwide, and there is no sign that this trend will abate.

This chapter has presented an overview of the terms and conditions of academic work and academic appointments internationally. Several clear trends emerge from this analysis:

> There has been a gradual change in the nature of academic appointments. The traditional notion of a professor who holds a job for life, focuses on teaching and research, and participates actively in institutional governance is giving way to alternatives.
>
> Despite the changes, institutional commitment to permanent or at least long-term academic appointments remains. However, new limited-term appointments and part-time positions are quickly proliferating alongside full-time, permanent appointments.
>
> Accountability and assessment of academic work are slowly becoming part of the academic career. The specific measurement of academic performance, particularly research and teaching, is central. Although these policies have attracted great interest, it is surprising how limited their actual implication has been worldwide.
>
> The senior faculty's traditional power over university governance has diminished. External bodies, specifically governing boards that are no longer dominated by professors, now exert more authority.
>
> In a few countries, such as the United Kingdom and the Netherlands, systemic reforms have included significant modifications of the traditional terms and conditions of academic appointments

and academic work. It is likely that other countries will eventually implement changes of similar scope. For example, several European countries are now considering whether to continue the civil service status of members of the academic profession.

The conditions of academic work are worsening. Salaries are not keeping pace with inflation, promotion is more difficult to achieve, accountability places more restraints on the traditional autonomy of the profession, and academic facilities in many countries are inadequate.

Even after the changes, the essential structure of academic appointments is unlikely to be altered in any revolutionary way. An academic ranking system will remain, although new titles and nomenclature are being introduced in some places. The "gold standard" of full-time professorial appointments with substantial job security will remain, although it is likely that fewer academics will achieve this level.

Organizationally, higher education institutions and systems and the academic profession are moving in a somewhat "American" direction. The United States, which has the largest and most comprehensive academic system in the world, has provided a model that other countries have carefully considered. American approaches to accountability—its course-credit system, the structure of academic ranks, performance-based salaries, periodic review of productivity, and other aspects—are often incorporated in plans for the reform of academic appointments in other countries.

Change is taking place, but from the perspective of most faculty, it is almost entirely negative—deterioration of salaries and working conditions, increased bureaucratization, and decreased professional autonomy. Academics worldwide, when asked about how they feel about their work, are pessimistic. Yet they maintain a strong commitment to the basic elements of the profession: teaching and research (Altbach and Lewis 1996). It may well be that changing circumstances, including the growing importance of accountability and assessment, are necessary if academic institutions are effectively to serve a diversified and expansive academic system.

The greatest challenge lies in safeguarding the academic profession as an attractive choice for intelligent and motivated teachers, scholars, and researchers. Paradoxically, at a time when there is universal agreement concerning the importance of higher education for the future of knowledge-based societies, the academic profession worldwide finds itself in a beleaguered state.

References

Albornoz, Orlando. 1991. "Latin America." In Philip G. Altbach, ed., *International Higher Education: An Encyclopedia.* New York: Garland.

Altbach, Philip G., and Lionel Lewis. 1996. "The Academic Profession in International Perspective." In Philip G. Altbach, ed., *The International Academic Profession: Portraits of Fourteen Countries.* Princeton, N.J.: Carnegie Foundation for the Advancement of Teaching.

Anderson, Martin. 1992. *Impostors in the Temple: American Intellectuals Are Destroying Our Universities and Cheating Our Students of Their Future.* New York: Simon & Schuster.

Arimoto, Akira. 1996. "The Academic Profession in Japan." In Philip G. Altbach, ed., *The International Academic Profession: Portraits of Fourteen Countries.* Princeton, N.J.: Carnegie Foundation for the Advancement of Teaching.

Bell, Linda A. 1999. "Ups and Downs: Academic Salaries since the Early 1970s." *Academe,* 85 (2): 12–21.

Ben-David, Joseph, and A. Zloczower. 1962. "Universities and Academic Systems in Modern Societies." *European Journal of Sociology,* 3: 45–84.

Castro, Claudio de Moura, and Daniel C. Levy. 2000. *Myth, Reality, and Reform: Higher Education Policy in Latin America.* Washington, D.C.: Inter-American Development Bank.

Chevaillier, Thierry. 2001. "French Academics between the Professions and the Civil Service." *Higher Education,* 41 (1–2: 49–75.

DeWeert, Egbert. 2001. "Pressures and Prospects Facing the Academic Profession in the Netherlands." *Higher Education,* 41 (1–2): 77–101.

Enders, Jürgen. 2000. "Down by Law? Employment and Working Conditions of Academic Staff in Europe." Paper presented at the International Conference on Employment and Working Conditions of Academic Staff in Europe, Kassel, Germany.

——— 2001. "The Chair System in Transition: Promotion, Appointment, and Gate Keeping in German Higher Education." *Higher Education,* 41 (1–2): 3–25.

Evans, G. R. 1999. *Calling Academe to Account: Rights and Responsibilities.* Buckingham, U.K.: Open University Press.

Farnham, David. 1999. "The United Kingdom: End of the Donnish Dominion?" In David Farnham, ed., *Managing Academic Staff in Changing University Systems: International Trends and Comparisons.* Buckingham, U.K.: Open University Press.

Finkelstein, Martin. 2001. "Understanding the Professoriate." In Philip G. Altbach, Patricia J. Gumport, and D. Bruce Johnstone, eds., *The Enduring Legacies: In Defense of American Higher Education.* Baltimore: Johns Hopkins University Press.

Gappa, Judith M., and David W. Leslie. 1993. *The Invisible Faculty: Improving the Status of Part-Timers in Higher Education.* San Francisco: Jossey-Bass.

Halsey, A. H. 1992. *Decline of Donnish Dominion: The British Academic Profession in the Twentieth Century.* Oxford: Clarendon Press.

Human Rights Watch. 1998. *Academic Freedom in Indonesia: Dismantling Soeharto-Era Barriers.* New York: Human Rights Watch.

Mora, José-Ginés. 2001. "The Academic Profession in Spain: Between the Civil Service and the Market." *Higher Education*, 41 (1–2): 131–155.

"More Good News, So Why the Blues?" 2000. *Annual Report on the Economic Status of the Profession, 1999–2000. Academe*, 86 (2): 12–36.

Moscati, Roberto. 2001. "No Longer at the Top? Italian University Professors in Transition." *Higher Education*, 41 (1–2): 103–129.

Neave, Guy, and Gary Rhoades. 1987. "The Academic Estate in Western Europe." In B. R. Clark, ed., *The Academic Profession: National, Disciplinary, and Institutional Settings.* Berkeley: University of California Press.

Schrecker, Ellen W. 1986. *No Ivory Tower: McCarthyism and the Universities.* New York: Oxford University Press.

Schuller, Tom, ed. 1991. *The Future of Higher Education.* Buckingham, U.K.: Open University Press.

Shattock, Michael. 2001. "The Academic Profession in Britain: A Study in the Failure to Adapt to Change." *Higher Education*, 41 (1–2): 27–47.

Shils, Edward. 1991. "Academic Freedom." In Philip G. Altbach, ed., *International Higher Education: An Encyclopedia.* New York: Garland.

——— 1997. "The Criteria of Academic Appointments." In *The Calling of Education.* Edited and with an introduction by Steven Grosby. Chicago: University of Chicago Press.

Sutherland, John. 2000. "Double Your Money." *Times Higher Education Supplement*, June 16, pp. 20–21.

Sykes, Charles J. 1988. *Profscam: Professors and the Demise of Higher Education.* Washington, D.C.: Regnery Gateway.

Task Force on Higher Education and Society. 2000. *Higher Education in Developing Countries: Peril and Promise.* Washington, D.C.: World Bank.

Trow, Martin. 1972. "The Expansion and Transformation of Higher Education." *International Review of Education*, 18 (1): 61–83.

7

Can Colleges Competitively Recruit Faculty without the Prospect of Tenure?

CATHY A. TROWER

*T*HE ACADEMIC LABOR MARKET is unlike any other for three reasons: (1) the existence of the tenure system, (2) the joint production of research and teaching, and (3) the differentiation of employers by quality. As Charlotte Kuh (1998) noted, "These three aspects of academic labor markets . . . should lead employers, especially prestigious ones, to be highly conservative in the award of tenure and to try to create non–tenure track positions to meet research demand" (p. 1). Kuh accurately predicted that the most rapid growth in positions off the tenure track would occur at research-intensive institutions where academic employers most need to "meet demand generated by research funding without incurring life-long obligation to an employee" (p. 1).

In many disciplines, tenure compensates for salaries lower than faculty could earn outside of academe (Bowen and Schuster 1986). According to Robert McGee and Walter Block (1991), "Professors who have tenure, or who are hired with the possibility of receiving tenure, will work for less money than professors who cannot hope to receive a guarantee of lifetime employment" (p. 547). Without tenure, institutions of lesser prestige could not afford to match salaries that would be required to attract and retain able faculty (Miller 1970). Indeed, conventional arguments hold that were it not for tenure, academe in general (with the possible exception of wealthy, elite institutions) would be

182

at a disadvantage to attract men and women of ability (American Association of University Professors 1977; Keast and Macy 1973).

Some institutions without tenure (e.g., Florida Gulf Coast University, Hampshire College, Evergreen State College), however, have recruited a highly credentialed, diverse, and competent faculty without paying a salary premium (Chait and Trower 1997; 1998). Other institutions (e.g., the Boston University School of Management, Greensboro College, and Webster University) offer various inducements for faculty to forgo the tenure track.

Some faculty actually prefer academic life without a tenure system (Chait and Trower 1997). David Breneman (1997) argued that tenure probably makes the most sense at selective, prestigious institutions. In any event, two questions arise: (1) Why not give junior faculty the choice of tenure or non–tenure track appointments, even at preeminent institutions? and (2) What would an institution have to offer to attract young scholars to be "non-tenured by choice" (McPherson and Schapiro 1999)?

This chapter presents findings from an empirical study of job choice among young scholars. Consider the following:

> If two teaching positions paid the same salary, had identical duties, and were identical in every other way—student body, prestige, geographic location, fringe benefits—but one position carried a guarantee of lifetime employment and one did not, which position would one choose? The answer appears to be obvious. Because most people are risk-averse, they would choose the position that included a guaranteed job for life, other things being equal. Therefore, the possession of tenure has some value. (McGee and Block 1991, p. 546)

While the answer to the question posed above is self-evident, what if salary, geographic location, or departmental prestige varied? What if (as in real life) there were no "guarantee" of tenure? Would the answer then be so clear?

While no single research study can unequivocally and definitively address such a complex issue, this chapter provides some answers to complicated questions about the trade-offs involved in job choice. The first sections present contextual background for the labor market of doctorally qualified individuals in various disciplines. After discussing the factors that candidates for faculty appointments considered important when deciding where to work, I present findings from a survey that varied those factors systematically and measured the likelihood an offer would be accepted. The results suggest that colleges and universities can indeed competitively recruit faculty off the tenure track, especially if two quality of life factors are met: an attractive geographic location and a preferred balance of research and teaching. More so than salary, institutional prestige, the likelihood of receiving tenure, the length of the contract, and the department's rank, location and work balance mattered. An attractive locale and meaningful work are magnets for young scholars and can entice them onto non–tenure track lines.

Background

The number of doctorates awarded in the United States has increased for thirteen consecutive years to total 42,683 in 1998 (Sanderson et al. 1999). The highest percentage of doctorates was awarded in the life sciences (20%), followed by the social sciences (17%), the physical sciences (16%), education (15%), engineering (14%), the humanities (13%), and business and other professions (6%).

In 1998, 71% of doctoral recipients with definite plans after commencement indicated that they would join the workforce as opposed to pursue further education through postdoctoral research or a teaching program. This decision, however, depended on the postgraduation norms and expectations of various disciplines. Postdoctorate positions are most common in the life sciences (61.2%) and the physical sciences (46%). In the sciences, Allen Sanderson and his colleagues note, "the historical trend is generally away from immediate career employment in favor of postdoctoral programs" (Sanderson et al. 1999, p. 26).

Academe remained "the most common employment destination of new doctorates who had definite commitments within the United States . . . (50% of the respondent population in 1998)" (p. 26); however, this percentage represented a decline, from 57% in 1978. The "industry/self-employed" sector on the *Survey of Earned Doctorates* increased most over the same time period, from 14.8% in 1978 to 24.5%

in 1998. Employment in the government sector declined from 12.3% in 1978 to 8.2% in 1998 (Sanderson et al. 1999).

According to the most recent Integrated Postsecondary Education Data System (IPEDS) report, more than half of all instructional staff in higher education work in part-time or full-time, tenure-ineligible positions (U.S. Department of Education 2000; see Chapter 5). Of the total instructional workforce in academe today, 43% work part time and, of the full-time faculty, 31% are ineligible for tenure, either because it is not offered at their institution or because they were hired onto a nontenure track.

Young scholars are much more likely than their senior counterparts to be off the tenure track (National Center for Education Statistics 1997). (See Table 7.1.) According to Martin Finkelstein, Robert Seal, and Jack Schuster (1998, pp. 55–56):

> The new-generation[1] faculty are . . . much less likely to be tenured: 23.9% compared with 73% of the more experienced cohort. An additional 42.9% of the new faculty and 10.5% of the senior faculty are "on the tenure track but not tenured." The combination of tenured plus tenure-eligible categories demonstrates the "tenure gap": 83.5% of the senior cohort but only 66.8% of the new-entry cohort. . . . [T]he new entrants are more than twice as likely not to be in the tenure stream.

Full-time non–tenure track positions are becoming the norm in many fields. "Among new career entrants, natural scientists (25.5%)

Table 7.1 Tenure status: percentage of new (N) versus senior (S) faculty

Program area	Tenured		Tenure track		Not on tenure track		No tenure for faculty status		No tenure system at institution	
	N	S	N	S	N	S	N	S	N	S
Professions	22	67	43	13	19	9	6	3	10	8
Humanities	23	76	41	8	18	5	8	3	10	8
Natural sciences	29	79	45	8	14	5	5	3	7	5
Social sciences	25	81	50	9	16	3	3	2	6	5

and social scientists (24.5%) are much less likely to be off ladder than faculty in the humanities (36.1%) and the professions (36.7%)" (p. 58). Part-time faculty are most prevalent in the fine arts (50.9%), business (46.5%), education (45.3%), and the humanities (44.8%).

According to Kuh (1998), the average annual growth rate from 1981 to 1995 in full-time non–tenure track positions occupied by faculty with doctorates was 3.88% in the physical, life sciences, and engineering, 3.48% in the social and behavioral sciences, and 2.81% in the humanities. The corresponding average annual growth rates for full-time, tenure track positions were 1.30%, 0.80%, and 0.65%.

During the same fourteen-year span, the percentage of adjunct positions staffed by Ph.D.s in the physical sciences, the life sciences, and engineering increased at an annual average of 11.2%, and in the social and behavioral sciences at a rate of 7.04%. In the humanities the rate was 2.15% (Kuh 1998). The average annual increases in part-time faculty were similar in the physical sciences, life sciences, and engineering category (3.93%) and in the social and behavioral sciences (3.83%). However, the percentage of part-time faculty in the humanities decreased by 0.68% in average annual percentage terms between 1981 and 1995.

The job market for Ph.D.s varied markedly across and even within fields. One might assume therefore that a doctoral graduate's propensity to accept a postdoctoral appointment or a non–tenure track position or await a tenure track offer would also vary. In the life sciences, postdoctoral appointments were the norm (66% in biology) whereas in English they were rare (4%). Employment in business/industry differed from 70% of physics doctorates to 6% in history. Doctorates in sociology were most likely to enter the academy as faculty members (83%), engineering Ph.D.s least likely (11%).

Within the academy, the outlook for doctoral graduates in geology, mathematics, economics, English, political science, and psychology was bleak compared to the academic labor market for chemistry, computer science, physics, business, history, and sociology. The employment outlook, norms, and markets for the various disciplines certainly shape job choice among recent graduates—whether to accept employment in academe or out and whether to accept a postdoctoral, tenure track, or non–tenure track position.

The Project on Faculty Appointments designed a study to examine job choice among young scholars. While the employment picture varies by discipline and while job choice is a complex process, the survey results shed light on the factors, in addition to discipline, that influenced the decision.

The Faculty Recruitment Study

Research Questions

The primary research question was "Does the chance of tenure significantly influence decisions about where to work?"—a vital question about which many have speculated. We also wanted to know: (1) What factors within an institution's control influence the choice full-time faculty make about where to work? and (2) Under what terms and conditions will candidates accept a full-time position with little or no prospect of tenure? Three sources were used to answer these questions: focus group interviews, a web-based survey of both first- and second-year faculty and doctoral candidates nearing completion of their degrees, and interviews and hiring data collected at Florida Gulf Coast University (FGCU), an institution that in its first year (1997–98) hired 92 full-time faculty members without tenure.

Focus Groups

Focus group research is by its very nature exploratory. It is typically used as a starting point to understand complex issues. This type of research is neither descriptive nor causal. It does not require random sampling and cannot be generalized to larger populations. It was instructive to use focus group interviews in order to gain insight into how young scholars approached the academic job search and to learn what variables were especially important to them as they considered academic employment and weighed various offers. Before designing an empirical study, we wanted to know how doctoral candidates and new faculty viewed tenure and non–tenure track positions.

Six two-hour focus group sessions were conducted across the nation: two with doctoral candidates in math and philosophy, two with first- and second-year faculty in the arts and sciences, and two with first- and second-year faculty in professional schools (e.g., business, education,

engineering).[2] Potential participants were identified through lists provided by disciplinary associations and universities. Each prospective
participant was first contacted by e-mail, then by phone, in order to
balance the groups by gender, discipline, and, for faculty, type of contract (tenure track or non–tenure track). We conducted focus group interviews with 20 doctoral candidates (8 females and 12 males) and 40
faculty (25 from professional schools, 15 from the arts and sciences; 20
females, 20 males; 8 with non–tenure track, 32 with tenure track appointments). Those selected represented a range of institutions, from
large research universities to prestigious liberal arts colleges to public
comprehensive universities.

Focus Group Findings

Job choice was a complicated decision influenced by the nature of the
position itself, the personal preferences and characteristics of the candidate, the department's quality, and the prestige of the institution.
Faculty and doctoral candidates most often considered whether the position was tenure track or non–tenure track, the length of the appointment (if non–tenure track), the mix of research and teaching, and the
workload. Faculty also considered the chances of earning tenure, but
this was not as important as other factors, in part because it was so unpredictable. Most doctoral students never even thought to ask questions about the success rate of junior faculty in achieving tenure.

Secondary factors were salary, benefits, sabbaticals, release time, limited service requirements, potential for mentoring, and performance
evaluation criteria. In the case of non–tenure track positions, faculty
preferred longer to shorter terms in most cases; one-year contracts
were particularly unattractive.

The type of appointment, whether on or off the tenure track, was
important to doctoral candidates and new faculty alike, but views on
this varied greatly, making it difficult to generalize. For some, unable to
imagine academic life without it, tenure was crucial in the job choice
process. For others, tenure was far less important than were other factors, such as location, the mix of teaching and research, and the quality
of the department. Still other focus group participants were ambivalent
on the matter of tenure and struggled with market realities and other
"practical" matters. One doctoral candidate remarked, "This isn't

about an ideal right now. Sure, tenure would be great, but I need a job. I have loans to repay, a family to feed, and a life to live. I can't waste too much time searching for the perfect offer that might never come along."

The academic employment market for doctoral candidates in philosophy and mathematics was unfavorable for different reasons. In philosophy, there were more candidates than positions, and in mathematics there were few tenure track jobs. Thus, both groups were realistically skeptical about their chances. Mathematicians enjoyed a better employment market outside of higher education and were slightly more open to non–tenure track positions. One math major commented, "Given the tight job market for faculty in math, there is no shame in taking a non–tenure track position." Candidates in philosophy agreed: "The market is so tight that I'm planning on applying for anything for which I'm reasonably qualified." "The market is tight; you go where you get an offer, tenure track or not." Four of twelve mathematicians and two of eleven philosophers would under no circumstances accept a non–tenure track offer.

While most doctoral candidates preferred the tenure track, some anticipated advantages to non–tenure track positions:

"I would actually prefer to bounce around for a few years. If I were offered a tenure track job now, it probably wouldn't be at that great a school. So I'll bounce around, get some experience, publish some papers, and then seek a tenure track job."

"Tenure track job ads scare me to death. When you read them, it looks like you have to balance what amounts to three full-time jobs, and all for $30,000."

"If I take a tenure track job now, I'm locked into that for quite a while. It might be somewhere that I don't ultimately want to be, some school where I don't feel that there are lots of opportunities."

"I think it's more important for me to be someplace where I can do my best thinking and writing and publishing, even if that's a non–tenure track position. Ultimately, this would put me in a better position to pick and choose later on, rather than be in a long-term relationship at a place that may not be nurturing."

"Even the tenure track is no guarantee. It's like this guillotine waiting to come down at the six-year point. If you don't have tenure, you bounce around on one-year contracts and you can't do that for more than ten years. Even if you're willing to do that, people won't keep hiring you year after year forever."

"I would definitely consider a multiyear non–tenure track position if there were no stigma attached to this type of employment arrangement."

"I would evaluate whether a non–tenure track [position] could lead to greater satisfaction with one's work. Tenure is a painful process. It equals pressure. You want to be happy, you don't want tenure."

"Having a non–tenure track position at a good school is better than a tenure track one at a bad school."

Whether or not the position was tenure track or non–tenure track was clearly important to the doctoral candidates in the focus groups, but it was not always the most important consideration. While doctoral candidates speculated about what they were likely to do, first- and second-year faculty discussed what they had actually done. Of the faculty in the focus group interviews, 20% held non–tenure track positions, and half of all faculty interviewed were at master's or baccalaureate institutions. Most of the interviewees had had at least two offers when they accepted their current positions.

Interestingly, when asked to name the most important factor in their decision about which post to accept, very few faculty talked about the opportunity for tenure or even whether the position was tenure track or non–tenure track:

"Tenure wasn't really a big thing with me once I found out what the culture is here; that is, people have been here a long time on and off the tenure track. And, not to sound cocky or anything, but I've always figured that if I need to find another position, I can, period. I'm not the kind of person to stay somewhere for twenty years anyway."

"Tenure really isn't a guarantee anyway. If they want to fire you, they will, regardless of tenure."

"Tenure was the least of my concerns. I didn't even ask what my chances were, since I might leave for industry at some point anyway."

"From what I've been reading, tenure is just another old sacred cow that might get slaughtered. Tenure is like the Social Security system; I'm not going to count on it. I was much more interested in where the job was and what I'd be doing than in whether it was tenurable or not."

But for some faculty, as for doctoral candidates, the type of appointment was crucial:

"I only considered tenure track offers. Even if I had been offered a non–tenure track position at a more prestigious institution, I would have made the choice that I did."

"Tenure was crucial to me. I don't want to move around and I had student loans to repay. I want to know that I have security."

Part of the appeal of tenure was that doctoral candidates and faculty alike saw it as a symbol of status and legitimacy, signifying quality, peer recognition, and professional autonomy.

"Tenure is a sign of validation; it shows perseverance, like the doctorate. It's the green card. It's also about peer recognition . . . you've been deemed worthy by your peers."

"It's a commitment on the part of the institution. Most of us made significant sacrifices to be here, but until you receive tenure you have no commitment from the institution and no status either."

"Tenure is important because you don't have to consistently prove yourself once you have it. You can even crash and burn on your research and have it not be the end of your career."

"In philosophy, tenure is essential. Academic freedom is everything. Besides, there aren't any legitimate non–tenure track jobs out there."

"If you want autonomy, you must have tenure. At least violations of your autonomy are less likely once you have tenure."

Many doctoral candidates were socialized throughout graduate school to covet tenure; they were taught that non–tenure track appointments were second-class, less conducive to a research career, and less secure:

"There's a certain stigma attached to non–tenure track jobs. My advisor said to never even consider one."

"My advisors strongly encouraged me to take a tenure track position at the most prestigious institution I could in order to maxi-
mize my ability to conduct research, whether or not I thought I
could actually get tenure there. If I didn't, it would be a stepping-
stone to tenure elsewhere, especially if the institution were really
prestigious."

"It's part of the graduate school experience. No one's advisor says,
'Gee, I hope you go out there and land a non–tenure track job!'"

"I really want a tenure track job. It's what I've striven for all these
years. It's what my family and advisor expect. It would be such a
letdown for everyone if I can't find one."

Clearly, faculty advisors played an instrumental role in shaping doctoral candidates' views about tenure track and non–tenure track positions.

Both faculty and doctoral candidates reported that the balance between teaching and research was especially important in deciding
where to work. Most candidates in mathematics and philosophy
wanted to do both: "I'm looking for a balance of responsibilities, not
where you are judged solely on research." "I like research, but teaching
is also important to me. I want to be at a place where teaching is taken
seriously by the institution, where teaching is part of the mission." "I
want an equal combination of teaching and research."

Whether they preferred teaching (e.g., "I want to be in a teaching-
oriented college with tenure"; "small classes, teaching focus") or research (e.g., "definitely a research institution with the opportunity to
publish"; "support for research . . . I'm really much less interested in
teaching"), doctoral students clearly felt that what they would be doing
was often more important than where they would be doing it.

While second to location, faculty also expressed the importance of
the mix of work:

"I took this job because of the teaching I could do here."

"I chose the place that was most interested in my research, and the
fact that it is a research institution will push me to stay current."

"[I liked having] the ability to do both teaching and research in
equal amounts."

"The 80–20 research/teaching split was what they offered and what
I wanted."

Several doctoral candidates felt that workload would be influential in their decision, especially the number, type, and variety of courses to be taught and the number of preparations in any one semester. Faculty members said: "I liked that there was a reasonable teaching load and that I could teach the classes I liked"; "I wanted [a light] teaching load and time for research as well as protection from service activities until I get tenure."

Most doctoral candidates cited salary as being far less important than other considerations, either because salaries were generally low or because salary ranges at the institutions under consideration were more or less uniform. None of the faculty identified salary as the most important determinant.

Beyond the type of contract on or off the tenure track, the workload and mix of responsibilities, and the salary, new faculty and doctoral candidates discussed a number of factors that might best be categorized as personal preferences and characteristics. These factors included the geographic location of the institution, the candidate's demographic characteristics (e.g., gender, age, income, marital/partnership status, children, race), and discipline.

For both doctoral candidates and faculty, geographic location (which encompassed concerns such as dual-career opportunities, affordable housing, cultural activities, crime rate, caliber of schools, and quality of life) figured heavily in the job choice process. Over half the faculty interviewed mentioned location as the single most important determinant of job choice. In contrast, only two doctoral candidates rated location as a top priority.

While not often mentioned by faculty or doctoral candidates in focus groups, a person's gender, age, race, marital status, or discipline might affect the choice of where to work. In order to ascertain whether differences in job choice occurred based on demographics, we gathered and analyzed these data in the survey.

Departmental quality and characteristics were very important to 22% of faculty and 32% of doctoral candidates. These criteria included who their colleagues would be, whether there would be mentors and support for their research, the department's rank, the degree of specialization required, the role of the department within the institution (e.g., courses for majors versus service courses), and whether the department functioned collaboratively and collegially. Other less frequently cited factors were opportunities for interdisciplinary work and for professional development.

Finally, the quality of the institution was a factor in job choice, although much less so than other attributes previously discussed. In terms of institutional prestige, one doctoral candidate noted, "I would take a postdoc at a prestigious institution over a tenure track position at a less prestigious one." Several felt that the stability of both the department and the institution was important.

Selection Grid Findings

In order to test the appeal of a non–tenure track position, participants completed a hypothetical exercise to rank twelve factors associated with such a job offer. It was stipulated that academic freedom and due process would be contractually guaranteed. Table 7.2 shows the rank orders by group.

Table 7.2   Inducement rankings, by group

Inducement	Ranking, by group					
	A	B	C	D	E	F
3–5 year renewable contract	1	2	6	4	1	7
10-year renewable contract	2	1	3	2	2	3
15% annual salary premium	4	4	2	1	3	3
One course reduction per semester	5	3	8	8	5	2
Courses limited to graduate or honor students; small class size	3	5	11	10	10	1
Sabbatical every 5 years	6	6	5	8	9	5
A paid-up annuity equal to 25% of annual salary	9	7	6	5	7	9
Travel grants up to $5,000 per year	7	8	4	6	4	6
Research funds equal to 1/3 of salary per year	8	8	1	3	5	8
Personal, expert investment counseling	12	12	12	12	12	11
Mortgage subsidy equal to 3 percentage points below market	10	11	9	11	11	10
Undergraduate college tuition payments up to $10,000 per year per child	11	10	10	7	8	11

Group A: Doctoral candidates, mathematics, San Antonio
Group B: Doctoral candidates, philosophy, Berkeley
Group C: Faculty, A&S and professional, Baltimore
Group D: Faculty, professional, Raleigh-Durham (education, engineering, law)
Group E: Faculty, professional, Harrisburg (business, education)
Group F: Faculty, A&S, Berkeley (philosophy)

The two student groups (columns A and B in Table 7.2) ranked the twelve items quite similarly, preferring some assurance of a multiyear contract, although mathematics majors preferred the three- to five-year contract and philosophy majors preferred the ten-year contract. The third factor among mathematicians was courses limited to graduate or honor students, or small class size. Third among philosophy majors was a one course reduction per semester. Both groups ranked fourth the 15% annual salary premium. Least valued by both groups were expert investment counseling, a mortgage subsidy, and undergraduate tuition payments for children (this perhaps reflected the relatively young age of those in these groups and the likelihood that they had few if any children).

There were few differences in rankings between the two groups of faculty in the professions (columns D and E) and no difference about the three least attractive inducements. Both groups ranked small classes tenth, a mortgage subsidy eleventh, and investment counseling twelfth. Group D, a mix of faculty in education, engineering, and law, placed the 15% salary premium first, followed by the ten-year contract and research funds. Group E, made up of business and education faculty, ranked the three- to five-year contracts first and the ten-year contract second, followed by a 15% annual salary premium, travel grants, and research funds.

Among the arts and sciences faculty, those in philosophy (Group F) were the outliers. Their top choice was small class size or honor/graduate students, followed by one course reduction per semester, a ten-year contract, and a 15% annual salary premium. Like doctoral candidates, the philosophers (Group F) and other faculty in Group C, which was a blend from arts and sciences and professional schools, ranked tuition payments, a mortgage subsidy, and investment counseling low on the list. Group C preferred research funds equal to one third of their salary per year, followed by a 15% annual salary premium, a ten-year contract, and travel grants.

Because there was a great degree of variance among individual rankings, a composite picture may be misleading. Incentives were not equally applicable across all focus group participants (e.g., a job candidate in a child-free home would not be concerned with undergraduate tuition payments; a single person living in an apartment would not be worried about a mortgage subsidy). In addition, perhaps the numbers or percentages attached to the variables were not high enough to attract respondents. In other words, a mortgage subsidy equal to 5 percentage points below market instead of 3 or travel grants up to $7,000 per year instead of $5,000 might have changed the rankings.

Selection Grid Discussion

Part of the difficulty with this exercise for some doctoral candidates, most notably philosophy majors, was that they could not conceive of a world without tenure. Some could not imagine what sort of institution would operate without a tenure system. For others, accepting a non–tenure track position at an institution that also offered tenure track positions was tantamount to career suicide. A philosophy major stated:

> It is not so much that we absolutely insist on security, but the reality is that academic life has so little going for it. There is only this one absolutely gratuitous benefit, which is that you have this absurd amount of security, which almost no one else in the workforce has. And I guess some people wouldn't mind giving that up if there were some other compensation. But just the idea of setting it aside and all other elements of academic life remain moderately crappy . . . the way they are . . . that would seem like I just gave up a whole lot. If I thought that there could be ten-year renewable contracts, that the overall pay would be higher and the teaching load a little lighter, then the trade-off seems more reasonable.

At least two of his peers disagreed:

> I refused to rank these things. Without knowing why I am not being offered tenure and who is guaranteeing my academic freedom, I can't even begin to assess what it would take, basically, for them to buy me off.

> This is like putting a price on academic freedom, and in philosophy you just can't do that. I might teach something that is very controversial and if I'm on contracts, even with this supposed guarantee of academic freedom, I could get fired if I piss someone

off. I just don't see a replacement for tenure, even with economic benefits and academic freedom.

The math majors, while less idealistic in their outlook on academic freedom, were equally unable to envision a non–tenure track job as attractive. Four out of twelve would not accept such a position under any circumstances, but the others allowed that some job is better than no job. One participant, who completed the ranking exercise only reluctantly, said, "You need to think about this as a balance between perks and respect. Peer respect is important to me. People will ask, 'Why didn't you get a tenure track position?' You could come off as shallow if you said that you took it because it offered more money. So many faculty in mathematics have worked for so long for so little money that they would find this kind of thinking troubling." Another mathematics major declared, "I would be suspicious of a non–tenure track position, especially at an institution that had tenure track ones. The existence of non–tenure track positions might mean that this department was anticipating difficulties." Several math majors, however, stated that non–tenure track jobs were a market reality and probably the wave of the future, so why not adapt and negotiate the best possible terms under the circumstances.

Faculty expressed similar views, but most seemed to be more comfortable than doctoral students with the non–tenure track option. (Recall that eight of the faculty focus group members actually held such positions.) Several believed that a non–tenure track position at a prestigious institution was an excellent stepping-stone to a tenure track appointment elsewhere and in many cases was better than a tenure track post at a less distinguished school. Some saw the non–tenure track possibility as appealing if it focused on research. One said, "I'd take a non–tenure track job if it allowed me to do what I want, period. None of the things on the list matter to me." For others, the benefit of a non–tenure track job was almost the opposite: it meant not having to publish or perish. Faculty disposed to accept a non–tenure track job wanted safeguards for academic freedom, some measure of economic security, and assurances of the financial viability of the department and the institution. Most felt that the decision to accept a non–tenure track job was influenced by age, marital status (younger, single scholars would be more apt to take a non–tenure track offer), and discipline. In certain fields, one participant exclaimed, "Qualified people line up for those jobs!"

Several faculty members, self-described as risk averse, opted for the tenure track at less prestigious colleges. Others discounted non–tenure track positions because such faculty were treated as second class, regardless of the institutional prestige. For still others, the attitude was "I've worked too hard for anything but a tenure track position." One faculty member insisted, "A non–tenure track position is not consistent with a high-quality research career. I wouldn't consider taking one."

The focus group interviews disclosed a great deal about how doctoral candidates approached the job market and about what affected the actual decisions made by first- and second-year faculty. Based on focus group responses, we designed two surveys, one for doctoral candidates and the other for first- and second-year faculty, in an attempt to understand still better the decisions faculty make about where to work and to investigate whether institutions can recruit faculty without the prospect of tenure. The survey instruments were pretested, revised, transferred to an electronic format, retested, modified again, and then distributed over the web.

Survey

We requested from deans and department chairs the names and e-mail addresses of first- and second-year full-time faculty, both tenure track and non–tenure track, and doctoral candidates who graduated or anticipated graduating between May 1999 and June 2000 from the top departments in three professions, six science disciplines, and six humanities/social sciences disciplines. Top departments were selected based on U.S. News & World Report's (1999) "America's Best Graduate Schools, 2000 Edition." The top departments were targeted because we assumed that these scholars probably had the most job offers.

Letters to deans or department chairs yielded lists from 429 top departments at sixty-five of the most selective institutions. In all, 88% of the institutions and 59% of the departments agreed to participate. We received the names and e-mail addresses of 1,304 faculty members and 5,776 doctoral candidates. After these lists were cleaned we were left with a usable sample of 1,186 faculty and 5,225 students.

The response rate was 58% for faculty and 38% for doctoral candidates. The five institutions with the most respondents, in descending order, were the University of Wisconsin, UC-Berkeley, University of Minnesota, Columbia University, and UC-Santa Barbara. In alphabetical order, there were also respondents from Arizona State, Brown, California Institute of Technology, Carnegie Mellon, Cornell, Harvard, Johns Hopkins, MIT, Northwestern, Ohio State, Penn State, Princeton, Rice, Stanford, University of California (Davis, Irvine, Los Angeles, San Diego), University of Chicago, University of Illinois, University of Iowa, University of Massachusetts, University of Maryland, University of Michigan, University of Missouri, University of North Carolina, University of Pennsylvania, University of Southern California, University of Texas, University of Virginia, Washington University, and Yale.

A section of both surveys was designed specifically to answer the following questions: Can colleges competitively recruit faculty without the prospect of tenure? What factors are important in the decision? What trade-offs among those factors do faculty candidates make when deciding where to work? Factorial design and conjoint analysis were used to measure the trade-off functions between levels of attributes of potential job offers.[3] That is, through conjoint analysis we could systematically vary or hold constant each attribute and measure the change in job choice patterns for individual decision-makers, a process that revealed preferences among variables and how each attribute affected choice behavior.

Survey respondents examined sixteen choice sets, each with two job offers. The first eight required respondents to choose a tenure track option, a non–tenure track option, or "neither." The second eight allowed respondents to choose one of two non–tenure track options or "neither." In all sixteen cases, faculty's choosing "neither" meant that they would remain in their current position. Doctoral students' choosing "neither" meant that they would continue their job search rather than accept the positions described.

Survey Results

Both faculty and doctoral students preferred tenure track to non–tenure track positions; however, both would accept a non–tenure track position under certain conditions. Two quality of life issues mattered most in the decision: geographic location of the institution and the balance of work.

Faculty

To understand whether any demographic variables (e.g., race, gender, marital status, employment status of spouse/partner, income, discipline, type of appointment) affected job choice, we held each offer constant at the default setting (shown with an asterisk in Table 7.3). The

Table 7.3 Choice set attributes and levels (asterisk denotes default)

Attribute	Levels
Balance of work	* Matches your preference Significantly different from your preference
Likelihood of tenure or contract renewal	Greater than 85% chance * 71%–85% chance 50%–70% chance Less than 50% chance
Geographic location	Somewhere you would really like to live * Somewhere you would be comfortable living Somewhere you would be marginally satisfied living Somewhere you would not like to live
Departmental ranking	* Top 10 in your discipline Between 11 and 20 in your discipline Between 21 and 40 in your discipline Not in top 40 in your discipline
Institutional prestige	Top 10 in the U.S. * Between 11 and 20 in the U.S. Between 21 and 40 in the U.S. Not in top 40 in the U.S.
Salary	At least 25% above average for your discipline At least 10% above average for your discipline * About average for your discipline At least 15% below average for your discipline
Contract length	10 years * 5 years 3 years 1 year

default setting was the level of each attribute that would act as a starting point when interpreting the survey results.

When given a hypothetical choice between a tenure track and a non–tenure track position, there was a 51% probability that first- and second-year faculty would stay in their current position, a 37% probability that they would choose the tenure track offer, and a 12% probability of choosing the non–tenure track job. The appeal of each offer varied greatly by the faculty member's current status as being on either a tenure track or not, and somewhat by discipline. The relative importance of the attributes in this exercise, across all faculty surveyed, was geographic location, work balance, contract length, departmental ranking, chances of tenure/contract renewal, salary, and institutional prestige. (See Table 7.4.)

When the choice was between two non–tenure track positions, faculty were even more likely to stay put; the probability of rejecting both non–tenure track offers was 62%. Still, 38% of the faculty would leave their current position to accept one of these offers if the terms were right. The importance of attributes shifted slightly in this scenario: salary became relatively more important, and the likelihood of contract renewal became relatively less important when the choice was between two non–tenure track positions.

Two demographic characteristics most influenced which faculty were likely to accept another offer: current status vis-à-vis the tenure track and discipline. Overall, respondents in non–tenure track positions were much more likely than tenure track faculty to accept a different offer, and faculty on both types of appointments were more

Table 7.4 Relative importance of job factors for faculty in choice set exercise

Factor	Tenure track vs. non–tenure track offers	Choice of 2 non–tenure track offers
Balance of work	2	2
Chances of tenure or contract renewal	5 —	— 6
Geographic location	1	1
Department ranking	4	4
Institutional prestige	7	7
Salary	6	5
Contract length	3	3

likely to accept a tenure track offer over a non–tenure track one. (See Table 7.5.)

Faculty in the professions were slightly more likely to continue in their present position than to accept either a tenure track or a non–tenure track offer, and faculty in the social sciences and humanities were most apt to stay with their present position when faced with a choice between two non–tenure track offers. (See Table 7.6.)

When current position (on or off the tenure track) and discipline were considered together, tenure track faculty in the professions were most likely to stay with their current position and non–tenure track faculty in the social sciences and humanities were least likely to stay. Faculty in the social sciences and humanities, whether on or off the

Table 7.5 Probability of faculty accepting a tenure track or a non–tenure track offer, or one of two non–tenure track offers, by type of current appointment

Offer	Current appointment	
	Tenure track	Non–tenure track
Scenario 1 (tenure track and non–tenure track offer)		
Stay with current appointment	.50	.29
Accept tenure track offer	.42	.50
Accept non–tenure track offer	.09	.21
Scenario 2 (two non–tenure track offers)		
Stay with current appointment	.80	.56
Accept one of two non–tenure track offers	.20	.44

Table 7.6 Probability of faculty accepting a tenure track or a non–tenure track offer, or one of two non–tenure track offers, by discipline

Offer	Professions	Sciences	Social sciences and humanities
Scenario 1 (tenure track and non–tenure track offer)			
Stay with current appointment	.41	.39	.37
Accept tenure track offer	.43	.48	.50
Accept non–tenure track offer	.16	.14	.12
Scenario 2 (two non–tenure track offers)			
Stay with current appointment	.68	.70	.71
Accept one of two non–tenure track offers	.32	.30	.29

tenure track, were more likely than their counterparts in the professions and in the sciences to accept the tenure track offer. (See Table 7.7.)

Because the remaining demographic variables—gender, race, age, marital/partnership status, whether or not the spouse or partner was employed, and income—affected only slightly the likelihood of accepting various offers, those small differences are not presented here.

What Is the "Right" Offer for Faculty?

A Decision Support System[4] revealed different probabilities in job offer choices when the levels of the various job attributes were altered (rather than holding them constant at default levels). Varying the two most important factors, geographic location and work balance, uncovered important distinctions.

The impact of geographic location can be illustrated by examples for two groups of faculty members in the professions, one group on the tenure track, the other group not. (See Figures 7.1 and 7.2.) In both cases, Scenario 1 was the default setting, where the geographic location was "comfortable" for the three possibilities. In Scenario 2, the location of the current position was marginally satisfactory, but the tenure track and non–tenure track offers were located where the faculty member had a strong desire to live. In Scenario 3, the tenure track offer was located where the faculty member did not want to live, but the other offers remained in very desirable locations.

In the case of the tenure track faculty member in the professions, the

Table 7.7 Probability of faculty accepting a tenure track or a non–tenure track offer, by type of appointment and discipline

Current appointment	Discipline	Likelihood of accepting tenure track offer	Likelihood of accepting non–tenure track offer	Likelihood of accepting neither offer (staying)
Tenure track	Professions	.37	.09	.55
	Sciences	.40	.07	.53
	Social sciences/humanities	.44	.06	.49
Non–tenure track	Professions	.47	.21	.32
	Sciences	.52	.18	.31
	Social sciences/humanities	.56	.16	.28

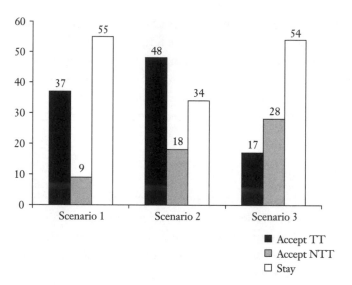

Figure 7.1   Probability of position acceptance: professions, on tenure track

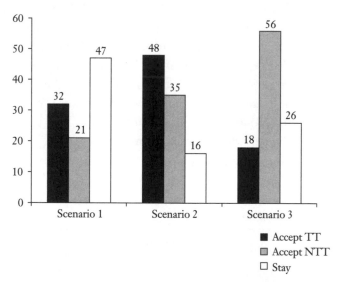

Figure 7.2   Probability of position acceptance: professions, on non–tenure track

likelihood of accepting a tenure track offer in a most attractive location (given an only marginally satisfactory current location) shifted from 37% to 48% and down to 17% when the tenure track offer was in an unattractive location (Scenario 3). In Scenario 3, the likelihood of accepting a non–tenure track position in an attractive location increased from only 9%, when all else was equal, to 28%. A faculty member currently employed in the professions in a non–tenure track position (Figure 7.2) was more likely (56%) to accept the attractively located non–tenure track offer, even over the tenure track one (18%) in an unattractive locale.

The same pattern, although not as extreme, occurred when the balance of work shifted from preferred to not preferred. Taking a faculty member in the sciences as an example, Scenario 1 was the default where the balance of work matched one's preference for all three job possibilities. In Scenario 4, the balance of work for the tenure track offer differed from the stated preference but all else stayed the same, and in Scenario 5, both the current position and the tenure track offer differed from stated preferences. For faculty on the tenure track, changing the non–tenure track offer to a balance of work that matched one's preference was not enough to attract many takers; the likelihood of acceptance moved only from 7% to 12%. (See Figure 7.3.)

However, in the case of faculty currently employed in a non–tenure track position, an offer of a tenure track position was enough to entice them, even with a balance of work that was not preferred. The probability of accepting the tenure track offer was 46%. (See Figure 7.4.)

To find the point where non–tenure track faculty were indifferent between a tenure track and a non–tenure track offer, we changed the length of the non–tenure track contract from three years to ten years (Scenario 6) and held all else equal to the previous exercise. The probabilities shifted from 52% to 39% for the tenure track offer and from 18% to 38% for the non–tenure track one. If the contract offer were sweetened even more by offering a 10% salary premium and a ten-year contract (Scenario 7), the scale finally tipped. Non–tenure track faculty in the sciences accepted the tenure track offer 37% of the time, the non–tenure track offer 41% of the time, and stayed put 22% of the time. Scenario 8 shows what happened with a ten-year contract at a 25% pay premium. The probabilities shifted very little, to 36%, 43%, and 21%. (See Figure 7.5.) There was no better deal that would cause a shift in probabilities for tenure track faculty, unless both geographic location and balance of work changed to a considerable degree.

For tenure track faculty members in the social sciences and humanities, the lure of tenure was especially strong. Quite an offer would be necessary to entice a scholar on the tenure track to a non–tenure track position. Figure 7.6 displays probabilities for a variety of scenarios, beginning with the default (1) where the probabilities are 44% (ten-

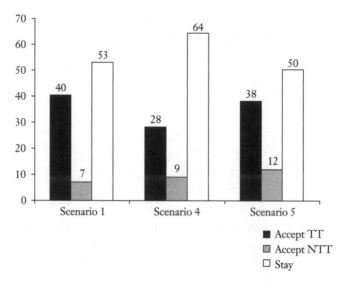

Figure 7.3 Probability of position acceptance: sciences, on tenure track

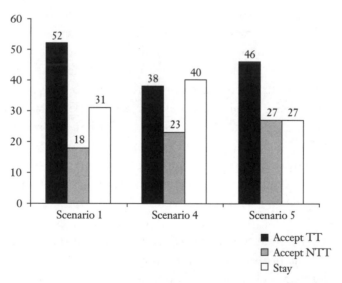

Figure 7.4 Probability of position acceptance: sciences, on non–tenure track (Scenarios 1, 4, 5)

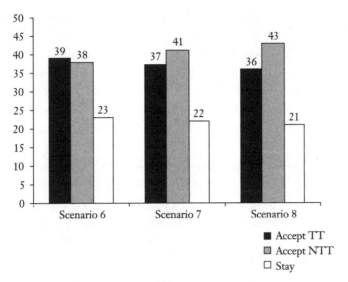

Figure 7.5 Probability of position acceptance: sciences, on non–tenure track (Scenarios 6, 7, 8)

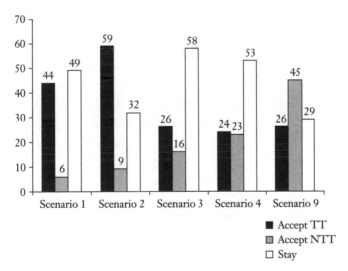

Figure 7.6 Probability of position acceptance: social sciences/humanities, on tenure track

ure track), 6% (non–tenure track), and 49% (stay with current position).

In Scenario 2, the current location was only marginally satisfactory, and the tenure track and non–tenure track offers were both in most attractive locales. The probabilities of a move shifted to 59%, 9%, and 32% respectively. In Scenario 3, when the location of the tenure track offer is unattractive, the probabilities changed to 26%, 16%, and 58% respectively.

To find the point of indifference between the tenure track and the non–tenure track offer, we shifted the length of the contract to ten years while holding all else at Scenario 3 levels; the probabilities changed to 24%, 23%, and 53% (Scenario 4). Finally, to discover what would increase the likelihood that a tenure track faculty member in the social sciences or humanities would accept a contract offer, we tested Scenario 9. In this offer, both the current position and the tenure track offer were in unattractive locations and the balance of work in both cases differed from the faculty member's preference. The contract offer, on the other hand, matched work preference, was situated in the most attractive location, and was for ten years. Under these "ideal" conditions, the probabilities shifted to 26%, 45%, and 29%. No pay premium was required; however, if salary were increased 10% over average on a three-year contract, the probabilities changed to 30%, 37%, and 33% respectively.

When presented with a non–tenure track offer, faculty currently on the tenure track under default conditions were very immobile. Discipline made no difference in the equation. At the default setting, where all was equal, tenure track faculty were 80% likely to stay put. If the balance of work in their current positions differed from their preference, and they were offered a contract appointment that matched their work preference, then the 80% likelihood of staying dropped to 73%. If the work balance matched their preference, but the location of their current position was only marginally satisfactory, the probability of staying dropped to 65%. However, if there was *not* a desirable work balance in the current tenure track position, *and* the current locale was unattractive, *and* a contract was offered with a match in balance in an attractive location, the probability of staying was only 20%.

Doctoral Candidates

When doctoral students were presented with hypothetical choices between a tenure track and a non–tenure track offer (all at default settings), they were twice as likely to accept the tenure track offer. They
chose the tenure track offer 54% of the time, the non–tenure track offer 26% of the time, and neither offer 20% of the time. For those who
chose the tenure track over the non–tenure track offer, geographic location of the institution figured most prominently in the decision, followed by the balance between research and teaching, the perceived
chances of achieving tenure, and the ranking of the department, salary,
and institutional prestige.

The relative importance of the variables differed for those who chose
the non–tenure track position over the tenure track one. Geographic
location and balance of work remained first and second; however, the
department's rank was third and the chances of contract renewal was
fourth. The other variables remained unchanged. (See Table 7.8.)

When the choice was between two non–tenure track offers, doctoral
candidates would accept one or the other 74% of the time. When the
choice was between two non–tenure track offers, the relative importance of the job factors varied slightly with salary fourth, chances of
contract renewal fifth, contract length sixth, and institutional prestige
last. Location and work balance remained most significant.

As was the case with faculty, no demographic variables significantly

Table 7.8 Relative importance of job factors for doctoral students in choice set exercise

Factor	Choose tenure track over non–tenure track offer	Choose non–tenure track over tenure track offer	Choice of two non–tenure track offers
Balance of work	2	2	2
Chances of tenure/contract renewal	3	4	5
Geographic location	1	1	1
Department ranking	4	3	3
Institutional prestige	6	6	7
Salary	5	5	4
Contract length	—	7	6

influenced these patterns. There were differences by discipline. Students in the social sciences and humanities were most likely to accept the tenure track offer—64% of the time compared with 52% in the professions and 48% in the sciences. (See Table 7.9.) Students in the sciences opted to remain on the job market 30% of the time compared with 26% in the professions and 19% in the social sciences and humanities.

When the choice was between two non–tenure track positions, there was little difference in probabilities of acceptance by discipline. Those in all disciplines were as likely to accept neither offer, with a slight preference in the social sciences and humanities for taking one of the non–tenure track offers.

What Is the "Right" Offer for Doctoral Candidates?

By systematically varying the most important attributes, we were able to see which offers most appealed to doctoral candidates. The examples that follow are for doctoral candidates in the social sciences and humanities; however, data from the model indicated that the behavior of candidates in the sciences and in the professions would be quite similar.

When presented with a tenure track and a non–tenure track offer, doctoral candidates preferred the tenure track most of the time. Holding everything constant at default levels (in a comfortable locale), a candidate in the social sciences or humanities would accept the tenure track offer 78% of the time, the non–tenure track offer 20% of the time, and neither 2% of the time. Figure 7.7 illustrates the impact of

Table 7.9 Probability of doctoral students accepting a tenure track or a non–tenure track offer, or one of two non–tenure track offers, by discipline

Offer	Professions	Sciences	Social sciences and humanities
Scenario 1 (tenure track and non–tenure track offer)			
Accept neither offer	.26	.30	.19
Accept tenure track offer	.52	.48	.64
Accept non–tenure track offer	.22	.22	.17
Scenario 2 (two non–tenure track offers)			
Accept neither offer	.50	.50	.46
Accept one of two non–tenure track offers	.50	.50	.54

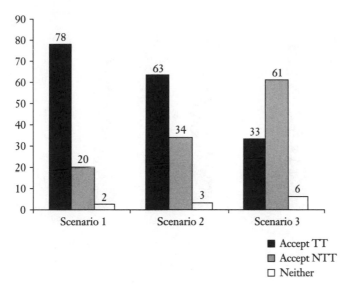

Figure 7.7   Probability of position acceptance: social sciences/humanities, doctoral candidates (Scenarios 1, 2, 3)

geographic location on job. In Scenario 2, where the tenure track offer was in a marginally satisfactory location, the probability the offer would be accepted dropped to 63%. When the location of the tenure track offer was somewhere the candidate did not want to live (Scenario 3), the likelihood of acceptance was 33% whereas the likelihood of accepting the contract offer, in a comfortable place, was 61%.

When the location remained at the default level (comfortable) for both offers, but the balance of work for the tenure track offer changed to "not preferred" (Scenario 4), the likelihood of accepting the tenure track position dropped from 78% to 57% and the probability of accepting the contract offer rose from 20% to 39%. (See Figure 7.8.) When the location for both offers was comfortable, but the balance of work for both offers was not preferred (Scenario 5), the probability of accepting the tenure track offer was 74% versus 21% for the non–tenure track position, and 5% for neither—quite close to the default probabilities. This suggests that while balance of work was important in job choice, it was not nearly as important as geographic location. Taken together, though, the impact was especially strong.

When the tenure track offer changed from a preferred to an unpreferred balance of work, but in a comfortable location, and the non–ten-

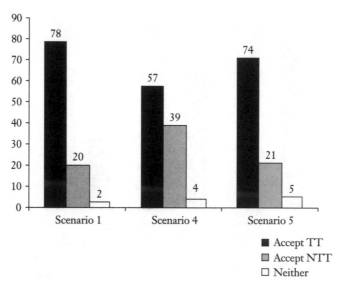

Figure 7.8 Probability of position acceptance: social sciences/humanities, doctoral candidates (Scenarios 1, 4, 5)

ure track position offered a preferred balance of work in an especially attractive locale (Scenario 6), the probabilities of 78% (tenure track), 20% (non–tenure track), and 2% (neither) changed to 44%, 53%, and 3% respectively. When the tenure track offer was in an unattractive location and the balance of work was not preferred, and the non–tenure track offer was in a most attractive locale and the balance of work was preferred (Scenario 7), the probabilities change to 9% (accept the tenure track position), 86% (accept the non–tenure track position), and 5% (accept neither). (See Figure 7.9.)

The same sort of choice behavior was likely to occur when doctoral candidates faced a choice between two non–tenure track offers. (See Figure 7.10.) In Scenario 8, contract offer 1 matched work preferences and location preferences, and contract offer 2 matched work preferences but in an unattractive location. The probability of accepting offer 1 was 82%, offer 2 was 10%, and neither was 7%. Location made a large difference. When contract offer 1 matched work preferences in an attractive location and contract offer 2 did not match work preferences but was still attractively located (Scenario 9), the probabilities of acceptance were 65% for offer 1, 29% for offer 2, and 6% neither.

When the choice was between two non–tenure track positions, the

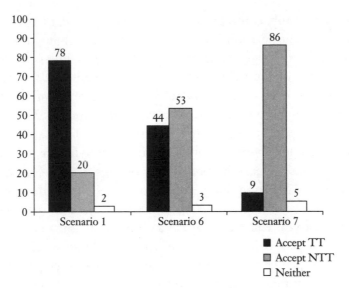

Figure 7.9 Probability of position acceptance: social sciences/humanities, doctoral candidates (Scenarios 1, 6, 7)

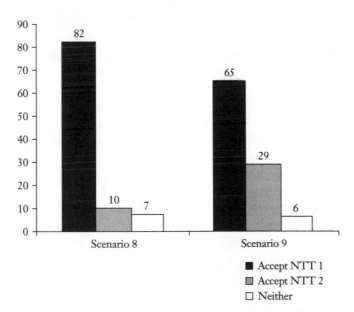

Figure 7.10 Probability of position acceptance: social sciences/humanities, doctoral candidates, two non–tenure track offers (Scenarios 8, 9)

department's rank, contract length, and salary played a larger and different role in the decision. Top-rated departments can lure top scholars without offering longer contracts or pay premiums, unless the location is undesirable or the balance of work is unattractive. A top-rated department wins even with a salary at 85% of the average of other offers, and a one-year contract against an unrated department's 25% pay premium and a ten-year contract (69% versus 21%). This explains in part why research universities can attract so many non–tenure track faculty.

With all else equal, the probability of accepting a contract offer moved from 37% for a one-year contract, to 46% for three years, to 51% for five years, and to 55% for ten years. The difference between five- and ten-year contracts suggests a diminishing rate of return on extended contracts. Salary had very little effect, all else equal; the probability of acceptance moved from 45% at 85% of average pay to 47% at a 25% pay premium—only 2 percentage points for a substantial pay differential.

Overall, survey results indicated that first- and second-year faculty, and doctoral candidates, would accept non–tenure track positions over tenure track slots if the former were in locations candidates desired and when assignments offered an attractive balance between teaching and research. Conditions being equal, however, most faculty most of the time would choose the tenure track position over the non–tenure track position hands down.

Institutions That Have Recruited Faculty without Tenure

While the survey measured hypothetical offers, some institutions without tenure have actually recruited faculty members. Located in Fort Myers, Florida Gulf Cost University hired 92 faculty for the academic year 1997–98: 9 professors, 29 associates, 45 assistants, and 9 instructors. Of this cohort, 47% were women and 23% were minorities. Slightly more than 75% of FGCU's new hires had doctorates compared with 67% at the University of Central Florida and 70% at both the University of South Florida and the University of West Florida, all peer institutions. Of the faculty with doctorates at FGCU, 59% earned their degrees from institutions in the Association of American Universities, generally regarded as the nation's premier research universities. In addition, 15% of FGCU's faculty relinquished tenured positions and 24% vacated tenure track positions elsewhere (Chait and Trower 1998).

We cite FGCU because substantial data are available, not because it is a typical institution. However, FCGU's experience indicates that a university can recruit a well-credentialed faculty without any prospect of tenure and without offering a salary premium. It may very well be that for FGCU faculty (as with faculty in the survey), the magnets of an attractive location and meaningful work were sufficient to offset the lack of tenure.

Major Findings

Tenure Track Preferred to Non–Tenure Track

This study demonstrated that the possibility of tenure was a powerful draw for most new scholars. All else equal, most faculty and doctoral candidates, when afforded a choice, will more often than not select the tenure track. The appeal of tenure was first and foremost about economic security and far less about academic freedom, although faculty wanted that, too.

The lure of tenure also had to do with socialization and status. Young scholars in most fields learned from professors, mentors, and peers that the only "legitimate" academic path was the tenure track. Those without tenure (whether part-time or in nontenurable positions) were often made to feel second class. They were excluded from campus governance and relegated to the periphery of the academic enterprise. These realities are likely to continue unless and until there is a critical mass of full-time scholars who do not have tenure, whether by choice or by design.

Faculty and doctoral students expressed similar views about academic life on the tenure track compared to term contracts. Tenure track faculty, non–tenure track faculty, and doctoral candidates all felt that the tenure track offered more employment security, induced more stress, entailed greater pressure to conduct research, afforded more mobility, allowed greater involvement in campus governance and more influence in one's department, and conveyed more status. These three groups also agreed that the chance to work outside of academe was unaffected by one's "track."

Tenure track faculty and doctoral students believed that professional autonomy and academic freedom were greater on the tenure track. However, non–tenure track faculty viewed these facets of academic life, as well as the pressure to excel in teaching, as about the same for both types of appointment.

Overall, faculty (93%) and doctoral students (88%) agreed that tenured and tenure track positions commanded more respect, and most faculty (73%) and students (66%) agreed that tenure was vital to protect academic freedom. On balance, then, the tenure track was preferable.

Geographic Location and Work Balance Most Important

Despite the appeal of the tenure track, the survey disclosed that faculty and doctoral candidates would select a non–tenure track position under certain conditions related to quality of life: geographic location and the balance between teaching and research. Location and work balance were more important than salary and contract length to candidates for faculty appointments. If an institution were attractively situated (in the opinion of the candidate), and if the scholar were offered a preferred portfolio of responsibilities, then all else was relatively unimportant, even whether the position was on or off the tenure track, if the tenure track did not offer those same advantages.

Implications

Location, Location, Location

If candidates do not perceive an institution to be attractively located, faculty recruiters will have to be creative if they are to attract top candidates. A candidate committed to life in California, say, for family reasons, cannot easily be seduced to Connecticut. However, a location that might be seen as "too rural" could be marketed on the basis of affordable housing, an easy commute, beautiful parks, good schools, and within hours of urban amenities.

The most ingenious institutions can even turn a cold climate to some advantage. One institution in northern Minnesota, for example, actually brings candidates to campus in the winter and involves them in the Winter Festival, ice skating, sledding, and skiing. All too often, academics are so focused on selling the quality of the department, the possibility of tenure, salary, and perquisites that they miss the chance to entice faculty, even without a tenure track line, by other marketing strategies that they may have used to attract students. Quality of life can be improved through such things as on-site day care, a state-of-the-art indoor recreational facility, or a picturesque pedestrian mall with boutiques, a coffeehouse, eateries, and a splendid bookstore. Materials from the local chamber of commerce may be as or more influential than the faculty handbook, and may be read with equal or greater interest.

The Work Matters

Colleges with vacancies should ascertain what mix of work top candidates really want. To the extent that their preferences for teaching, research, and service can be accommodated, the chances of successful recruiting increase, regardless of whether the position is tenure track or not. Some institutions, like the University of Iowa, allow senior faculty to adjust their work portfolio to match personal preferences and departmental goals. Why not permit and encourage junior faculty to do the same? Perhaps institutions could offer new faculty opportunities to teach senior level or honors courses, or take a mini-sabbatical after three years to conduct research and publish the results. It should also be possible to limit service commitments for the first several years of employment.

Find the Right Combination

If employment contracts or faculty policies do not allow flexibility in work assignments for new faculty, the institution will have to "sell" other features, like the quality of the department, the chances for tenure or contract renewal, or salary. Search committees, department chairs, and deans should recall that what may have been important twenty or thirty years ago may matter less today. Some institutional incentives that have proven attractive to young scholars in the past have included lighter teaching loads, limited service activities prior to tenure, summer stipends, graduate students to help with research,

research start-up funds, assistance with grant applications, equipment and lab facilities, moving expenses, and tuition remission. The greater presence of women and minorities in faculty positions suggests new realities and new incentives. With the increasing number of dual-academic career households, institutions may want to offer shared or split appointments and think of ways to attract both partners. Women scholars are unlikely to have a stay-at-home spouse or partner; they may have children or want children, and they want to lead a balanced life. Therefore, the traditional "up or out" tenure system, hardly designed with them in mind, may not be attractive.

Do Not Underestimate the Lure of the Outside Offer

While this study did not measure choice behavior when an outside offer was in play, many scholars have more options today than ever before. The business/industrial sector has been especially active in making offers to academics and new Ph.D.s. Law firms have undergone remarkable change from the days of "up or out" partnerships. Almost *half* of the nation's largest law firms have replaced the conventional "up or out" system with various forms of tiered partnerships to afford firms and attorneys more latitude. Law firms recognized that with women accounting for 40% of law school graduates, conditions and expectations would have to change.

Keep the Best, Even in Non–Tenure Track Positions

Non–tenure track faculty were more likely to opt for another offer than were faculty in their first or second year on the tenure track. Therefore, institutions should assure, to the extent possible, that their non–tenure track faculty are satisfied (see Chapter 5 in this volume). In addition, this study showed that when doctoral candidates chose between two non–tenure track offers, the length of the contract was especially important and mattered more than salary.

It is certainly possible, although not easy, to competitively recruit junior faculty without tenure, especially when the institution offers an attractive location and a preferable balance of work at a top-rated department. Candidates for faculty positions will consider non–tenure track positions when these attributes are satisfied. It appears that contract positions will more likely be accepted in those disciplines where non–tenure track positions are the norm, where outside labor markets for those with doctorates are thin, or where outside labor markets (e.g., business, engineering) offer faculty a fallback position. In addition, this study has shown that some candidates actually prefer a non–tenure track alternative.

While employment decisions of young scholars are complex and difficult to predict, insights important to faculty recruitment specifically and to the health of the academy more broadly can be gleaned by understanding better what influences the choices academics make about where to work.

Notes

I am grateful to everyone who assisted with various aspects of this research project, including Jordan Bach, Janice Ballou, Jared Bleak, Robert Brennan, Richard Chait, Lara Couturier, James Honan, Cathy Lachapelle, Jordan Louviere, Robert Meyer, Heidi Neiman, KerryAnn O'Meara, Cheryl Sternman Rule, Colin Rule, Matt Taylor, Dave Volpe, the faculty and doctoral candidates who participated in the focus groups, pretested the survey, and completed the survey, and the deans and department chairs who supplied e-mail lists.

1. "New-generation" faculty were defined as having seven years or less in a full-time faculty position and as having teaching, research, or administration (program director, department chair, or academic dean) as their principal activity.

2. The focus group interviews were conducted by Janice Ballou of the Eagleton Institute of Politics, Center for Public Interest Polling, at the State University of New Jersey, Rutgers.

3. In factorial designs, the researcher is able to examine the effects of several factors simultaneously by forming groups based on all possible combinations of the levels of the various treatment variables. Conjoint analysis is utilized to determine the contributions of predictor variables and their respective values to the determination of decision-maker preferences and to establish a valid model of judgments that is useful in predicting the acceptance of any combination of attributes (Hair et al. 1992).

4. The Decision Support System was developed by Memetrics, an internet start-up based in Sydney, Australia.

References

American Association of University Professors. 1977. "Academic Freedom and Tenure: 1940 Statement of Principles and Interpretive Comments." *AAUP Policy Documents and Reports.* Washington, D.C.: American Association of University Professors.

Bowen, Howard R., and Jack H. Schuster. 1986. *American Professors: A National Resource Imperiled.* New York: Oxford University Press.

Breneman, David W. 1997. *Alternatives to Tenure for the Next Generation of Scholars.* New Pathways Working Paper Series, no. 14. Washington, D.C.: American Association for Higher Education.

Chait, Richard, and Cathy A. Trower. 1997. *Where Tenure Does Not Reign: Colleges with Contract Systems.* New Pathways Working Paper Series, no. 3. Washington, D.C.: American Association for Higher Education.

———— 1998. "Build It and Who Will Come?" *Change,* 30 (5): 20–29.

Finkelstein, Martin J., Robert K. Seal, and Jack H. Schuster. 1998. *The New Academic Generation: A Profession in Transformation.* Baltimore: Johns Hopkins University Press.

Hair, Joseph F., Jr., Rolphe E. Anderson, Ronald L. Tatham, and William C. Black. 1992. *Multivariate Data Analysis with Readings,* 3rd ed. New York: Macmillan Publishing Co.

Keast, William R., and John W. Macy, Jr. 1973. *Faculty Tenure: A Report and Recommendations by the Commission on Academic Tenure in Higher Education.* San Francisco: Jossey-Bass.

Kuh, Charlotte. 1998. "Off-Tenure Track Employment and the Labor Market." Paper presented to the Workshop on Higher Education, National Bureau of Economic Research, National Research Council. November.

McGee, Robert W., and Walter E. Block. 1991. "Academic Tenure: An Economic Critique." *Harvard Journal of Law and Public Policy,* 14 (2): 545–563.

McPherson, Michael S., and Morton Owen Schapiro. 1999. "Tenure Issues in Higher Education." *Journal of Economic Perspectives,* 13 (1): 85–98.

Miller, John Perry. 1970. "Tenure: Bulwark of Academic Freedom and Brake on Change." *Educational Record,* 51: 241–245.

Modern Language Association. 1998. "Data on the Job Market." MLA Surveys of Ph.D. Placements. Available online: *http://www.mla.org.JILData_98.htm.*

Sanderson, Allen, Bernard Dugoni, Thomas Hoffer, and Lance Selfa. 1999. "Doctorate Recipients from United States Universities: Summary Report 1998." Chicago: National Opinion Research Center.

Shoun, Janel. 1999. "As Faculty and Staff Leave FGCU, Officials Vow to Monitor the Situation." *Naples Daily News,* May 31.

———— 2000. "FGCU Faculty Concerned Again about Job Security." *Bonita Daily News,* June 5.

U.S. Department of Education, National Center for Education Statistics. 1997. "Instructional Faculty and Staff in Higher Education Institutions: Fall 1987 and Fall 1992." NCES No. 97–467. Washington, D.C.: U.S. Department of Education, Office of Educational Research and Improvement.

———— 2000. *IPEDS Fall Staff Survey in Postsecondary Institutions,* 1997 electronic data file, final release (February).

U.S. News and World Report. 1999. *America's Best Graduate Schools: 2000 Edition.* Washington, D.C.: U.S. News and World Report.

Wilson, Robin. 2000. "A New Campus without Tenure Considers What's Missing." *Chronicle of Higher Edcation,* May 12, p. A18.

8

Can Faculty Be Induced to Relinquish Tenure?

CHARLES T. CLOTFELTER

SUPPOSE ONE BELIEVES it would be desirable to reduce the number of faculty with tenure. How might this be accomplished? Short of an edict of unimaginable effectiveness or a catastrophe of unparalleled severity, the only realistic route to a significant weakening of the reign of tenure is by way of voluntary relinquishment—by faculty members who have tenure to give it up. In order to assess how realistic a possibility that is, this chapter poses the following question: Under what circumstances would a faculty member voluntarily relinquish tenure? At a university where tenure is available, what incentives or added features, if any, might make contracts as attractive to faculty as tenured positions? Beyond the cynical view that "everyone has a price," the question must be viewed from the standpoint of a prototypical faculty member.

Posing the question of whether faculty might be willing to relinquish tenure is meant to imply nothing about the ultimate desirability of adopting such policies. Rather, I aim to examine a question that in principle is amenable to empirical analysis, and I offer some perspectives and observations that may be useful in answering it. This chapter implicitly treats tenure as a condition of employment quantitatively similar to other conditions, such as workload, promotion in rank, and remuneration. In that light, tenure's value to faculty can be assessed.

Not everyone will agree with these assumptions; some may believe

221

that this question simply should not be asked, because tenure is a basic right, like freedom. From this perspective, to ask how much someone would want to forgo tenure is tantamount to asking the price of freedom. Similarly, some may argue that tenure has an externality value, so that if one person gives it up, its value to others is diminished. For proponents of either of these views, the cold calculations discussed in this chapter will be unhelpful, distasteful, or both; but for anyone willing to weigh the costs against possible benefits, this chapter provides a framework for deliberation and debate.

To obtain insight into the question of what it would take to induce faculty to relinquish tenure, four focus groups of tenured faculty were convened. In forming the groups, an effort was made to include representatives of research universities as well as other types of institutions, and to have some variety of disciplines, largely because nonacademic alternatives would be expected to differ according to these categories. With an eye to attracting busy faculty for the required two-hour period, two different meeting dates and sites were used, one in conjunction with the annual meeting of a regional professional association and one in a location easily accessible to a large number of institutions. Two groups consisted of economists, one from research universities and one from other types of institutions. A third group consisted of faculty in business and engineering at research universities in the Research Triangle area of North Carolina, and the fourth group was comprised of humanities and social science faculty from liberal arts colleges in North Carolina. The four groups included a total of 26 faculty members.

Before turning to the views expressed in those focus groups, I begin by considering the desirability of alternatives from the perspective of colleges and universities and distinguish relinquishment of tenure from other changes that might be instituted. I then consider aspects of alternative systems likely to interest potential candidates for relinquishment. After a discussion of the findings from the focus groups, I conclude with a discussion of the feasibility of reducing the number of tenured faculty through relinquishment. Because of the importance of institution-specific details, the complexity involved in making decisions under uncertainty, and the high stakes that would be involved in the relinquishment of tenure, posing hypothetical questions can be expected to yield only clues, not conclusions. Nevertheless, the views of faculty in the focus groups do provide a number of insights that institutions would be well advised to consider.

What's in It for the Institution?

At least three motives might underlie an institution's desire to reduce the number of tenured faculty. One motive is to increase the administration's flexibility to allocate faculty positions in the future, especially in response to shifts in student demand for courses. Second, administrators might believe that faculty on contracts would have greater incentives to produce research and teach better. For example, the dean whose school devised the nontenure option that is discussed later in this chapter opined, "We fully expect that the simple fact of real accountability will motivate faculty members to be productive" (Lataif 1998b). Third, the administration may want simply to change the allocation of authority within the institution. As Michael McPherson and Morton Schapiro (1999, pp. 92–97) argue, tenure is an outward manifestation of real faculty influence on important issues related to the management of the institution, especially as regards research and teaching. Eliminating tenure would surely shift the balance of power between the faculty on the one hand and the board and administration on the other.

From the perspective of a college or university, the desirability of enticing faculty to relinquish tenure is a relatively straightforward financial calculation. Since the demise of mandatory retirement in 1994, the award of tenure to the typical assistant professor carries an obligation of thirty to forty more years of compensation. Given assumptions about the expected real growth in compensation, the probability that the professor will leave before retirement, an estimated retirement age, and the standard mortality tables, a reasonable estimate of the expected present value of the institution's obligation to that faculty member can be made. For a thirty-two-year old freshly tenured associate professor with a $70,000 salary, for example, the university faces an expected obligation on the order of $2.7 million in present value terms, assuming he retires at age seventy. If he retires at seventy-five, the expected obligation is $3.0 million. By contrast, the university assumes an obligation of only $700,000 if it gives a ten-year contract to this same associate professor.[1] The difference between these two present values represents one simple estimate of the cost of tenure. These figures apply only to the payroll costs, and do not count other support costs routinely associated with faculty.

Such a financial calculation ignores two important features. First, the no-tenure route presumably offers the institution much more flexibility to replace an unproductive faculty member. Thus, one benefit of inducing a fallow faculty member to relinquish tenure would be the expectation of increased productivity achieved through the improved research and teaching by the faculty member's replacement.[2]

Second, relinquishment of tenure will have a complex effect on the quality of peer evaluations and the incentives for faculty to be productive. As Michael McPherson and Gordon Winston (1993) argue, the "up or out" nature of tenure decisions serves as a serious and effective prod to the productivity of assistant professors, a benefit to both institutions and candidates. Furthermore, H. Lorne Carmichael (1988) contends that because the evaluators are typically tenured, they are sufficiently secure to promote the best candidates rather than worry that to do so could threaten their own continued employment. Studies of institutions without tenure (Chait and Trower 1997) indicate that very few faculty are denied renewals. More broadly, Martin Finkelstein, Robert Seal, and Jack Schuster (1998) have worried that loyalty to institutions, important to many aspects of institutional governance, will wither with a decline in the proportion of tenured faculty. "Loyalty," they write, "dissipates in both directions" (pp. 107–108).

Unlike the calculation of reduced financial obligation, the effect on neither selectivity nor loyalty can be readily quantified. College and university leaders may decide that their institutions would benefit if faculty could be induced to surrender tenure. Even some faculty—both active and prospective—might stand to gain were such a scenario realized. If institutions offered, as an alternative to tenure, contracts with an attractive package of salaries and benefits, some faculty might respond favorably. Furthermore, if alternative arrangements could reduce the cost of higher education, students and their families would benefit as well. In the remainder of this chapter, I set aside the question of whether an institution should attempt to induce faculty to relinquish tenure and focus instead on whether such an approach is feasible. That tenure can be eliminated is not in question; a few colleges have done so (see Mallon, Chapter 9 in this volume), but the list of those that have dropped or never had tenure, or instituted inducements to forgo tenure, is a short one and does not include many prominent institutions.

Relinquishment of Tenure

In this chapter, "relinquishment" applies to tenured faculty (or faculty offered tenure) who voluntarily accept some form of term contract in place of indefinite tenure, not in lieu of termination or on the threshold of retirement. Whether offered to tenured faculty collectively or selectively, and whatever the package of proffered compensation may be, the practice is considered relinquishment if both parties intend that the faculty member continue in essentially the same role, only on a nontenured basis. This type of relinquishment differs from a two-track system, where faculty are provided a choice, either at the time of initial employment or the time of the tenure decision, between a position based on a tenure decision and one based on a term contract. To be sure, such a two-track system can be combined with an effort to induce faculty with tenure to relinquish it. Relinquishment also differs from planned or early retirement, where faculty members commit to a definite and usually accelerated schedule to retire in return for compensation of some kind. Effective in January 1994, retirement cannot be mandated. Thus, any planned retirement is by definition a voluntary relinquishment of tenure, but not the kind at issue in this chapter.

Tenure as We Know It Today

Just like any other choice, a professor's decision about whether or not to relinquish tenure would depend on the available alternatives—in this case, a comparison between two work situations. While a professor will normally have a clear picture of life under tenure, the nontenure alternative will be comparatively much more uncertain. To set the stage for the choice, I will describe each alternative. Doing so will reveal a degree of uncertainty even with regard to the tenure option.

Tenure represents a guarantee by an institution of continuous employment for a faculty member without any mandatory termination date. Technically, the guarantee is conditional: on most campuses, a tenured faculty member can be fired for "adequate cause" (for example, demonstrable or gross incompetence), "moral turpitude," the discontinuation of an entire academic program, or a state of financial exigency. The guarantee is one-way because faculty members always retain the right to resign, subject to due notice. Furthermore, tenure usually carries an implicit, and sometimes explicit, promise by the institution not to decrease the faculty member's normal salary. Although a faculty member's performance can affect salary and, more rarely, workload and lab and office space, the standards of performance effectively imposed on tenured faculty members are typically quite minimal.[3] As McPherson and Winston (in Finkin 1996) observe, "The obverse of close attention to the academic worker's performance prior to tenure is the marked inattention to performance after tenure" (p. 105).

The combination of minimal performance standards and the inability to set a mandatory retirement age leaves open the possibility that faculty members could continue to occupy positions long after their productivity and effectiveness have waned, blocking the way for freshly trained scholars to take their places. The extent to which this has become a problem is not yet clear, though there are some early indications of blockage, at least at research universities. Analyzing data from three North Carolina universities, Robert Clark, Linda Ghent, and Juanita Kreps (1998) find precipitous declines in the retirement rate at age seventy, along with significant reductions in the percentage of faculty under age forty.[4]

As serious as the effects of a slowdown in faculty retirement might prove to be, this is not the only, or necessarily the most important, reason why institutions might wish to reduce the number of tenured faculty. Probably more important, most colleges and universities cannot afford to disregard changes in student demand or withstand financial difficulties.

Despite the prevalence of tenure, administrators are not entirely powerless to resist the effect of its strictures. In the last few decades, some universities have lengthened the probationary period, an action that slows the rate of growth among the tenured ranks. Institutions have also hired faculty in large numbers, full- and part-time, off the tenure track (see Baldwin and Chronister, Chapter 5 in this volume). Such personnel, with titles such as instructor, lecturer, research professor, and postdoctoral fellow, now comprise more than half of all teaching and research positions nationwide (Roey and Rak 1998).

Another way colleges and universities can respond to the costliness of tenure would be through post-tenure reviews that could culminate in dismissal for cause. For example, a proposal considered by Boston University in 2000 would require annual face-to-face meetings for all faculty to evaluate their work, with provisions for lighter teaching loads for those faculty who do the most research, and for part-time status for those whose work was found wanting (Greene 2000). Like the tenure process itself, however, such consequential post-tenure review procedures would consume significant resources, mostly in the form of faculty time for additional peer reviews. The system would presumably also have to be structured so that the standards by which faculty are judged are both reasonable and fully disclosed. As long as such a system were applied equally to all tenured faculty, irrespective of age, it would appear to offer a better basis than now exists for institutions to reward tenured faculty differentially and, in the extreme, to fire them for cause. Tenure under such a regime could well look quite different from tenure as it currently exists in most institutions.[5] If the likelihood that a tenured faculty member would voluntarily relinquish tenure depends, as I believe it does, on the quality of life with tenure as opposed to the expected quality of life under a contract, a major change, such as the introduction of serious post-tenure reviews (with a non-zero probability of adverse consequences for poor performance), would affect that decision.

What Does the Alternative Look Like?

Any decision to relinquish tenure involves a comparison between two work situations: present conditions under tenure and the anticipated conditions under a term contract. Although the future cannot be known with certainty under either scenario, the alternative situation surely entails greater uncertainty than the status quo. Faced with the option of relinquishing as valuable a job attribute as tenure, a reasonably cautious professor would want more details about the alternative before making the leap. Discussed in this section are several points of comparison that appear to be pertinent, if not important, to most faculty members presented with the choice between a tenured and a non-tenured position.

Length of the contract. Undoubtedly, the length of a contract is one of the most important factors in this comparison. Whereas tenure means "without term," virtually any term appointment less than one's actuarial life expectancy, plus a decade or so, will seem like a reduction in the number of years of assured employment. Contracts could cover one year or extend to ten or more. The Philadelphia College of Textiles and Science, for example, recently instituted multiyear contracts as an alternative to tenure. A plan might contain the presumption of a series of renewable contracts, such as 1, 3, 3, 3, 5, 5, 5, for a total of 25 years. Under the option of "rolling contracts," the term of employment renews each year. Unless the faculty member is notified of termination (a so-called negative trigger), the length of the contract remains constant.

Duties associated with each option. A second important point of comparison relates to the duties assigned to faculty on each track. For instance, the amount and type of teaching could differ. Usually, non–tenure track faculty teach lower-level, survey, and service courses. Some schools and departments vary course loads, even among the ranks of tenured and tenure track faculty, as a function of research productivity. Such a practice would be relevant to any faculty member's comparison of tenured appointments. With respect to administrative duties and governance, the differences have been even starker, with nonregular faculty often disenfranchised and virtually absent from the governing councils of colleges and universities. Although neither inherent nor necessary, such differences are typical, and they are almost certain to enter into the calculus of faculty who might be choosing between the two tracks. Other duties normally associated with faculty positions, especially committee assignments and student advising, are also likely to be at least marginal considerations.

Salary differential. Labor economics offers a vast body of research suggesting that people must be offered compensating wage differentials in order to accept jobs that are in some way unappealing. In the present case, where an employer hopes to persuade a faculty member with tenure to choose a position without it, one expects the latter option to carry the higher salary. How much that differential proves to be looms as an important variable.

Other differences in conditions, benefits, and status. Beyond salary differentials, there are nonwage aspects of jobs, such as the quality of office and lab space and the frequency of sabbatical leaves, that can significantly affect the relative attractiveness of academic positions.

So too might less tangible features, especially the symbolic status accorded to faculty on contracts versus colleagues with tenure. Any hint of second-class citizenship will be readily discerned and could markedly affect job satisfaction. This presents less of a problem for faculty who relinquish tenure; for these faculty some certification of "tenure-worthiness" might increase the attractiveness of the contract alternative.

Reviews of job performance. Another element of comparison between tenured and contractual positions concerns performance evaluations. By and large, tenured faculty have been subjected to fairly cursory annual reviews, and any salary adjustments at stake are typically small. Not surprisingly, many tenured professors find the relative freedom from scrutiny and discipline inherent to this approach to be a most attractive feature. Life would be different if colleges and universities were to adopt vigorous regular reviews of tenured faculty, even if the principal threat were embarrassment rather than salary reduction or dismissal for cause. However rigorous the renewal reviews for faculty on contracts, such a change in the evaluation process for tenured faculty would tend to make tenured positions comparatively *less* attractive than before post-tenure review.

Procedures for not renewing contracts. What kind of documentation would the institution have to provide in order not to renew the contract of a faculty member working on a contract basis? In the case of program discontinuation or financial exigency, what rules would determine the order in which tenured and nontenured faculty would be terminated? Is there an appeals process? How successful might a lawsuit be against the institution? Perhaps the central issue related to non-renewal is whether there is a presumption of renewal or a presumption of nonrenewal. If it is written or understood that renewal is to be expected given satisfactory performance, one might well have more confidence in the safety of a contract position than if there were no presumption at all of renewal. On this question, the legal realities may be less important than faculty members' perception of the prospects.

How widespread are contracts? Would the option of taking an enhanced contract over a conventional tenured position be offered across the board, or would the choice be left to, and tailored to, the individual? A similar dichotomy applies to universities' efforts to induce faculty to retire: while some institutions have made blanket offers, often crafted in complex ways, other, mainly private, institutions pursue separate negotiations with individual faculty members. In the case of relinquishment, either approach, across the board or case by case, could apply equally well.

A Specific Alternative: Dual Tracks at the BU School of Management

While this chapter has necessarily been speculative thus far, a very real alternative to tenure exists at the Boston University School of Management.[6] There, a two-track system includes a provision that allows faculty to forgo or relinquish tenure. Instituted in 1996, the plan creates a separate option, a ten-year renewable contract and a salary premium of 8% to 10%, for professors who have, or are otherwise eligible to have, tenure. Faculty on ten-year contracts retain the rights and responsibilities enjoyed by tenured faculty members, including voting on tenured appointments. In addition, academic freedom is contractually guaranteed, and any alleged violations are afforded strict due process. The contracts are renewable: the school intends to subject candidates for renewal to the same peer-review process currently used for tenure candidates, with "tenurability" as the standard for renewal. This plan resembles Simon's (1991) proposal to offer faculty who pass the tenure hurdle the choice between a conventional tenured position and a term contract with a higher salary. For professors hired with tenure, the choice is indeed a pure one. Each professor can choose tenure or a ten-year renewable contract at a higher salary.

The Boston University plan modifies the choice for other faculty in two ways. First, newly hired faculty are eligible to opt for the contract track, but only after three years of employment, enough time to allow both the candidate and the university to make a fully informed choice. After that three-year period, faculty who choose the alternative track immediately receive a salary increase and agree, in return, to accept a ten-year contract instead of tenure, if they are judged to be tenurable by the school's tenure and promotion committee at the end of the initial probationary period. Second, for tenured professors already on board, the school reserves the right not to make the offer. This seems to be a prudent exception, because an administration may frequently find no advantage in increasing a faculty member's salary for the next ten years. In any case, the Boston University plan serves as a tangible example of a policy that seeks to induce faculty to relinquish their tenure. The fact that, among incoming junior faculty, about half of those offered the contracts accepted them certainly implies that faculty will, under the right circumstances, forgo tenure, and by extension, suggests that relinquishment is more than a theoretical possibility.[7]

The Focus Groups

In order to gain insight into the likely responses of faculty to offers involving relinquishment of tenure, several focus groups of tenured faculty were convened. As noted earlier, they were designed to differ by discipline and type of institution. Potential participants were contacted by e-mail or phone and told that tenure would be the discussion topic. All participants were paid a modest honorarium. Table 8.1 summarizes the composition of the four focus groups. In all, 26 faculty attended one of the four focus groups.

Two groups (denoted A and B in Table 8.1) consisted of economists who, by virtue of their discipline alone, would be expected to be comfortable with the concept of trade-offs and an assessment of alternative conditions of employment. One group of economists (A) came from research universities, and the other (B) was made up of faculty from comprehensive universities and liberal arts colleges. A third focus group (C) consisted of faculty in engineering and business schools from research universities in North Carolina. It was thought that faculty in these fields would be more likely than most faculty to have prospects for professional employment outside of higher education. A fourth

Table 8.1 The focus groups

Group	Discipline	Institution type	Number of participants
A	Economics	Research universities	4
B	Economics	Comprehensive universities, liberal arts colleges	6
C	Engineering, business	North Carolina research universities	12
D	Humanities, social sciences	North Carolina liberal arts colleges	4
			Total = 26

focus group (D) was composed of members of humanities and social science departments at small liberal arts colleges in North Carolina. During the focus groups, which met for two hours each, participants were asked general questions about tenure, followed by more specific questions on what inducements might lead the participants to forsake tenure.

Despite efforts to include faculty from various categories, the participants in these focus groups clearly were not representative of all faculty. The range of disciplines was limited in order to afford participants some common ground for discussion. Moreover, the acceptance pattern showed selection bias on at least one dimension: the participants tended to be older than the average tenured faculty at their institutions. Attendees might also have had distinctive attitudes toward tenure. One participant speculated that the focus group participants probably enjoyed academic life in general and for this reason might be more inclined to spend two hours discussing issues related to higher education.

The focus group discussions were insightful, not just about tenure but also about life in an academic workplace. Before considering the participants' views on tenure and the feasibility of voluntary relinquishment, it is instructive to summarize their opinions about the work environment of the tenured professor. As is so often the case in other situations, some of the most important facets of one's work world go unmentioned simply because they are so obvious, and therefore so unremarkable, to those who inhabit that environment. Yet, for the purpose at hand, such facts may be critically important.

Four generalizations are noteworthy. The first conclusion to be drawn from the focus groups is that the work environments of tenured professors differ markedly by type of institution to a much greater extent than among institutions of a given type. For example, while the duties, compensation, and physical environs of professors of political science may differ somewhat among research universities, the differences are sometimes dramatic between private research universities and small liberal arts colleges or public comprehensive universities— for example, in salary, fringe benefits, teaching load, expectations about research, participation in institutional governance, opportunities for sabbatical leave, office equipment, and prestige.

The starkest contrasts revealed in the focus groups were in teaching load and sabbatical policies: faculty at research universities teach less and have more ready access to sabbatical leaves. Professors at research universities also enjoy a more financially secure world on two counts. First, a national job market for active researchers means opportunities for mobility. By contrast—and several participants raised this point— once someone attains tenure at a non-research institution, job mobility seems to disappear. In addition, some of the less prestigious colleges and universities face a rather bleak financial outlook. One participant, for example, teaches at an institution where enrollments had declined by 50% in recent years. Finally, and although the sample was admittedly small, it may be noted that every case in which a participant displayed anger toward his or her institution involved a faculty member at a college or non-research university.

A second important feature about academic life that emerged from the observations of focus group members was that some tenured faculty members can indeed be described accurately as deadwood. A pejorative term that surfaced unbidden in at least two of the sessions, "deadwood" refers to a state of relative incompetence decried by critics of tenure and dreaded by senior professors. From the perspective of focus group participants, deadwood arises not from the gradual diminution of mental powers over time, but as a result of the relentless advances in knowledge and technique embodied in the continual flow of assistant professors with newly minted Ph.D.s into the professoriat. To be sure, the rate of advance and therefore of technical obsolescence differs by field, but the phenomenon is widespread in the academy. As one economist stated, "The standards keep changing all the time," leading many tenured faculty to be relieved that they are not now candidates for tenure. "The irony is that 80% of us couldn't make it," commented another participant. A third offered a description worthy of *Profscam* (Sykes 1988):[8] "There are a lot of faculty who don't do anything anymore. They don't keep up with the literature. They don't keep up with teaching methods. Plus, students complain, semester after semester, about poor teaching, and yet the administration doesn't do anything about getting rid of them because they've been tenured for years and years." Still another participant offered the opinion that tenured faculty can be "fuzzier about expectations" for themselves even as assessments of junior faculty must be rigorous and precise. The apparent result of the drift toward deadwood is a lock-in effect whereby tenured faculty become "stuck," or professionally immobile.

A third familiar aspect of academe revealed by the focus groups concerns the unusual degree of discretion most faculty members have at work. Academic departments are much more like voluntary associations than business firms to the extent that faculty have relatively broad discretion over research agendas and the content and pedagogy, if not the selection, of course offerings. Moreover, the focus groups highlighted that governance and administrative chores are largely undertaken voluntarily. While an egalitarian ethic shapes the distribution of chores within a department, each individual generally decides whether to be a good citizen and whether to assume his or her "fair share" of work. Under these conditions, a dean or department chair often has to cajole—or shame—faculty into serving on committees and performing other administrative tasks. One focus group participant recalled the store of personal "capital" he had to expend as a department chair to persuade his tenured colleagues to serve the department's needs. Indeed, several participants stressed the ability to say no to such administrative requests as a principal benefit of tenure. As one participant noted wryly, "Tenure is a great thing to have. The problem is that your colleagues have it, too."

A fourth ever present, yet often overlooked, characteristic of academia that emerged from the focus groups was the tight linkage between tenure and prestige, although no participant stated it quite that explicitly. Tenure and prestige are closely connected because all of the most renowned colleges and universities offer tenure, because virtually all of the nation's most eminent professors hold tenure, and because tenure appears to be harder to achieve at the most distinguished institutions. George Johnson (1999, Tables 9 and 10) notes that tenure probabilities tend to be higher in higher-paying fields. Like higher salaries, tenure appears to be one means by which the market rewards those in high demand. By contrast, almost all of the institutions that have eliminated tenure occupy the lower tiers of status within academe. As with other professions, prestige matters to professors, and tenure symbolizes elevated status.

These four generalizations—differences across institutions, the presence of deadwood, the degree of professional autonomy, and the correlation between tenure and prestige—all bear on the question of whether faculty will relinquish tenure.

What Matters

A central purpose of the focus groups was to ascertain what, if anything, would induce tenured faculty to relinquish tenure voluntarily. At one point in each session, participants were asked to consider a list of items as part of a hypothetical compensation package that would be offered in return for relinquishing tenure. (See Table 8.2.) They were asked to rank the items in order of desirability. Participants were told that in this hypothetical situation relinquishment of tenure would not jeopardize academic freedom, which would be contractually guaranteed, or any of the rights and privileges tenured faculty currently enjoy (except voting on tenured appointments). Near the end of each session, participants were asked to take account of all the possible items and to state whether or not some combination of incentives would prompt them seriously to consider relinquishing tenure. The participants' reactions to this proposal ranged from bemused interest to outright resentment. Some participants, including a majority from professional schools, were willing to talk about what package might suffice to compensate for the loss of tenure. Others, including almost all faculty from liberal arts and comprehensive colleges, were unwilling even after gen-

Table 8.2   Ranking of possible inducements to be added to the employment contract

	Ranking, by group		
Inducement	A	B	C
15% annual salary premium	1	1	4
A paid-up annuity equal to 25% of annual salary	2	2	2
10-year renewable contract	9	3	1
3-year renewable contract (rolling contract)	8	4	3
Research funds equal to 1/3 of salary per year	6	5	5
3–5 year renewable contract	3	6	9
One course reduction per semester	6	7	8
Travel grants up to $5,000 per year	5	12	6
Sabbatical every 5 years	3	11	12
Courses limited to graduate or honor students; small class size	12	8	7
Mortgage subsidy equal to 3 percentage points below market	10	10	10
Undergraduate college tuition payments up to $10,000 per year per child	11	9	13
Personal, expert investment counseling	13	13	11

tle encouragement to entertain the idea seriously.[9] Owing to the general reluctance of the fourth focus group to engage in the ranking exercise, Table 8.2 presents summaries for just three groups.

The list of possible inducements included straight salary increases, additional fringe benefits, additional financial support for academic activities (e.g., travel), and modifications in work conditions (e.g., reduced teaching, more frequent sabbaticals). In the main, the participants deemed the form of compensation to be less important than its monetary value, in effect favoring a cafeteria plan over specific benefits. Table 8.2 shows the preferences that three of the four groups expressed. Two groups cited the 15% salary increase as the most potent inducement, while one group judged the ten-year contract to be most attractive. The second choice of each group was a paid-up annuity. At the bottom of the lists were fringe benefits of small value to participants, such as tuition remission and mortgage assistance. Evidently few of the participants had college-age children or were contemplating home purchases. The economists, not unexpectedly, showed the greatest ease in translating the various items into a single basis for comparison (the present discounted value) and viewed this exercise as a particularly interesting aspect of the entire discussion.

The question posed to the focus group participants was inherently complex. A microeconomist might be able to model the choice as a decision under uncertainty, but not without making a number of assumptions about the probability of various job attributes and fringe benefits. Central to the theorist's model would be an individual's degree of risk aversion.[10] As a practical matter, the greatest obstacle any faculty member would face when asked to apply the model would be to imagine what his or her work situation would be like under a term contract, and especially what the chance of nonrenewal would be. This would be a difficult enough forecast to make in a real-world plan such as Boston University's, especially before any track record had been established about the odds for reappointment for contract professors. One can imagine schemes designed to compensate for the lack of a track record with regard to tenure probabilities, such as a salary figure tied to actual future tenure rates. However, such schemes could easily become too complicated, unworkable, or both. For the participants in these focus groups, for whom the alternative was altogether hypothetical, it is easy to understand if some participants simply could not take the choice seriously. Thus it is exceedingly difficult from such focus group encounters to learn very much useful information about explicit trade-offs involving specific job attributes. Nonetheless, the discussion yielded five useful conclusions relevant to the topic at hand.

Job Security

Professors are well aware of the value of the job security that tenure entails. Although this security is not absolute, it is sufficient to insulate tenured faculty from some of the threats or forces that impinge on employees in most industries. Protection against the threat of being fired or expressing unpopular views, a common justification for tenure, is a benefit keenly appreciated by the faculty in the focus groups. When asked about the benefits of tenure, several participants offered stories from their own careers in which tenure allowed them to express what they perceived as unpopular views without fear of reprisal. (Interestingly, all of these stories came from professors in research universities.) Another benefit tenure provides is protection from trendiness and pressure to conform in the marketplace of ideas. One participant noted the fickleness of funding agencies and their tendency to turn away from certain lines of work; tenure offers protection against these shifts. Finally, and perhaps most significantly, tenure provides a measure of freedom in the workplace. Tenure means not having to jump when one's boss issues a directive. Put another way, it transforms the meaning of "boss." This transformation to a large extent explains the reliance in the academic workplace on volunteers to get essential jobs done, as noted earlier.

Age

Although it probably should have been obvious beforehand, it became clear after listening to the focus group sessions that age is a powerful predictor of attitudes toward relinquishment. Comments by participants about the number of years before retirement or whether tuition benefits could apply to grandchildren made clear that one's stage of career colors the relative value of various incentives. Thus, the prospect of a ten-year renewable contract looks quite different (and less desirable) to a thirty-five-year-old professor than to a fifty-year-old professor who plans to work for another ten years. Indeed, as faculty approach the traditional age of retirement, relinquishment of tenure more and more resembles planned retirement. In light of typically high productivity during the early stages of a career and the anticipation of retirement in later years, it is not unreasonable to conclude that tenure may be of greatest value to faculty in the middle years, especially if family responsibilities loom largest then as well. Such reasoning has one clear implication for the likelihood of success for plans to induce faculty to relinquish tenure: relinquishment will tend to be easier to induce as a faculty member ages.

Institutional Details

There is no better illustration of the "devil in the details" axiom than speculation about whether faculty would relinquish tenure. There was lively discussion in the focus groups about what kinds of offers might make relinquishment tempting, but those discussions were peppered with questions and speculation about what the details of the contractual arrangement would be, particularly questions about who would conduct evaluations for renewal and what criteria would be employed. One participant expressed what was implicit in the comments of several: that the only acceptable basis for nonrenewal would be "for cause," which does not differ fundamentally from provisions under a traditional tenure system. Focus group discussions assumed that evaluations for contract renewal would be based on the same criteria employed for tenure decisions. In that case, the participants preferred peer reviews to administrative evaluations. For one economist whose appointment was in a business school, "peer" implied evaluation by other economists, not by business faculty more generally, and certainly not by university administrators. For relinquishment to have appeal, a professor would have to have a great deal of self-confidence and confidence in the legitimacy of the evaluation process. One participant noted, "I have confidence in myself, not in my evaluators."

Who Else Would Be on Contracts

More than a few participants commented that the desirability of relinquishment would depend on how many other tenured faculty at the same institution relinquished their tenure and, for some, how many other institutions adopted a similar plan. In this case, there was thought to be security in numbers. Institutional prestige entered into the equation as well. Most agreed that if the most preeminent universities installed such plans, other institutions would likely follow suit. As long as nontenure options were confined to less distinguished institutions, however, contracts would not be as readily accepted elsewhere.

Intangible Aspects

In "Economics and the Environmental Muddle," Stephen Kelman (1981) addressed the question of why economists had not been more successful in persuading policymakers to follow their approach to environmental problems, which relies on price incentives rather than regulations to discourage and limit the amount of pollution. Interviews revealed that many people in policy positions were offended by the economists' readiness to "put a price" on anything, including the quality of the environment.

Participants in the focus groups, most notably noneconomists from non-research institutions, had a similar reaction about tenure. To them, the offer to buy tenure was distasteful, almost repugnant, because this approach threatened to change the nature of their role in the institution. Tenure was for them the tangible manifestation of the fact that they were not mere employees. Because of this special position, they were willing to work for less, for the love of the institution, although not always without resentment. (One said, "We are already getting ripped off.") One faculty member from a small college wondered aloud about the tenured faculty there: "What is the difference between you and any other hired hand?" Tenure, according to this professor, allows faculty to resist the supposed consumer orientation of administrators. This professor concluded, "I don't like being treated like I'm an employee." To these individuals, attempts to induce faculty to relinquish tenure would be further proof that business values were replacing academic ones. One participant from a small college labeled such attempts "manipulative" and "dirty," saying, "I don't want to be bought off."

In considering the feasibility and prudence of plans to induce faculty to relinquish tenure, such views cannot be brushed aside lightly. Because of tenure's importance to the faculty's self-image and its pivotal role in the academic enterprise, the very attempt to induce professors to relinquish tenure may threaten important bonds of loyalty and, not incidentally, ignite a political powder keg. These negative effects may be more likely to occur in smaller, less selective, less affluent colleges, where institutional loyalty, as opposed to disciplinary affiliation, arguably looms larger as a motivator of faculty behavior. Similarly, academics who regard tenure as a right, rather than merely a condition of employment, may look askance at the economist's predilection to see the possibility of monetary trade-offs everywhere.

Is Relinquishment a Pipe Dream?

What, then, are the implications of these observations and considerations for the feasibility of policies to induce faculty to relinquish tenure? I offer three.

Prevailing Norms an Impediment

The focus groups revealed a deep reluctance on the part of tenured faculty to entertain the possibility of giving up tenure. Certainly the desire for economic security accounts for a large part of that reluctance; however, the norms and meanings that surround academic tenure are important, too. In academic labor markets, tenure acts as a signal of high quality, a fact not easily held constant in hypothetical discussions with focus groups. Because virtually all prominent scholars have tenure, and because tenure is the most desirable job attribute in academia, it would be surprising if tenure were not associated in people's minds with high quality. To be sure, a few celebrated faculty members hold nontenured appointments at distinguished universities, although not many of these are renowned as researchers. Thus, a faculty member's acceptance of a term contract, however laden with perquisites, runs the risk of a self-imposed label as a scholar of the second rank, unless this faculty member has already achieved or been offered tenure. If more faculty were to relinquish tenure or forgo an offer of tenure, especially at top-tier research institutions, then this stigma could largely be erased. In this case, the power of emulation might take over, transforming what had been a mark of shame into a neutral or even attractive attribute. Similarly, if those accepting nontenured appointments could obtain, as at

Boston University, some parallel indication of tenure-worthiness at the time of the appointment, the quality-signal role of tenure might be reduced or eliminated. As this discussion serves to illustrate, the social or marketwide context will be an important element in the acceptance of these alternative positions.

Institutional Circumstances and Behavior as Factors

If the probability that faculty will relinquish tenure depends on their assessment of the risks entailed in a contract, the actions of administrators can exert enormous influence over the attractiveness of the option. If administrators establish a track record of reasoned reviews and few surprises for contract renewals of formerly tenured faculty, the chances that professors will opt for relinquishment will increase. In contrast, arbitrary action will reduce the number of takers and raise the price of the inducements. Faculty who have worked in an institution for a while can be expected to know about job characteristics. New hires who are given the choice of tenure or contract can be expected to become knowledgeable about these relevant facts, including not only the salary levels but also the required duties, the relative status in the two tracks, and the actual probability of nonrenewal facing those on contracts. While this may seem like a tall order, it is not uncommon for candidates for positions to amass considerable information before making a decision, and it does not seem unreasonable that this would be true in the present application as well.

Institutions can wield great influence over the success of any attempts at inducement. Imagine the first questions that are likely to occur to tenured faculty on learning their institution will attempt to induce faculty to relinquish tenure. "Why are they doing this?" "What would my prospects for continued employment be if I were to accept their offer?" In seeking answers to questions such as these, faculty are likely to consult their best sources of information—their institution's stated objectives, conditioned by the institution's past behavior, as well as the experience of similar institutions. A university with a consistent track record for candor and credibility will be better positioned to convince its faculty that its motivation is institutional flexibility rather than simply covert reduction in faculty size.

The importance of detail and institutional reputation also affect the equation. As is the problem faced in general by experimental analysis and hypothetical survey questions, decisions made in the absence of full information or, indeed, without the prospect of actual consequences must necessarily be suspect. One may ask faculty members the hypothetical question of whether they would consider a no-tenure alternative, but the answers given, in the absence of real information about each alternative, must be taken with a grain of salt.

Some Faculty More Willing Than Others

It is safe to say that some groups of faculty will respond more readily to offers of alternative conditions of employment than others. Professors with better job prospects inside and outside the academy would seem more likely to accept contract positions, since they would be more marketable in the event of nonrenewal. Thus faculty in professional schools, where more nonacademic labor markets operate, might be more apt to relinquish tenure than colleagues with few or no options other than college teaching. The availability of external funding could also translate into different response rates by field. In the sciences particularly, external support, rather than tenure, is the ticket to security. Therefore, one might expect active scientists, in addition to all professors who could readily find employment outside the academy, to be more likely to relinquish tenure for a price. And surely there will also be differences by age. As noted earlier, the closer to anticipated retirement, the more likely a professor will equate an offer of relinquishment with planned retirement. The element of uncertainty is in effect removed.

At the very least, considerations such as these should make it clear that an institution considering a policy to induce faculty to relinquish tenure would be well advised to consider all the policy's costs as well as all the benefits. Since the costs—especially the effects on loyalty, quality, and institutional governance—are apt to be difficult to measure, the prudent academic administrator would do well to tread very carefully into this terrain.

Notes

I am grateful to Richard Chait, Jerry Green, Charlotte Kuh, Michael Lawson, Paula Stephan, and Gordon Winston for helpful comments and discussions, to

Janice Ballou for conducting focus groups, and to the faculty who participated in those focus groups. The views expressed here are mine, however, and do not necessarily reflect those of the Harvard Project on Faculty Appointments, any of the individuals mentioned above, or any institution.

1. These calculations are expressed in constant dollars, ignoring inflation, and are carried out using mortality rates for white males. Real salary is assumed to grow at 1.5% per year over inflation, the probability that the faculty member will take another job is assumed to be 2% a year, the fringe benefit rate is assumed to be 22%, and a discount rate of 2% is utilized.

2. Evidence presented by Albert Rees and Sharon P. Smith (1991, pp. 70, 66) suggests that while research activity generally declines with age, teaching effectiveness in the social sciences does not, and that in the humanities and natural sciences does so only gradually.

3. Currently, the notion of serious post-tenure review, which might result in dismissal for poor performance, remains a largely untested concept.

4. Estimated probit equations imply that, other things held constant, the probability of retirement for a seventy-year-old faculty member fell from 50% before 1994 to 8% in 1994 and after for those under the state's defined benefit retirement plan, and from 24% to 5% for those under other retirement plans (Clark, Ghent, and Kreps 1998, Table 7). The proportion of faculty under the age of forty in the three institutions fell from 28% in 1988 to 18% in 1997 (Table 1), a change that would have been a function of the age profile of faculty as well as by any changes in age-specific retirement rates.

5. The American Association of University Professors (AAUP) has weighed in on this issue, opposing plans that use such reviews as the basis for reevaluation of tenure status; but that is the very kind of plan that has the potential to change the faculty member's calculus enough to affect the probability of relinquishment.

6. This section is based on Lataif (1998a, 1998b) and a conversation with Associate Dean Michael Lawson of the Boston University School of Management, March 11, 1999.

7. According to an October 14, 1999, memorandum from Dean Louis Lataif, a total of nine faculty members (50%) have accepted the Alternative to Tenure contracts thus far. This figure had not changed as of March 13, 2000.

8. *Profscam* (Sykes 1988) is a well-known treatise critical of the academy.

9. To explain his unwillingness to rank the alternatives, one participant in this group wrote, "I disagree with the whole idea of relinquishment of tenure." Another wrote, "None of these arrangements would make me relinquish my tenure."

10. Risk aversion can be viewed as the premium a person would pay to have a sure source of income rather than an uncertain source of income with the same expected value. The more risk averse an individual, the greater this required premium. Consider, for example, a faculty member whose future income and non-monetary benefits from his current position are worth a total of $500,000 in today's dollars and whose best alternative employment yields only $300,000. If the chance of losing his position were 10%, the expected value of future employment benefits would be 0.9 ($500,000) + 0.1 ($300,000), or $480,000. To a risk-neutral person, the chance of dismissal would be valued at $20,000 (that is, $500,000 versus $480,000). To a risk-averse person, it would have an even higher cost.

References

Carmichael, H. Lorne. 1988. "Incentives in Academia: Why Is There Tenure?" *Journal of Political Economy*, 96 (3): 453–472.

Chait, Richard, and Cathy A. Trower. 1997. *Where Tenure Does Not Reign: Colleges with Contract Systems*. New Pathways: Working Paper Series, no. 3. Washington, D.C.: American Association for Higher Education.

Clark, Robert L., Linda S. Ghent, and Juanita Kreps. 2001. "Faculty Retirement and the Impact of the Elimination of Mandatory Retirement at Three North Carolina Universities." In Robert L. Clark and P. Brett Hammond, eds., *To Retire or Not? Retirement Policy and Practice in Higher Education*. Philadelphia: University of Pennsylvania Press.

Ehrenberg, Ronald G., Michael W. Matier, and David Fontanella. 2001. "Cornell University Confronts the End of Mandatory Retirement." In Robert L. Clark and P. Brett Hammond, eds., *To Retire or Not? Retirement Policy and Practice in Higher Education*. Philadelphia: University of Pennsylvania Press.

Finkelstein, Martin J., Robert K. Seal, and Jack H. Schuster. 1998. *The New Academic Generation: A Profession in Transformation*. Baltimore: Johns Hopkins University Press.

Finkin, Matthew W. 1996. *The Case for Tenure*. Ithaca, N.Y.: ILR Press.

Greene, Elizabeth. 2000. "Committee Urges Boston University to Demand More of Professors." *Chronicle of Higher Education*, October 27, p. A14.

Hammond, P. Brett, and Harriet P. Morgan, eds. 1991. *Mandatory Retirement for Tenured Faculty*. Washington, D.C.: National Academy Press.

Johnson, George. 1999. "Trends in the Relative Earnings of Tenure Track Faculty: 1973–1995." Paper presented at the National Bureau of Economic Research Higher Education Working Group, Department of Economics, University of Michigan. April 30–May 1.

Kelman, Stephen. 1981. "Economics and the Environmental Muddle." *Public Interest*, 64 (Summer): 106–123.

Lataif, Louis E. 1998a. "Lifetime Tenure and a Working Alternative." *The Manager*, Spring: 38–40.

——— 1998b. "A Realistic Alternative to Traditional Tenure." *Chronicle of Higher Education*, June 26, p. B6.

Leatherman, Courtney. 1998. "AAUP Offers Guidance on Post-Tenure Reviews." *Chronicle of Higher Education*, June 26, p. A13.

McPherson, Michael S., and Gordon C. Winston. 1993. "The Economics of Academic Tenure: A Relational Perspective." In Michael S. McPherson, Morton Owen Schapiro, and Gordon C. Winston, eds., *Paying the Piper: Productivity, Incentives, and Financing in U.S. Higher Education*. Ann Arbor: University of Michigan Press.

McPherson, Michael S., and Morton Owen Schapiro. 1999. "Tenure Issues in Higher Education." *Journal of Economic Perspectives*, 13 (1): 85–98.

Rees, Albert, and Sharon P. Smith. 1991. *Faculty Retirement in the Arts and Sciences*. Princeton, N.J.: Princeton University Press.

Roey, Stephen, and Rebecca Rak. 1998. *Fall Staff in Postsecondary Institutions, 1995*.

Washington, D.C.: U.S. Department of Education, Office of Educational Research and Improvement.

Simon, Julian. 1991. "A Solution for the Tenure Problem." *Cato Journal*, 10 (Winter): 835–838.

Sykes, Charles J. 1988. *Profscam: Professors and the Demise of Higher Education.* Washington, D.C.: Regnery Gateway.

Trower, Cathy A. 1998. *Employment Practices in the Professions.* New Pathways: Working Paper Series, no. 13. Washington, D.C.: American Association for Higher Education.

9

Why Is Tenure One College's Problem and Another's Solution?

WILLIAM T. MALLON

$\mathcal{A}$CADEMIC TENURE has been called the "third rail" (Magrath 1997) and the "abortion issue" of the academy (Chait 1997). Even a cursory examination of scholarly journals, the *Chronicle of Higher Education*, or the op-ed pages of the nation's newspapers explains why. Discussions about tenure are more often impassioned arguments than empirical analyses. One way partisans make the case for or against tenure is through conjecture about what would happen if colleges abolished tenure. For example, one vitriolic critic of tenure argued that "the replacement of lifetime tenure with fixed-term contracts would, at one stroke, restore accountability, while potentially freeing the vast untapped energies of the academy" (Sykes 1988, p. 258). Conversely, many tenure stalwarts have claimed that an institution that relinquished tenure could not attract top-notch recruits, thus severely impairing the quality of faculty (e.g., Cotter 1996; Finkin 1996).

Two problems arise from these assertions. First, both sets of claims, until now, have been speculative. Proponents and opponents of tenure have been inattentive to the colleges that have actually undertaken what pundits have only pondered. A number of institutions of higher education have eliminated tenure, while others have replaced contracts with tenure. Do the conventional arguments for and against tenure apply at these colleges? Why is tenure one college's problem and

246

another's solution? This chapter addresses these questions with data rather than assumptions and anecdotes.

Second, the typical litany of benefits and drawbacks to both tenure and contract systems tends to be rationally based. A rational model posits that college and university leaders would examine tenure and the alternatives and then logically choose the appropriate employment system based on a dispassionate cost-benefit analysis. Thus, advocates of change have argued that contract systems are better than tenure because contracts more readily enable adjustments to the labor force and ensure greater performance accountability. Conversely, champions of conventional practice have maintained that tenure is superior to contracts because, among other reasons, the onetime, "up or out" evaluation process guarantees more rigorous reviews than periodic contract renewals. This attention to the rational strengths and weaknesses of both policies ignores important nonrational, symbolic, and ambiguous properties of tenure. In truth, colleges have abolished and instituted tenure for symbolic as well as substantive reasons.

This chapter presents research on three colleges that recently moved from contracts to tenure and three that moved from tenure to contracts. After a brief review of the study design, we consider the bases for each policy change and the similarities and differences among the institutions' rationales. The chapter concludes with practical implications about policy shifts in either direction.

Research Design and Methodology

A multiple case-study research design (Yin 1994) was used to investigate the questions posed in this chapter. Three sources were constructed to identify colleges that moved in one direction or the other: (1) media accounts in the *Chronicle of Higher Education* and other newspapers; (2) summaries of American Association of University Professors (AAUP) investigations as reported in *Academe*; and (3) archives of the Harvard Project on Faculty Appointments. These sources identified seventeen colleges that abolished tenure and eight that instituted tenure. The sample for this study was narrowed to include six institutions—three colleges that moved from contracts to tenure (Group I) and three that moved from tenure to contracts (Group II). Because most sites requested anonymity, all six were assigned pseudonyms, and individuals are identified only by position.

A brief description of each institution follows, with 1999 statistics for the size of the full-time faculty and full-time student enrollments.

Group I: contracts to tenure

> *Accomac College* (110 faculty, 1,500 students), the only public institution in the study, abolished tenure in 1971 and instituted multiyear contracts instead. The college reinstated tenure in 1993.
> *Grace College* (58 faculty, 1,100 students), a Roman Catholic institution, moved to tenure in 1991.
> *Lakeview College* (225 faculty, 5,800 undergraduates), an independent, nonsectarian institution, adopted tenure in 1997.

Group II: tenure to contracts

> *Blessed Trinity College* (75 faculty, 1,025 students), a Roman Catholic institution, eliminated tenure in 1982. Since then, all nontenured faculty have been on annual contracts.
> *Rowlette College* (50 faculty, 650 students) technically discontinued tenure in 1973, but the institution did not formally adopt a multiyear contract system until 1986.
> *Scott College* (85 faculty, 1,350 students), an independent institution with an explicit Christian mission, abolished tenure in 1993.

Previously tenured faculty at all three institutions in Group II retained that status when the colleges moved to contracts. At the time of this research, then, both tenured and nontenured faculty members were employed at the colleges.

Four colleges—two that moved in each policy direction—served as primary research sites (Accomac, Lakeview, Rowlette, and Scott). At these institutions, the researcher interviewed a large number of faculty, administrators, and trustees over the course of two to three days and obtained extensive written documentation, including faculty handbooks, policy drafts, minutes from faculty and board of trustees meetings, and reaccreditation reports. Grace and Blessed Trinity served as secondary sites,[1] where the researcher interviewed a limited number of

key informants during a one-day visit. In all, this study entailed 41 interviews and 8 follow-up telephone conversations or e-mail exchanges.

Why Did Colleges Move from Contracts to Tenure?

Colleges moved to tenure for substantive reasons—for example, to improve the faculty evaluation process. But these colleges also used tenure as a talisman, hoping its cachet would bring credibility to the faculty and prestige to the institution.

Faculty Quality

Interviewees at two of the three Group I colleges—Accomac and Lakeview—asserted that tenure was a solution to problems of faculty quality. Both institutions had initiated plans to increase their visibility and
reputation regionally and nationally. Administrative and faculty leaders
believed that a tenure system would help achieve a higher-quality faculty in two ways: tenure would be an incentive for faculty recruitment,
and the tenure-review process would be more rigorous than the contract-renewal process so that only faculty with strong records of teaching and research would remain at the college.

Recruitment. Accomac and Lakeview's attitude about tenure was akin
to the way a peahen judges a peacock. The peahen has no absolute
measure of the peacock's breeding value, so she relies on the size and
magnificence of the peacock's feathers. Feathers are a proxy value for
breeding superiority.

Faculty and administrators at these colleges were unsure how prospective faculty members compared the attractiveness of their college
to others. Many at Accomac and Lakeview believed that new recruits
used tenure as a proxy value for institutional quality. They believed that
faculty candidates perceived institutions without tenure as prospective
suitors with short, drab feathers. Interviewees at both schools maintained that the shift to a tenure policy would lead to better faculty
hiring. At Accomac, administrators wanted to employ faculty with
stronger credentials and greater potential for scholarship. At Lakeview,
faculty historically were hired from industry and the arts, not from
conventional academic paths. Its goal was to attract more "traditional"
faculty with doctoral degrees and college teaching experience. In both

cases, administrators and faculty believed that the lack of tenure weakened the institution's hold on first-choice candidates, although these conclusions were more impressionistic than empirical. Nevertheless, without systematic, hard data on why recruits accepted offers elsewhere, search committee members focused on the apparent differences between other colleges and their own. As one Accomac professor put it, "We went through a number of hiring processes and we would lose people. . . . You watch your candidates go to institutions with tenure and you draw some conclusions about that."

Faculty evaluation. Tenure was also thought to enhance faculty quality through systematic reliance on performance evaluation. Interviewees indicated that contract systems did not lead to the dismissal of mediocre faculty members. "We terminated three people in the last fifteen or twenty years," reported the Lakeview provost. Faculty and administrators at Accomac referred to the contract system as de facto tenure. The president noted, "With only one exception I can think of, no one was pushed out." The problem with contracts, maintained an Accomac professor, was that "it's easier to say yes to someone under a contract system than under a tenure system." The provost agreed: "It was hard enough to turn someone down who's been part of the community for five years, let alone ten or fifteen." These institutions believed that the more stringent evaluation processes associated with a tenure system would solve the problem of lax performance reviews because tenure would "increase the rigor by which people move into a protected employment category" (Lakeview board chair). If more faculty were "weeded out" during the probationary period and tenure-review process, then presumably the quality of the faculty would improve.

The new evaluation procedures led to increased rigor for some faculty, but not for all. On the one hand, the new policy raised the standards for new faculty members. At Accomac, for example, junior faculty on the tenure track were expected to produce more scholarship of higher quality than peers at the college ten years earlier. An analysis of the Accomac faculty handbooks (see Table 9.1) indicates that evaluation standards are indeed stricter under the new tenure policy than under the previous contract provisions.

On the other hand, the move to tenure contributed to the very problem that it was supposed to solve—lack of rigor in faculty evaluation—because large numbers of faculty were grandfathered into the new tenure systems without any review. Fully 67% of Accomac faculty and 83% of Lakeview faculty were automatically awarded tenure without performance evaluations, a fact that some faculty members at the colleges found unsettling. An Accomac professor remarked: "We had to grandfather 50 faculty into tenure. They received no review. . . . It's dangerous to suddenly take a whole lump of people and create a tenure system, when they might be here another thirty or forty years. So you create a division. Junior faculty feel like they're carrying the institution on their backs."

At Accomac, tenure was intended as a mechanism to increase the standards for faculty scholarship. In this instance, the handbook indicates that new faculty must produce scholarly publications to earn tenure, a standard not applied to grandfathered colleagues. But tenure was awarded en masse to senior faculty at Accomac and Lakeview without any performance review.[2] Automatic tenure was politically necessary because, in effect, faculty already had employment security under contracts. Senior faculty would not have agreed to the new tenure systems without a guarantee of immediate job security. After many years under the contract system—in which they were not held to stringent standards—these professors did not want to face the possibility of being denied tenure. While politically expedient, the grandfathering of large numbers of faculty created an irony: in order to improve the rigor of the evaluation process for future faculty, the colleges first had to disregard rigor for the current faculty.

Table 9.1 Differences in acceptable forms of scholarship in Accomac College's faculty handbook under the contract policy (prior to 1993) and tenure policy (after 1993)

Accepted "professional activities" under contract policy	Accepted "professional activities" under tenure policy
Publications (without any stipulation of type or scope)	Scholarly publications; "articles on intellectual topics in journals, magazines, or newspapers"
"Actively participating in professional conferences or conventions"	Presentations of papers at professional meetings
"Taking new coursework or training in one's field to remain current and competent"	"Studying or training that expands competence . . . into *new areas*" (emphasis added)

Power and Influence in Campus Governance

Faculty at Lakeview and Grace colleges, but not Accomac, also wanted tenure because they wanted greater power. These colleges had histories of having autocratic presidents as well as faculty who were unsocialized to the traditions of shared governance. At Grace College, a professor recalled that the president routinely "treated the faculty with utter contempt" and that most faculty accepted "submissiveness to authority." The faculty as a whole did not initiate the move to tenure at Grace because "we were used to someone else governing; we didn't want to self-govern." However, a small group of faculty leaders believed that, at an institution where most faculty lacked doctorates, "it was necessary to adopt tenure to develop a sense of confidence on the part of faculty."

Lakeview had a history of very powerful department chairs—considered part of the administration—who, according to one professor, had "enormous and virtually unhampered discretionary powers" to make faculty appointment and retention decisions. Moreover, Lakeview faculty members were apathetic about governance. A faculty leader said, "Truthfully, it was rather difficult to get faculty engaged in the issues here." Faculty advocates of tenure insisted on a collegewide tenure-review committee in order to assure that faculty generally played a greater role than department chairs in tenure decisions. With the new committee, faculty had more power, department chairs less. A professor stated, "Let's be clear. This is about power. It's about power over who gets to make the decisions."

After tenure was adopted, a Lakeview professor proclaimed, "Tenure, to a certain extent, has helped lessen that autocratic management style" of department chairs. With the creation of the faculty tenure-review committee, stated a colleague, "much of the power shifted from where it used to be. It has invested the faculty with power." At Grace College, however, observers noted that although power did shift, some faculty were ill prepared for the responsibility. A strong faculty supporter of tenure reflected, "You can have tenure and still have poor governance. Some faculty, now with tenure, became arrogant. The once-submissive misused their power and unfairly denied tenure to people they didn't like." The provost agreed, saying, "The faculty has not understood governance yet."

Institutional Isomorphism

A third reason for the shift from contracts to tenure can be attributed to the power of isomorphism, a phenomenon that drives one organization to resemble others with the same set of environmental circumstances. Viewed through the lens of institutional isomorphism (DiMaggio and Powell 1991), tenure prevails in American higher education for three reasons: (1) external organizations, like the AAUP, and cultural expectations within academe pressure colleges and universities to offer tenure; (2) colleges mimic the best-known and most successful institutions of higher education, which all offer tenure; and (3) most prospective faculty are socialized, explicitly or subtly, to accept tenure as normative.

The colleges that embraced tenure did so for isomorphic reasons. Grace College was pressured to adopt tenure by the AAUP, which censured the college in 1990 for the president's dismissal of a faculty member. Shortly thereafter, the president resigned. The board of trustees and a new administration, said a faculty member, "saw censure as a disgrace. There was a sense of embarrassment. It got a lot of play in the press." The AAUP required that the college adopt a tenure system in order to be removed from the censure list. According to a professor, "The impetus for tenure was to erase the stain of censure. It was not about faculty pushing for employment security." In this case, a powerful outside agency pressured the college to conform to standard practice. The impetus for tenure did not come from within the institution. A professor noted, "We weren't out to get tenure; we were out to get the president. Without the AAUP's censure, we wouldn't have tenure. If the AAUP hadn't pressed the concept, the faculty would not have."

Accomac and Lakeview colleges embraced tenure to emulate other more prestigious colleges. The Accomac president wanted the college to be recognized as a premier liberal arts college. To achieve that goal, the president began a "Campaign for National Prominence." According to the provost, the president "felt that if Accomac was going to become a first-rate liberal arts institution, it probably ought to be like other prestigious colleges in most respects," including a low student-faculty ratio, selectivity in admissions, and tenure. Faculty and other administrators shared this sentiment. A faculty member noted, "The college wanted to be more traditional and more mainstream." The

Accomac provost commented, "We needed to be comparable to our so-called peer institutions. . . . There's something funky about an institution that doesn't have tenure." At Accomac and Lakeview, this isomorphic pressure was linked to institutional maturation. Accomac wanted to shed its image as a countercultural college. A Lakeview trustee commented, "Lakeview has moved from a somewhat iconoclastic, unique, we're-not-like-all-of-those-other-places institution into a large private college that increasingly craves to be welcomed into the educational mainstream."

The third isomorphic tendency, at play at Accomac and Lakeview, involved professional norms. Individual faculty members at these colleges were socialized—tacitly, if not explicitly—as graduate students to regard tenure as the universal currency of professional legitimacy. Faculty members without tenure did not possess the coin of the realm. Most faculty asserted that tenure solved the problem of professional recognition and peer status. A Lakeview professor stated that tenure "would give us recognition outside the institution. It provided credibility to the outside." The lack of tenure was a "glaring omission in the faculty's status among their peers." Unlike Accomac and Lakeview, Grace College did not seem influenced by this phenomenon. Most faculty at Grace were indifferent to tenure until the AAUP compelled the college to accept the policy. The least prestigious of the three colleges, Grace was the least affected by professional norms.

As these rationales illustrate, the Group I colleges embraced tenure for both substantive and symbolic reasons. For Accomac and Lakeview, advocates forecasted tangible improvements to faculty quality because of more stringent evaluations. For all three sites, tenure conveyed important symbolic messages about institutional legitimacy, whether measured by peer practice or by the AAUP. Tenure signaled status and credibility.

Noticeably absent from these expressed motivations were the traditional purposes of tenure: academic freedom and economic security. Faculty members at all three sites reported little threat to job security under contracts; their interest in tenure was not predicated on increased economic protection. Additionally, faculty did not couch the shift to tenure as a matter of academic freedom. One Lakeview professor's comments were typical: "If you can find anybody on campus to say, 'I'm glad we got tenure because I thought my academic freedom was at risk,' I would fall out of my chair. I have never, ever heard that."

These three institutions found compelling reasons to embrace academic tenure. Every interviewee—faculty, administrator, and trustee alike—maintained that the shift to tenure was a good step for their institution. Why, then, would three other colleges head in the opposite direction?

Why Did Colleges Move from Tenure to Contracts?

As reported by faculty, administrators, and trustees, Blessed Trinity, Rowlette, and Scott colleges eliminated academic tenure largely for the very same reasons the other institutions embraced it. While some of the rationales relate to substantive outcomes in employment policy, others attend to the symbolic nature of tenure in the academy.

Improvements to Faculty Quality

Nationally, a common argument for faculty tenure is Darwinian: only the strongest survive. Tenure was envisioned as a means to promote a rigorous, momentous, "up or out" decision, where only faculty with superlative track records would be rewarded with permanent employment (Commission on Academic Tenure 1973; Finkin 1996; Machlup 1964). The experiences of Blessed Trinity, Rowlette, and Scott colleges suggest that survival of the fittest does not occur at all institutions. At these colleges, nearly all faculty members received tenure without formal application or in-depth review by peers or supervisors. Longtime faculty members recounted stories of receiving tenure casually and even unexpectedly:

> "After my fourth year, I went to the dean's office to pick up my new contract. I told the dean, 'I'm supposed to get tenure this year.' So the dean picked up the phone and told his secretary, 'Sandra, Steve gets tenure this year.'" (Scott College)
>
> "The contract I had to sign [gave] a rank and a salary, and then there was a section that said 'comments.' And under 'comments,' it said 'tenure.' That's all. Just one word." (Rowlette College)

"The only information needed in one's dossier was a résumé and
student evaluations. The real interest was in the department
chair's recommendation. . . . The tenure and promotion process
was a piece of cake." (Blessed Trinity College)

Scott College exemplifies how the informal tenuring process became
a problem. Some Scott faculty members who, in the eyes of many,
should not have received tenure, did so anyway. Subsequent adminis-
trations and board members complained that some of these professors,
unworthy of tenure to begin with, became even less productive thereafter. Faculty members also criticized these tenured colleagues as "not
carrying their weight," "no longer doing anything constructive," and
"semiretired." Under a system where virtually every faculty member
received tenure, often without formal reviews, the policy did not insure
a high-quality faculty, as proponents had envisioned. Instead, Scott
found that poor-quality teachers, "unaccountable" to both administrators and faculty colleagues, were subject to removal only through bur-
densome procedures and only for extreme incompetence. As a result,
administrators and trustees labeled tenure "the problem" and abolition
of tenure the solution. Once tenure was eliminated, recalcitrant professors could theoretically be compelled to improve under threat of
nonreappointment.

Not every Scott interviewee saw a clear cause and effect relationship
between tenure and questionable faculty quality. Several people identified an inadequate evaluation process as the root cause of "deadwood."
The academic dean noted that tenure "had caused damage to this institution" not because of an inherent flaw in the concept, but because of
"the way in which it had been handled. It had been mishandled at this
institution." One professor lamented, "If we could have implemented
[an] evaluation system fifteen or ten years ago, then maybe the tenure
issue would not have been a problem. . . . I think the issue was that it
was too easy to get tenure and we tenured people we shouldn't have."
As these sentiments suggest, tenure was really a secondary concern. It
was labeled a problem only after the college developed a tradition of lax
evaluation standards and cumbersome dismissal procedures.

Faculty members at these Group II colleges observed that the evaluation process became more standardized under the new policy of term
contracts, hardly a surprise given the lack of standards under the tenure

policy. But interviews and faculty employment data also suggest that the new contract policy produced no greater selectivity than the tenure system. At Scott College, since tenure was abolished in 1994, none of the 54 faculty members who have undergone contract-renewal or post-tenure review has been dismissed, although 3 departed voluntarily after receiving negative evaluations. Similarly, in the ten-year period following the implementation of multiyear contracts (1988–1999), Rowlette College did not renew 5 of 67 faculty members' contracts for performance-related reasons. In the eighteen years since tenure was eliminated at Blessed Trinity, none of the approximately 60 full-time faculty members hired has been released for performance-related reasons. These data corroborate research that found that "contract systems, *in practice*, mirror tenure systems on the dimension of economic security" (Chait and Trower 1997, p. 6).

On the one hand, the expected solution—namely, the abolition of tenure—did not solve the problem of faculty evaluation. While the contract-renewal process at these three colleges led to several separations, over 93% of faculty at each institution reviewed under the new contract system remained. If the goal were to induce some modest degree of turnover, these colleges could have simply tightened their standards for tenure. On the other hand, at least at Scott College, the abolition of tenure was an important ceremonial event that prompted faculty to be more attentive to issues of performance. The president stated, "I think [the elimination of tenure] had a halo effect. . . . It caused people to think, 'Well, if they can get rid of tenure, they can get rid of me.' . . . If discontinuing tenure doesn't send a signal that accountability is taken seriously, I don't know what does."

The discontinuance of tenure at Scott sent a powerful symbolic message that the college was addressing the problem of faculty accountability, even though the policy change did not in practice produce much faculty turnover. The mere shift in policy signaled that the college was willing to take radical strides to confront concerns about faculty performance.

Financial Reasons

Most colleges without tenure are financially brittle institutions—small, unheralded places with limited resources and tight budgets (Chait and

Trower 1997). In light of that image, conventional wisdom holds that colleges relinquish tenure because of financial necessity—trustees and administrators are wary of tenured appointments with lifetime obligations to people and programs.

Two of the three Group II sites fit this model. (Scott College, with a $200 million endowment, does not.) Blessed Trinity and Rowlette are both tuition-dependent institutions; each has an endowment barely over $4 million. Both colleges became concerned with tenure because of fiscal problems. Rowlette suffered a major financial crisis in 1973, when faculty and staff endured three months without pay. Concerned that the college could not withstand long-term financial obligations of any kind, trustees placed a moratorium on tenure. A trustee explained that tenure "became an issue because it costs the institution $1.5 million to tenure each professor. It was an enormous expense for the college to incur." At Blessed Trinity, the president noted that "everyone comes back to the dollar." The board of trustees was worried about "a large number of high-salaried faculty in departments with low student enrollment" so that "the institution becomes unable to reallocate resources."

Did the contract system solve these institutions' fiscal problems? Blessed Trinity went through a period of expansion from 1982, when tenure was discontinued, to the mid-1990s; the full-time faculty increased 38%. The argument that tenure might cause fiscal hardship amid a period of enrollment growth seems implausible. However, in the mid-1990s, an enrollment dive in one department precipitated the release of two nontenured faculty members. As Richard Chait and Cathy Trower (1997) concluded: "Most institutions without tenure view contracts as an important hedge and a valuable last resort to protect economically brittle, tuition-dependent colleges against catastrophic losses in enrollment and related financial hardships. . . . Contract systems insure institutions against disaster. *If* enrollments plummet, *then* the college can downsize comparatively expeditiously" (p. 9).

It is less clear if the shift to contracts helped Rowlette's financial position. After the board of trustees abandoned tenure in 1973 because of financial concerns, the institution suffered financial exigencies in 1984 and 1994. In each case, several tenured faculty members were released while many nontenured professors were retained. The faculty argued that tenure did not constrain labor force adjustments during financial crises, and thus the trustees' "nervousness" with tenure was unwarranted. "The board's decision to stop awarding tenure," a professor said, "was supposed to be related to fiscal issues, but I didn't see the point in that, since the college has always been able to let go of tenured faculty members in times of crisis." Furthermore, there is no evidence that the faculty on contracts were released any more easily. Faculty and administrators referred to the contract system as "virtual tenure" and, for all practical purposes, viewed the two employment systems as equivalent in terms of economic security. Therefore, the extra flexibility that trustees envisioned did not materialize. A former president remarked, "I don't think the board thought about the implications of a long-term contract system—that it was, in some ways, a tenure system."

Since Rowlette fired tenured faculty because of financial circumstances, and since contract faculty were no more likely to be dismissed, why was tenure seen as the problem and a contract system the solution? Rowlette's decision to move from tenure to contracts for fiscal reasons was based more on perception than on lessons learned in practice. Trustees relied on a perceived difference between tenure and contracts rather than an actual difference. Trustees equated tenure with lifetime job security; yet they also assumed "that a contract is a contract—that you could end it or break it." Without evidence that contracts were substantively better than or even different from tenure, decision-makers relied on the presumption that a multiyear contract system was short-term and flexible and that tenure was lifelong and rigid. As policy was actually practiced, neither impression proved to be correct.

Anti-Isomorphism

Group I colleges implemented tenure in part because of isomorphic pressure to resemble institutions with tenure. At Blessed Trinity, Rowlette, and Scott colleges, countertendencies prevailed. These colleges exhibited anti-isomorphism: a force that insures an institution does not resemble others in the environment. Evidence in these cases suggests several types of anti-isomorphism.

Financial distraction—we can't afford to be like them. A family in severe financial hardship focuses on basic necessities, not on keeping up with the Joneses. Blessed Trinity and Rowlette, but not Scott, experienced a similar anti-isomorphic tendency. As noted above, these colleges were preoccupied with fiscal concerns, so they focused on survival rather than on "luxury items" like tenure. Trustees originally stopped awarding tenure because they were fearful of long-term financial commitments; faculty did not noticeably react to the moratorium on tenure because they were distracted by more pressing financial matters, like low salaries.

Mission socialization—we don't want to be like them. Scott College, but neither Blessed Trinity nor Rowlette, exhibited another anti-isomorphic tendency: mission socialization. Because of Scott's religious and cultural mission, the college did not want to mimic those secular institutions that the president regarded as elitist and aloof. The board of trustees and the president prevented the college from adopting trends or values that the greater higher education community might take for granted—coeducational residence halls, for example. Also, the president disdained faculty prerogatives, such as shared governance and tenure, considered sacrosanct on other campuses. He remarked, "I resent people who see it as their duty to get inside a college with a special mission and make it like everybody else." Furthermore, the president and trustees wanted to demonstrate that they were capable of bold, aggressive leadership, and steadfastly at odds with the established norms of higher education. There is arguably no better way to make a statement of iconoclastic leadership in higher education by abolishing tenure.

Faculty zones of indifference—we don't care if we are like them. Another anti-isomorphic inclination at these three colleges—more an enabler of change than a reason for the policy shift—was that the faculties as a whole were indifferent to tenure. Observers noted that most faculty members at these institutions were uninterested in the national scene of higher education. They were similarly unconcerned about their institutions' reputation in national disciplinary associations or informal discussions.

Power and Governance

Scott College was a unique site in that the shift from tenure to contracts was part of several policy changes designed to reduce the faculty's voice in governance. Two years before tenure was discontinued, the board of trustees and the president mandated a new faculty governance system that eliminated elected faculty officers. The president believed that "the dean is the chief academic officer who should be in charge of the faculty. You cannot put them in charge of themselves. . . . I see the role of faculty more traditionally than at a lot of places. I think they should teach young people. That's what I think they should do. They shouldn't be running the college." By changing the faculty governance structure, the president consolidated power and, from his point of view, made the college more efficient. He also framed the shift away from tenure as part of this "power struggle." He found that, prior to the policy change, "some faculty were outright hostile to the institution. . . . So there was a struggle here, and it came down to power. That's reflected in governance and it's reflected in the security that faculty think gives them license to do whatever they want." After these modifications went into effect, decision-making became hierarchical. The president "makes the decisions," reported a faculty member. Another contended, "It became more of a dictatorship."

One might expect that the faculty would have resisted such moves, and indeed some did. A small number demonstrated on campus, attempted to organize a vote of no confidence, wrote editorials to the media, and contacted the AAUP. The majority, however, did not protest. Some faculty were simply uninterested in power and governance. One said, "The majority of people . . . believe in management, believe in authority of position. They believe their job is one of a professor and not one of making those major decisions, making administrative decisions." Others mentioned a more reluctant acceptance of their role: "Faculty do whatever they have to do to keep their jobs." A colleague said, "You just expect to be told how it's going to be and, if you don't like it, there's the front gate."

Did These Colleges Really Move in Opposite Directions?

These six institutions had multiple reasons for changing faculty appointment policies, some of which coincide with conventional wisdom (e.g., instituting tenure to improve faculty recruitment) and some of which do not (e.g., abandoning tenure to improve faculty quality). Three important themes cut across these institutions, regardless of the direction of the policy change. First, all six institutions were in part pursuing the same goal: a better system of faculty evaluation. Second, the six institutions share similar patterns of growth but diverge in their aspirations. Third, the presidents' previous on-the-job learning may have contributed to their willingness to support the policy shifts.

Faculty Evaluation

Paradoxically, the two sets of colleges moved in opposite directions in part to accomplish the same goal: to improve the process and tighten the standards by which faculty attained long-term, protected employment. For the vast majority of faculty, employment security at these colleges was never in jeopardy. Table 9.2 compares faculty evaluation outcomes at the six colleges under both the old and the new employment policies.

In both groups, faculty were rarely dismissed for performance-related reasons. Blessed Trinity, Rowlette, and Scott prior to their policy changes offered tenure to nearly all candidates, often without any review. The evaluation process did not foster a rigorous examination of performance and potential. Instead faculty, administrators, and trustees viewed tenure more as a mechanism to guarantee job security regardless of qualifications and less as a system to insure selectivity and quality control.

Similarly at Accomac, Grace, and Lakeview colleges prior to the policy changes contracts were regularly renewed for all faculty, so much so that faculty and staff routinely referred to the system as de facto or virtual tenure. These colleges did not exercise the flexibility that contracts theoretically permit. As the board chairman of Lakeview opined, "We had a system in place in which removing faculty was extraordinarily difficult. I find simply ludicrous the notion that the alternative to tenure is employees at will. Even schools that have rolling contracts have all sorts of problems with nonrenewal of contracts. . . . I came to see the contract system in much the same way as traditional tenure."

At all six of these sites the central problem was not an ideological battle over the principles of tenure but a more pragmatic concern common to many institutions of higher education: how can the college encourage a more demanding examination of faculty credentials and performance? This begs the question. Why not simply improve faculty evaluation procedures, a relatively uncomplicated matter, rather than completely overhaul the employment systems, a far more complex task? The answer lies in the symbolic nature of tenure. As Lee Bolman and Terrence Deal note, "Many organizational events and processes are important more for what they express than for what they produce" (1991, p. 244). Incremental modifications of faculty evaluation systems might have produced the stated objective but without the tacit message

Table 9.2   Faculty evaluation outcomes before and after change

College	Before change	After change
Group I		
Accomac	Between 1983 and 1993, contracts for five faculty members were not renewed.	Between 1994 and 1999, of 21 tenure candidates, 3 professors denied tenure and 4 others counseled to resign.
Grace	Faculty interviewees were unaware of anyone being denied a contract for performance-related reasons.	Between fall 1992 and fall 1999, 26 faculty members received tenure and 3 were denied. Additionally, 3 faculty members resigned prior to the tenure review; but, according to a current faculty member, "There is no way to substantiate that they elected to resign because of concerns about their ability to attain tenure."
Lakeview	Data unavailable, but the provost reported, "I think we've terminated 3 people in 15 years."	In 1999 (first year of new policy), all 8 candidates successfully earned tenure. All 9 professors who underwent post-tenure review received positive results.
Group II		
Blessed Trinity	According to faculty, "There was no campus ethos to get tenure"; those who applied routinely were awarded it.	In 18 years since tenure was abolished, none of the 57 faculty members hired has been dismissed for performance-related reasons.
Rowlette	Data unavailable, but interviewees stated that, prior to moratorium, tenure was rarely denied.	From 1988 to 1999, the college did not renew contracts of 5 faculty members for cause.
Scott	Data unavailable, but interviewees state that tenure was rarely denied.	Between 1994 and 1999, 10 of 12 junior faculty members awarded long-term contracts; the other two remained on annual contracts. Of 42 post-tenure or contract-renewal reviews, 39 successful and 3 counseled to resign.

to be derived from the shift to or from tenure. Decision-makers used the abolition or adoption of tenure as a powerful signal to indicate no more business as usual. The policy shifts transmitted messages about institutional identity to various groups that simple improvements in faculty evaluation could not. A complete overhaul to faculty employment policies was necessary to catch people's attention. So while the two sets of colleges moved in opposite directions, they undertook the same action—a fundamental and complete shift in existing policy—for the same purpose. The very act of overhaul, irrespective of direction, had greater impact than the substance of the change per se.

Institutional Maturity

A second theme that emerges from these colleges concerns institutional history and patterns of growth. All six developed from nontraditional origins, but the three Group I colleges "matured" to incorporate mainstream practices, including tenure, while the three Group II colleges deliberately remained on the fringe of American higher education.

The six institutions were chosen without regard to their origins or history. A quick glance at institutional characteristics did not reveal much similarity in historical roots: the oldest college, Accomac, began operation in 1840, while the youngest, Grace, was founded in 1958. Yet upon further investigation important parallels became evident. First, five of the six colleges started as secondary schools or women's colleges and then evolved into four-year coeducational baccalaureate institutions. The sixth, Rowlette College, began with a three-year curriculum for World War II veterans, also a nontraditional genesis. Second, all six institutions received full accreditation as four-year baccalaureate colleges between 1962 and 1974, a twelve-year span, despite the 118 years that separated the oldest from the youngest. (See Table 9.3.)

These facts emphasize how young these institutions are compared to the larger higher education community. They do not have long track records as full-fledged colleges. As a result, they share several common points of development. Many faculty members at the time of full accreditation did not come from traditional academic paths. At Scott College, for example, a professor noted that "even by the late 1970s, many faculty had been hired out of a secondary education mode." Similarly, a Rowlette professor described early faculty hires as "amateurish," and the Blessed Trinity president characterized the faculty as "inexperienced in higher education." Lakeview faculty were, for a long time, part-time practitioners, not full-time academics. Furthermore, many Lakeview faculty and administrators considered themselves "revolutionaries" who purposefully and proudly eschewed traditional symbols of academe such as rank, accreditation, and tenure. At Accomac, many faculty hired in the late 1960s promoted the idea of the college becoming, in the words of one longtime professor, a "hippic place" that discarded conventions like tenure and grading. In addition to employing a large cadre of faculty unsocialized to the dominant norms of higher education, these colleges developed organizational cultures more akin to high schools or two-year colleges: no system of shared governance, solid emphasis on teaching but little interest in scholarship, and an atmosphere emphasizing quality of life. The comments by a Scott College professor are typical:

> A lot of people like small colleges, like liberal arts colleges. A lot of people just want to teach; they don't want to do research. A lot of people want family environments. . . . I've been at [a large research university] and taught there—150 papers to grade, not knowing students' names—I didn't want that. It's nice to be in this environment, to know the students.
>
> Q: Is it a trade-off?
>
> Yes, it is. It's a quality of life issue, and it's an individual issue. I have three boys and I was responsible for raising them and I thought to myself, "Where else do I want to be but someplace that's

Table 9.3 Institutional background

Institution	Year founded	Founded as	Year accredited as a 4-year baccalaureate college
Accomac	1840	Women's high school	1968
Blessed Trinity	1954	Women's college	1962
Grace	1958	Women's college	1967
Lakeview	1890	Women's college	1974
Rowlette	1946	3-year college for veterans	1967
Scott	1909	High school	1971

supportive of that environment?" So, in my case, I said, "People can tell me what to do."

Numerous faculty at these colleges highlighted this organizational milieu, characterizing their institutions as "families" or a "Ma and Pa store."

Interviewees at Group I sites noted that their institutions moved away from this culture and "grew up" in various ways—by increasing the number of faculty with doctorates, encouraging scholarship and research rather than just teaching, and establishing faculty committees and other hallmarks of shared governance. Additionally, faculty, administrators, and trustees asserted that introduction of a tenure system was a mark of institutional maturity. Constituents at these three institutions envisioned tenure as a vehicle to demonstrate that the colleges had matured, moved into the mainstream, and shed their countercultural images. One Lakeview faculty member said that tenure was intended to "make the college come of age, to take the college into a mature stage of academic life." The president agreed. "I thought that creating a tenure system would be a good sign of the maturity of the college." The provost at Grace College sounded a similar note: "The tenure system gave the institution a sense of maturity; we had grown from a little girl's college." For these colleges, then, tenure was both a mechanism for promoting, and an outward symbol of achieving, a coming of age.

This yen for institutional maturity and stature was not discernible at Group II institutions. Observers noted that because faculty at these institutions were not professionally competitive they had little interest in the cachet of tenure. Tenure meant little to them when their institutions awarded it, and they were nonchalant when it was taken away. At Rowlette, a professor declared, "Call us demented, but there were a number of us on the faculty who just couldn't have cared less about tenure. . . . The faculty on the whole has remained consistently indifferent to this matter." A Blessed Trinity faculty member said, "I don't think faculty felt it was important when the college did away with tenure. There wasn't a strong faculty culture that supported an investment in academic tenure." A colleague emphasized that the familylike culture at the college was more important to faculty than any benefits from tenure: "There was a willingness to trade off tenure for another system.

Plus, the lack of tenure helps with the environment of collegiality because faculty are not willing to be competitive with one another. Faculty colleagues are not willing to sit in judgment of one another. We know each other too well."

These two sets of colleges shared similar institutional histories but "grew up" in different ways. In a sense, the colleges were at the awkward age of adolescence, two sets of teenagers with different aspirations. Group I colleges were like teenagers yearning to be recognized as adults. The move to tenure was the rite of passage to adulthood, the ceremony that demonstrated, especially to peers, that the faculty were now members of the club. Group II colleges were like other teenagers for whom membership in the club had little utility or import. Like adolescent nonconformists, they preferred not to play the games of the "in" crowd.

Presidential Learning

In these two different groups the presidents helped to define institutional values and ambition. The presidents at the colleges that moved to tenure had roots at institutions with tenure, while those at the tenure-to-contract sites came from less traditional professional backgrounds. The presidents' vision may have influenced shifts in policy, and their previous work experience may have influenced that vision.

The presidents at each set of institutions shared similar career backgrounds. At the Group I sites, they had been faculty members and administrators at four-year institutions with tenure. At the Group II colleges, one president previously served at another institution without tenure, one had been a high-school principal, and the third worked at an association of two-year colleges.

While it is not possible to determine cause-effect relationships between the presidents' previous posts and the move toward or away from tenure, it is noteworthy that the relationships exist because college presidents, according to Michael Cohen and James March, "observe the consequences of [their] actions and infer the structure of the world from those observations. They use the resulting inferences in attempts to improve their future actions" (1986, p. 199). Because each president nominally succeeded in prior positions, the lessons they learned in those posts contributed to a preference for one system over the other.

The president at Scott College, for example, concluded that the contract system at his previous institution did not pose any significant disadvantages and in fact made his job easier. He said, "I came from a college that did not have tenure . . . so I was comfortable with the trustees' attitude of wanting to eliminate tenure." Therefore, he "learned" that a contract system was a desirable alternative to tenure. Rowlette's president became familiar with nontenure systems while at the American Association of Junior Colleges, so he was comfortable when the board of trustees imposed a moratorium on tenure. Lakeview's president, however, came to his college having "learned" of tenure's importance to high-quality institutions. While he noted some of tenure's shortcomings, he also observed, "Having served as a president and as a chancellor in both public and private higher education for twenty years, I am more committed to tenure than ever." In his prior post as dean at an Ivy League college, the president at Accomac had a similar learning experience about tenure, including, he asserted, its positive effect on faculty recruiting. Academic tenure was inextricably linked to his concept of elite, high-quality institutions.

Symbolic Purposes

The most far-reaching impact of the changes at these six colleges was symbolic, not substantive, and cultural rather than operational. These institutions were wrestling with larger questions for which the answers were ambiguous or unknown. Participants at Accomac and Lakeview asked, "How do we improve quality and prestige?" At Blessed Trinity and Rowlette, trustees wondered, "How do we ensure financial stability in a tumultuous environment?" At Grace College, trustees and administrators asked, "How can we ensure that we are not scarred by scandal?" At Scott, the president pondered, "How can we achieve a proper balance of power?" The implementation or discontinuance of tenure became the answer to each of these questions. Why? Because "faced with uncertainty and ambiguity, human beings create symbols to resolve confusions, increase predictability, and provide direction" (Bolman and Deal 1991, p. 244). These colleges eliminated or implemented tenure as a means to communicate that they were attending to and solving problems, even though they had a host of alternative solutions and were unsure that the shift in tenure policy, one way or the other, could substantively solve the stated problems. Rituals and cere-monies—the traditional acts and routines that give meaning to human activity—serve four purposes: "to socialize, to stabilize, to reduce anxi-eties and ambiguities, and to convey messages to external constitu-encies" (Bolman and Deal 1991, p. 262). The shift in employment pol-icy at each site served one or more of these purposes. Participants at Accomac, Lakeview, and Grace asserted that tenure would move the college into the mainstream. Adopting tenure would clearly convey to the external higher education community that they were joining the club and would socialize new faculty to believe that the college was "normal." At Blessed Trinity and Rowlette, trustees sought financial and programmatic flexibility through the removal of tenure. The dis-continuance of tenure was an attempt to reduce anxiety about the col-lege's precarious financial position and to send a message to outside groups (such as creditors and donors) that the college was taking the necessary actions to protect its fiscal health. For Scott, the president believed that the act of abolishing tenure would send a message to fac-ulty that he was in charge and would compel them to be accountable to him. That act reinforced for both longtime and new faculty the hierar-chical decision-making norm.

In each of these cases, the tenure or contract system was not a so-lution that arose solely from a rational examination of alternative choices. Instead, these institutions, like other organizations, relied on myth and perception to fill the void of uncertainty and ambiguity. De-spite the colleges' substantive goals for altering their faculty employ-ment policies, they also shifted to or away from tenure to send a mes-sage about institutional identity—about "who we are."

Practical Implications

The colleges in this study are not representative of the spectrum of American higher education. Nevertheless, their experiences allow ex-trapolations (Patton 1990) on the meaning and practice of tenure more generally.

In terms of job security, contracts are in effect de facto tenure. In practice, there is little difference in job security between tenure and contract systems at these colleges. The three colleges that instituted contracts have retained over 90% of their faculty. When asked why faculty were not upset when tenure was discontinued at Rowlette College, a tenured professor replied, "It wasn't a gut issue. You didn't need tenure; you could stay here forever." Moreover, for some faculty members, a contract system is just as good as tenure. An untenured Rowlette professor asserted, "Faculty just didn't feel that tenure would enhance security in any way."

The adoption of a tenure system does not necessarily insure quality in the short term. By grandfathering large percentages of faculty, Group I colleges undercut the argument that tenure insures quality. Several institutions tenured large numbers of faculty with questionable credentials, and then these same individuals passed judgment on tenure for junior colleagues. In order to increase faculty quality over the long term, these colleges had to grandfather large percentages of faculty without any type of performance review. This was the political price institutions had to pay to adopt tenure.

Academic freedom is not necessarily dependent on one appointment policy or the other, but depends on institutional context and circumstances. At Rowlette and Lakeview colleges, participants maintained that academic freedom has always been protected, regardless of employment policy. In fact, faculty took pride in their institutions' serious commitment to openness, freedom, and truth. A Rowlette professor was emphatic that "there has never been a loss of academic freedom." A counterpart at Lakeview maintained that both before and after tenure was introduced "this has been a very open place, a rather liberal place. Nobody's threatened because of what they say or do." Academic freedom at these colleges depended on the interplay of personalities, not on the presence of tenure. As one professor maintained, "The seasons of caution here . . . wax and wane. It has more to do with the personalities of the president and the provost than with tenure or the lack thereof."

Academic freedom did not exist equally robustly on all campuses without tenure. While some faculty members at Scott claimed that their academic freedom was not diminished after tenure was eliminated, the college community narrowly defined the concept. The Scott faculty handbook stated that professors "should at all times seek accuracy, should exercise appropriate restraint, should show respect for others, should make explicit they are not institutional spokesman [*sic*], and should not make statements which are detrimental to the mission and/

or operation of the College." Under this definition, many Scott faculty did not define their loss of voice in campus governance as an abridgment of academic freedom. Those who believed in shared governance felt differently about the move away from tenure. Said one longtime professor, "I feel that people are reluctant to rock the boat too much."

What is most different at these colleges since they added or removed tenure? First, the colleges wanted to improve their faculty employment practices, and in some cases—at Accomac, Grace, and Scott colleges — the policy changes did indeed have that functional impact. Faculty evaluations at these colleges, for example, are more stringent for new faculty under the present system than was the case for faculty under the old policy, as evidenced by slightly higher turnover rates for performance-related reasons.

The more pronounced difference at these colleges, however, involves the latent function of the policy shifts. By using a process as a proxy for an outcome, all six institutions moved in a similar fashion. These shifts, both to and away from tenure, were façades—elaborate treatments that affected beliefs more than behavior and policy more than practice. The most significant consequence of the substitution in policy lies in the act of change itself. These big changes captured the attention of constituents, as if the colleges wanted to say, "Look at us. Now we're different." In proclaiming a difference, the institutions *were* different.

Adding or abolishing tenure was at the core a symbolic act, a play in which the performance was more important than the plot. While the rhetoric of tenure and contracts is typically argued on a rational basis, the experiences of these colleges suggest that shifting to or away from tenure is not so much about the plot—improved results and better outcomes—as it is about the performance—messages, ceremony, and spectacle.

Notes

1. The secondary sites were used to reach "data saturation, the point of data collection where the information you get becomes redundant" (Bogdan and Bilken 1992, p. 68).

2. At Grace College, 42% of faculty were automatically grandfathered. Grace has been omitted from this discussion, however, because interviewees did not claim that the move to tenure was a strategy to improve faculty quality.

References

Bogdan, Robert C., and Sari K. Bilken. 1992. *Qualitative Research for Education: An Introduction to Theory and Methods.* New York: Allyn and Bacon.

Bolman, Lee G., and Terrence E. Deal. 1991. *Reframing Organizations: Artistry, Choice, and Leadership.* San Francisco: Jossey-Bass.

Chait, Richard P. 1997. "Why Academe Needs More Employment Options." *Chronicle of Higher Education,* February 7, p. B4.

Chait, Richard P., and Cathy A. Trower. 1997. *Where Tenure Does Not Reign: Colleges with Contract Systems.* Washington, D.C.: American Association of Higher Education.

Cohen, Michael D., and James G. March. 1986. *Leadership and Ambiguity: The American College President.* 2nd ed. Boston: Harvard Business School Press.

Commission on Academic Tenure in Higher Education. 1973. *Faculty Tenure.* San Francisco: Jossey-Bass Publishers.

Cotter, W. R. 1996. "Why Tenure Works." *Academe,* 82 (1): 26–29.

DiMaggio, Paul J., and William W. Powell. 1991. "The Iron Cage Revisited: Institutional Isomorphism and Collective Rationality in Organizational Fields." In W. W. Powell and P. J. DiMaggio, eds., *The New Institutionalism in Organizational Analysis.* Chicago: University of Chicago Press, 63–82.

Finkin, Matthew W. 1996. *The Case for Tenure.* Ithaca, N.Y.: ILR Press.

Machlup, Fritz. 1964. "In Defense of Tenure." *AAUP Bulletin,* 50: 112–124.

Magrath, C. Peter. 1997. "Eliminating Tenure without Destroying Academic Freedom." *Chronicle of Higher Education,* February 28, p. A60.

Patton, Michael Q. 1990. *Qualitative Evaluation and Research Methods.* 2nd ed. Newbury Park, Calif.: Sage Publications.

Sykes, Charles J. 1988. *Profscam: Professors and the Demise of Higher Education.* Washington, D.C.: Regnery Gateway.

Yin, Robert K. 1994. *Case Study Research: Design and Methods.* 2nd ed. Thousand Oaks, Calif.: Sage Publications.

10

How Might Data Be Used?

CATHY A. TROWER

JAMES P. HONAN

*T*WO FUNDAMENTAL PRINCIPLES of the academy are to ground arguments in data and to draw conclusions from systematic analysis. Ironically, both the literature on the use of data in organizations and actual practice in academe suggest that policy discussions and decisions only sometimes honor these core tenets. When faculty employment, work life, or productivity is under consideration, anecdotes, impressions, and dogmatic beliefs are far more likely than data to serve as a catalyst and rationale for policy deliberation and formulation.

Two fairly recent events illustrate the exception and the rule respectively. During the late 1990s, tenure was under scrutiny in Arizona and Minnesota. Members of the Arizona Board of Regents believed that tenure was the root cause of several problems at the state's three public universities. "At the outset, members of the Arizona Board of Regents were becoming increasingly concerned about problems they perceived to result from the implementation of the tenure system at the State's three public universities," remarked Frank H. Besnette, Executive Director of the Arizona Board of Regents (1997, p. 1). Those problems included constraints on programmatic flexibility, innovation, redirection of faculty priorities, and actions against unproductive faculty members.

"A problem solving approach between the Regents and faculty members was considered the best way" to move forward in a way that would "prevent the kind of destructive cycle of accusation and counter-accusation between trustees and faculty members that has characterized much of the discussion about tenure nationally" (Besnette 1997, p. 1). A work plan was developed to design and implement a periodic audit of the operation and effectiveness of the universities' tenure systems. The tenure audit, conducted at all public universities in Arizona, provided data on tenure track faculty by race and gender, full-time and part-time faculty by age, and tenured, tenure track, and non–tenure track faculty by age. These data were then used to examine faculty workloads, the balance between teaching and service, and productivity (see Ervin 1998). With the implementation of a post-tenure review process, the Arizona institutions also now gather and distribute data about the outcomes of such reviews.

In Arizona's case, the data helped persuade the regents that tenure was not the root cause of the problems; data moved them in another direction. Once the board understood how faculty actually spent their time, and that there were safeguards in place to evaluate faculty throughout their career, the regents felt comfortable with the tenure system and its benefits.

Likewise, in Minnesota,[1] the Board of Regents became interested in the relationship of tenure to faculty productivity and institutional flexibility, particularly the institution's ability to redirect financial and human resources to meet emerging needs and priorities. Concern intensified when the state legislature withheld $6.6 million from the Academic Health Center pending reform of the tenure code. Daniel Farber recalled the events:

> No one ever said it would be easy to reform the tenure code at the University of Minnesota. But then no one ever said the process would become so messy either. By the time the process ground to a halt, four regents had left the board. . . . Tenure went from being an esoteric academic rule to front-page news, day after day. Because of the controversy, the system had come within a few dozen votes of becoming the nation's first major research university to unionize. Oh, and by the way, there also were some constructive changes in the tenure code. But the price was steep, in terms of

morale, political capital, and institutional vitality. (Farber 1997, p. 6)

Most participants in the process agree that reform of the tenure code at Minnesota was hampered by lack of data. The regents were troubled because data necessary to answer basic questions were not readily available. What happens to tenured faculty in the event of program closure at other research universities? How much of the budget is tied to tenure track versus non–tenure track lines? Part-time versus full-time faculty? How many tenured faculty are likely to retire in the next five years? From which departments? Do other medical schools tie base salary to productivity? What percentage of the faculty have tenure, by department? How does this compare to other research universities?

Former regent Jean Keffeler (1997b) noted:

Above all, a university should be a community in which inquiry and the pursuit of information are encouraged and protected, even when controversial, united by civility and high common purpose. Proponents and opponents of tenure reform ought to agree that the sorry proceedings . . . at the University of Minnesota demonstrated that we have a long way to go in meeting the true standards of intellectual and academic freedom at our university. If the goal was least change, most control, then we did well. The faculty and administration stonewalled the production of meaningful, timely information about tenure practices and faculty profiles. Precious little factual information about the Minnesota tenure situation was provided by the Regents, the administration, or the faculty. As a result, the general public was well informed about the tenure rhetoric and poorly informed about the tenure reality at the University of Minnesota. (p. 10)

By way of advice, Keffeler (1997a) said:

Provide your administration and trustees with information, not anecdotes . . . hard data, benchmark data, best practices information. Do anything that can be done to get beyond the natural insularity and myopia of the institution you serve, including its familiar social patterns and mythology. In Minnesota, there was too little information, too late. We allowed the process to jump to an emotional debate where no one wins. (p. 6)

Keffeler also said, "The process was never grounded in scholarly inquiry or data. Our intellectual standards were amateurish and would not stand the light of day in even a mediocre business" (1997b, p. 11).

The Arizona and Minnesota cases raise a number of important questions about the role of data-driven analysis in the review and formulation of faculty employment policies. Did data really make a difference in Arizona? Would the availability of systematic data and analysis have helped or hindered the process in Minnesota? In what ways? From whose perspective? Why did the reexamination of tenure in two states produce such radically different processes? While the presence or absence of data about faculty employment policies and practices was certainly not the only issue at work, and tenure remained intact at both universities, firsthand accounts suggest that the use of data helped turn a sensitive issue in Arizona into a policy consensus, grounded in fact, that effectively defused a potentially explosive situation. Faculty and administrators were able to persuade the regents that their institutions were flexible, could and did innovate, and employed productive faculty who taught large numbers of undergraduates. The absence of critical data in Minnesota created a void where rumors, opinions, and e-mailed messages swirled, with little or no data to support the opinions. Not coincidentally, perhaps, a few embers erupted into a mighty conflagration.

Do Data Make a Difference?

Based on the experiences of regents, legislators, faculty, and administrators in Arizona and Minnesota, as well as conversations with these constituents elsewhere, the Project on Faculty Appointments at Harvard University Graduate School of Education established an Information Resource Center to design, pilot, and distribute both a policy archive and a practice profile in order to assist parties to policy deliberations on faculty employment issues. The policy archive (discussed in Chapter 2) enables users to compare faculty employment policies of

250 colleges and universities. The practice profile provides institution-wide, longitudinal data on faculty personnel actions. A number of fundamental questions guided the development of these two data resources: Do better, more reliable data on faculty employment policies and practices change the substance and nature of policy discussions and personnel actions? If so, how? What data are used, by whom, and in what ways on campuses and within state agencies and legislatures? What problems arise when institutions attempt to collect, analyze, and disseminate such information?

While the archive can be an effective resource when institutions consider handbook revisions, it tells only one part of the story. We must also ask "What is the impact of policy on practice? How do policies affect the employment of faculty from point of entry to exit?" To better understand actual practice, the Project on Faculty Appointments worked with academic officers and institutional researchers from ten institutions to design and pilot a data template to track and report important faculty personnel actions over a five-year period. (In descending order of student enrollment, the ten are: University of Arizona, University of Cincinnati, University of Tennessee at Knoxville, University of North Carolina at Chapel Hill, Kansas State University, Oakland University, Ithaca College, Illinois Wesleyan University, Goucher College, and Bethany College.) Categorized by gender and ethnicity, the template includes data on type of appointment (e.g., full- and less than full-time; non–tenure track, tenure track, and tenured), tenure decisions, turnover, age, retirement projections, and the outcomes of post-tenure reviews. In October 1998 the ten institutions developed common definitions and a standard format.[2] Participants also identified a wide range of intended uses for the data, including plans to (1) revise faculty employment policies, (2) prepare trend analyses, (3) inform discussions of flexible hiring policies, (4) benchmark against peer institutions, and (5) clarify, confirm, or refute current beliefs and perceptions on campus about faculty employment policies and practices.

Assessing the Utility of Data

In autumn 1999 project staff visited the ten pilot institutions to meet with faculty, administrators, staff, and in some cases trustees and legislators, to discuss the collection and use of data on campus. This section highlights conclusions and common themes from the site visits.

Political Readiness Is Crucial

When undertaking a data collection process of this sort, political readiness is a vital element. Political readiness is largely determined by the who and the why. Who wants the data? For what purpose? Is senior leadership in charge of or at least supportive of the effort? This concept was wonderfully described by a provost who said, "Data don't just get up and walk around by themselves. If they don't align with some higher will, they'll just sit there. Those data are impotent, and they only become potent when somebody in charge wants something to happen."

The role of senior leaders varied widely among the ten institutions, ranging from coach to quarterback to spectator. At institutions where the president and/or provost led the process, the demand for the template data was higher than at institutions where senior administrators were only tangentially involved. In some cases, a senior leader (e.g., chief academic officer) actually made the case for collecting the data, presented the template data to campus constituents, and linked the information to policy formulation and decision-making. Remarks by a senior academic administrator during the data presentation on one campus demonstrate how leaders can set the tone for data collection and use:

> Our university is currently grappling with how it and its schools and departments might be redefined to meet future needs and demands. In order to do this, we need to know where we are and what we are dealing with. We also need to know how we stack up against other universities by looking at comparative data. We need to address questions such as: How are we doing regarding faculty diversity? What are the trends regarding faculty retention? To what extent are faculty leaving the institution and why are they leaving? How will we cope with increased accountability? How are we using our faculty resources? Now that we have this database on faculty employment issues, we can take a hard look at real data, not just base our arguments on what we think or feel. We are

now in a position to use data to make decisions that are good for faculty and good for the institution.

Likewise the provost at another institution openly expressed strong interest in the data: "The template data provide us with a snapshot of the institution and are directly linked to important issues concerning faculty employment. The data will be helpful in policy conversations with deans and department chairs, and I would like to see us collect at least some of the template data on an ongoing basis."

In a few cases, no data from the template were actually presented during the site visit; as a result, most constituents were not very knowledgeable about what data were collected or how they might be used in campus policy development or decision-making. In these instances, senior leaders were chiefly spectators. Data appeared to be relatively unimportant to them and were unlikely to be used in decision-making. At one institution, the provost noted that the president had "little use for data" to inform decisions. The attitude was "Why marshal data to make a case when the case can be better, or just as easily made, by anecdote or personal relationships?" Not surprisingly, data at this institution were in complete disarray. The institution had little or no technical expertise and no political readiness to collect information about faculty employment. In fact, in the past, decisions to implement phased and early retirement plans were made with little data about how many people were likely to participate or what these programs would cost.

At several institutions, administrators and faculty explicitly intended to link the template data to institutional governance, policy deliberations, and decision-making. For example, several deans and department chairs indicated that comparative, quantitative data on faculty appointment trends could help make a case for more resources for their department or unit. Others suggested that template data might be used to support strategic planning or might be incorporated into their institution's academic program review processes.

During one site visit, a senior academic officer articulated the ways in which the template data might directly tie to campus decision-making and policy formulation. In remarks to a group of deans, department chairs, and faculty, he stated: "We want to inform you and acquaint you with the data we have collected and would like you to share your insights and observations with us. As far as we're concerned, this is public information. I think these data have good potential to help us focus on important institutional issues and to provide guidance on some initiatives we are considering. The template data are a resource for future conversations that will take place here."

In other cases there was no intention among academic administrators and/or faculty to use the data systematically to support decision-making and policy formulation. At other institutions, the template data collection and campus discussion may have opened a small window of opportunity for informed review of faculty employment policies.

Particularly on campuses with no tradition of data-driven decisions, the very act of collecting data can provoke concern and suspicion. A department chair remarked, "I'm conscious of what the administration will do with these data now. I'm doubting the results, not the what, but the why. What and who is behind this?" A senior administrator on the same campus reported, "It seems like every time we gather data there is some suspicion; folks always wonder about the agenda." Others expressed concern about the accuracy of the data and the cost-benefit ratio of the effort. Some skeptics assumed the role of "data checkers." One remarked, "I probably wouldn't use the data, but if someone else might, I want to be sure that it's accurate."

On another campus, which had undergone recent scrutiny and policy oversight by trustees, the provost admitted, "If we were to have said [to the faculty] that these data were for the Board of Regents we would have encountered foot-dragging, but because this was a research project . . . people were excited about it." Said another provost,

> On our campus, there is an inherent fear of being overmanaged . . . a fear of the "corporatization" of higher education. There's a sense that "you," the administration, want to boil "us," the faculty, down to numbers and then make decisions based on them, and to a certain extent they're right! Data can be scary because they threaten faculty members' autonomy . . . a huge reason why people enter academe in the first place. To me, these data prove that we're interested in our faculty, in what they do. My job is to convince the faculty that I'm not going to use the data in ways that will restrict them or make them feel like they're clock-punchers.

At several institutions, little trust was expressed about the collection and use of the template data. At one site, doubts were repeatedly expressed about whether the central administration *could* actually collect accurate data on faculty employment issues and decisions. At another, there were concerns about how the data might be used, leading one faculty member to note, "We don't normally collect these data because too many people figure that it could only be harmful, never helpful, to do so." Without trust, intention, and leadership—the three elements of political readiness—the probability that data will matter drops precipitously.

Technical and Operational Readiness Is Vital

Technical readiness—an institution's technological capacity to collect the data—is another vital ingredient. What sorts of software are available for data collection and analysis? Are there staff members with the requisite expertise? Operational readiness is another essential factor. This reflects the quality and accuracy of existing data on faculty employment, both current and historical.

Technical and operational readiness differed greatly among the pilot institutions. The information systems and databases from which data were generated were questionable at several sites. In addition, the staff varied in size, competence, and available time. At some institutions "the data just weren't there"; at others, data on faculty were collected and maintained in multiple systems, in different formats, and in several locations (e.g., central administrative offices, school/college deans' offices, specific departments). One academic administrator noted: "We don't have a good institution-wide academic database; the deans and department chairs maintain faculty appointment data locally, but we don't do as good a job as we could centrally. Frankly, the information we need is not in one location."

In one extreme case, the provost's office lacked ready access to accurate data on a broad range of faculty employment issues. Instead, one administrator allowed, "data were all over the place." Some information was stored on a mainframe employee database, other data were maintained on personal computers by deans and department chairs, and still other records, on paper, were filed in the provost's office. As a result, officers could not determine the actual number of tenured and tenure track faculty appointed in the various colleges and departments in the most recent academic year. The provost speculated that the dearth of data might reflect a subconscious concern about what the data might indicate as well as a level of institutional indifference to data as a prerequisite to decision-making.

At another institution, the data collection challenges were more operational, but just as significant. In this case, the problem was that changes in the institution's human resource data systems resulted in different data files and formats across the five years covered by the template. Thus, some of the variation in the data was as much a result of data systems as actual changes in faculty appointment policies and practices.

This example points to an important data collection issue: many faculty data systems focus primarily on operational and administrative details (e.g., payroll, benefits, and employment status) rather than on data and analysis for policy development and decision-making. Consequently, gathering policy-relevant data on key faculty employment and work life issues presents substantial challenges for many institutions. These difficulties explain in part why key data on faculty appointments are not readily available to decision-makers. Of course, having technology, staff, and readily available data does not insure that the data will be used; that depends on political readiness, as previously discussed.

Definitions Are Problematic

Faculty employment issues are inherently complex, not only for professors and administrators, but especially for constituents with less frequent and direct campus contact (e.g., trustees, legislators). As a result, definitions matter, lest terminology further cloud an already complicated policy arena. Without a common vocabulary, meaningful comparisons across departments, schools, and institutions are unattainable. Accurate data based on clear categories and precise definitions are crucial to generate and analyze useful faculty employment data.

Agreeing on definitions presents an early and sometimes insurmountable challenge to data collection efforts. The very definition of what constitutes data is sometimes unclear. As C. O. McCorkle (1997) put it, "Management information takes many forms, including both quantitative data and subjective judgments of informed persons" (p. 3). Data on faculty employment issues can include anecdotes, descriptive statistical information, subjective judgments, comparative or interinstitutional statistics, benchmark analyses, descriptions of normative and nonstandard policies and practices, surveys, focus group information, financial and budget reports, and evaluation studies. Furthermore, some data are "official" or formal, and other data are "unofficial" or informal, yet both may matter, although not always with the same constituents.

The use of national or peer-group data on faculty employment can be limited because important terms and definitions were not sufficiently discussed and refined by decision-makers and data providers. One academic vice president noted, "What looks relatively simple gets quickly convoluted when you're not using similar definitions." "This is crucial," agreed a research university president. "Most discussions of faculty issues get bogged down by definitional problems, so that if you don't agree to terms you've got an unsolvable problem." He continued:

> There is a need to normalize the data, for example, research dollars per faculty member. Almost everything involves counting faculty, but the government, IPEDS, they all have different definitions, so every institution is counting differently. This is a big issue. While the lack of common definitions does not hamper our ability to make decisions relevant to ourselves, it does hamper our ability to see ourselves in a broader context. For example, the number of part-time faculty . . . is that a problem in and of itself? No, probably not, but what we need to know is does a certain number put us outside of the norm?

The inability to achieve common definitions for important terms strengthens the ability to resist change. As one faculty member observed: "One sure way to maintain the status quo is to say that something is indefinable; then it cannot be measured. It's possible that the academy likes having things that cannot be measured. I've seen this happen in many conversations of faculty productivity, work load, and quality. How do you measure them? Well, first you have to define them . . . and no one wants to do that!"

For meaningful comparisons, faculty data invariably involve counting (e.g., full-time and part-time faculty; tenured, tenure track faculty, and non–tenure track faculty; research dollars; salaries), and without common definitions the tallies have little value. The same problem would arise with the Consumer Price Index, the Dow Jones Industrial Average, or reports on corporate earnings. If everyone were to account differently, comparisons and conclusions would be impossible to draw.

Data on Faculty Employment Generates a Desire for More

Consistent with the literature on data as catalyst for further data collection (Feldman and March 1981; Weiss 1991b, 1999), as these data were produced faculty, administrators, and sometimes board members on many campuses requested additional data and finer-grained analysis. Most users wanted to "get behind" the numbers, to find out what they really mean. In all cases, the dissemination of quantitative data produced a desire for qualitative data to explain the findings and trends. For example, once differences between the number and percentage of women and minorities compared with white males who persist to tenure was known, additional questions emerged: Why is the persistence rate different? Why do women and minorities drop out on their way to tenure? Were they considered tenurable when they left, or were they likely to have been denied tenure? Are they leaving for better offers elsewhere? Did they leave academe altogether? Was there a chilly climate on campus? The template data at one institution, for example, suggested that women faculty resigned prior to the tenure decision at a significantly higher rate than men. After seeing the data, a faculty member declared, "If these numbers are right, then I think we're in a crisis." Other faculty members at the meeting recommended that the data on resignations be disaggregated by college and department to better understand what was happening. A professor suggested that follow-up interviews be conducted to determine why women were resigning prior to the tenure decision. In order to effect change on campus through policy changes, faculty and administrators needed a lot more than just raw numbers. However, the numbers themselves offered clues about what additional information was needed.

At another institution, the data showed that minority faculty were leaving at a higher rate than white faculty prior to the tenure decision. Said the provost, "It wasn't the data that made a difference in my thinking, but the data led me to meet with the African-American tenure track faculty. They made comments about the majority culture that measures success based on individual competitiveness. The minority culture measures success based on community ethics, collaboration, and furtherance of community. We needed the qualitative piece to put with the data."

In some cases, data that could be viewed as unfavorable produced demands for more data to clarify, justify, or refute the original information. The demand for additional data can be a challenge to "wrong" data, a way to filibuster, or even a way to disprove an unfavorable conclusion, much as objectionable research findings produce challenges to methodology. Even when the data are not disputed, demands for more data can arise because discussion of the extant data lead people to say, "Now that we know this, wouldn't it be great to know that?"

In a few cases, the template data neither confirmed nor refuted common beliefs or popular perceptions, but they generated more questions anyway. At an institution where the data disclosed that no one was denied tenure during the past five years, faculty and staff proposed a number of possible explanations. Could it be that the tenure criteria were faulty? Perhaps the administration was unwilling to make tough decisions? Maybe the institution has a highly effective "weeding out" process? Was it possible that the market was so favorable that the institution could pick and choose the very best junior faculty? Should the institution reconsider its tenure and promotion policies? No attempt was made, at least during this meeting, to resolve these widely divergent and apparently conflicting hypotheses. Provosts, deans, department chairs, and faculty wanted additional comparative data that would help the institution understand norms for certain policies, practices, and trends. In still other cases, the aggregated, institution-wide data from the template led to interest in data disaggregated by department, school, and/or discipline, and by race and ethnicity beyond the two categories used in this study.[3]

Some organizations suffer from "conspicuous overconsumption" of data on the premise that "if some data are good, more data are better." Organizations are most apt to fall prey to "data frenzy" where:

decision criteria are ambiguous;
performance measures are vague;

the success of a decision depends on other decisions that cannot be
   predicted or controlled;
institutions and occasions are closely linked to rational ideologies
   (Feldman and March 1981, p. 193).

These four factors epitomize academe and faculty work life, so it is
not surprising that on every campus we heard: "Now that we know the
numbers, it would be great to know what lies behind them." Armed
with quantitative information, decision-makers discussed what qualitative data could answer questions that the numbers raised. The first im-
pulse at many institutions was to gather still more data, about rank,
time in rank, workload, publication records, or some other aspect of
faculty employment.

What Is Measured Becomes What Matters

The very compilation and dissemination of data place certain faculty
issues into play. As Edgar Schein (1992), among others, has recognized,
what gets measured is what matters. Data make certain problems, like
the percentage of women and minorities in tenured and tenure track
positions, harder to ignore. In about half of the cases, the template
data catalyzed campus discussions of specific, problematic policy issues.
One faculty member said, "Seeing data like these allows us to look at
ourselves, to consider possibilities and explanations. It opens the door
for a conversation. It puts these issues into play." Confronted with hard
data, a department chair remarked that she knew intuitively that the
percentage of tenured faculty at her institution was high, "but not that
high." Equipped with the actual data, the chair proposed that this issue
become an agenda item for further discussion.
   How the data are gathered, which distinctions are made, and how
they are presented determine how they will be used. Because the template required institutions to report data by gender and race, certain
differences were spotlighted. Had we instead asked for data by department, but not by gender and race, departmental differences would have
been highlighted and gender/race issues would have been obscured.
The template data by gender and race identify possible dispropor-
tionate effects of faculty employment policies. For example, one institution's data revealed that the faculty's demographic profile barely

changed over five years. As one faculty member observed, "We have a completely stagnant faculty when you look at women and minorities. We've made no progress." The template data provided a similar insight at another institution, where a faculty member commented, "As I look at the data, gender equity is a glaring issue. This is really quite surprising. Many of us feel that we've made tremendous progress regarding gender equity, but the data don't support this view." There was discussion of the institution's relatively low number of faculty of color. A senior administrator mentioned that the institution had recently undertaken an initiative to recruit faculty of color, but added, "the numbers show we're not there yet."

In some cases, the data provoked discussion of complicated and persistent policy issues that remained unclear and unresolved. In one particularly noteworthy example where an institution with a tenure cap had recently downsized, the template data precipitated reconsideration first of the definitional aspects of the quota and then the utility of the policy altogether.[4] At another institution, the reality of part-time faculty became "all too clear" as campus constituents could no longer deny their existence in increasing numbers over the five-year period, especially when coupled with decreasing numbers of full-time tenured and tenure track faculty. At another institution, the data were used to identify a problem with women's resigning prior to the tenure decision at a much higher rate than men, and the data showed that the number of men and women taking phased retirement was much greater than expected. Where data raised red flags, institutions zeroed in on possible explanations and solutions.

While typically not articulated, the use of faculty employment data is clearly symbolic and acts as a signal to convey what is important at an institution. One provost said, "The very fact that we are collecting and disseminating these data signals the campus community that we are interested in faculty work life and factors that effect it." Said another chief academic officer, "This process is symbolic as well as rational. It shows that we are concerned about how women and minorities fare here." For at least three institutions, the process of collecting these data allowed administrators to bring faculty employment data together in one central location and provided a rationale for why this should be done.

Some leaders used the data collection process as a way to reinforce culture. What leaders measure is a sure sign of what is important in an institution (Schein 1992). This was especially evident at those institutions where the president and/or the provost played an active role in leading the data collection effort. These leaders were aware of their institution's involvement and prepared for the process. Said one provost, "We plan to use these data when we hire new faculty and staff as part of an orientation process." At another university, department chairs suggested that they would use the data in a similar capacity: to show prospective and probationary faculty factual data about time to tenure and tenure success rates.

Data Are Rarely Directly Linked to Decisions

Consistent with most prior research on the subject, we did not find direct links between data and policymaking. The literature presents a mixed picture of the value and role of systematic data and analysis for purposes of decision-making and policy development. Carol Weiss (1999) observed:

> Policy does not take shape around a single table. In democracies, many people have a hand in defining the issues, identifying the perspective from which they should be addressed, proffering policy solutions, and pressing for particular policy responses. Legislators[,] . . . civil servants, constituency groups, pressure groups, party leaders, potential beneficiaries of new policy, taxpayers, intellectuals . . . all take part in supporting and opposing new definitions, conceptual frames, and policy proposals. Almost never does the choice of policy hinge on the presence or absence of information. (p. 195)

Further, since decisions usually occur by "accretion," rather than at an official time and place (Weiss 1991a, 1999), no one can be certain which data, if any, affected which decisions.

Similarly, M. S. Feldman and James March (1981) determined that "the link between decisions and information is weak" because:

> Much of the information gathered and communicated by individuals and organizations bears little relevance to the decision.

Much of the information used to justify a decision is collected and interpreted after the decision has in effect been made.

Much of the information gathered in response to requests for information is overlooked when making the decision for which it was requested.

Regardless of how much information is available at the time a decision is first considered, more information is requested.

The relevance of the information provided is less conspicuous than is the insistence on information (p. 174).

Although tangible links between data and decisions are uncommon, data often do play a role—though rarely the lead role—in decision-making and policy formulation. At the very least, the presence or absence of data can influence how leaders and other parties frame problems and determine which issues to highlight or mute in policy discussions. Data thus can be used for various purposes. (See Table 10.1.) Of the twelve functions identified in the literature, three were particularly prominent in the pilot project on faculty employment data: monitor, compare, and substantiate.

One very important role played by data collected over time is to help organizations evaluate policies and practices, to *monitor* progress, and to make "marginal adjustments in strategies currently in use" (Weiss 1981, p. 188). Throughout our site visits, faculty and administrators discussed how important it is to have trend data—for example, on the number of part-time faculty. On one campus, an administrator discussed how the decision to hire part-time faculty was not made centrally. "Rather," he said, "the growth in numbers of part-time faculty was the cumulative impact of hundreds of separate decisions in separate departments. Snapshot data only provide one part of the picture. The trend data allowed us to see the cumulative picture and will allow us to continually monitor the situation."

A provost put it this way: "You have to keep adjusting the compass. Data show you where you are, and these trend data show you where you've been. But they are only one piece of the picture. We have to consider our technology, our clientele, and our institutional and programmatic strengths to decide on how best to approach the future. The data are part of monitoring what's happening, and they inform institutional adjustments."

Table 10.1 The role of data in decision-making and policy formulation

Function	Role of data	Sources	Questions answered/ statements made by the data
Catalyze	As a catalyst for further or improved data collection As a catalyst to rethink assumptions	Feldman and March (1981) Weiss (1991b, 1999)	Do we have the data we need? If not, what additional data should we collect? Are the data that we have appropriate? Are the data correct?
Compare	To put an institution's experience with a particular challenge or issue into a broader, comparative context	Weiss (1981, 1999)	How do other institutions handle this issue? How are other institutions doing with regard to X or Y? Are we in a better or worse position on X or Y than our peers?
Identify/warn	To identify a specific policy issue or problem To warn decision-makers that there is/may be a problem	McCorkle (1977) Trow (1964) Weiss (1981, 1991b, 1991c, 1999)	How do issues get "put into play" in policy processes? What causes issues to appear on a policymaker's radar screen? Do we have a problem here? (red flag)
Illuminate/enlighten	To illuminate policy changes and alternative decision options To shift the spotlight from one place to another	Trow (1964) Weiss (1981, 1991b, 1991c, 1999)	What are the potential policy options? What works or does not work?

Category	Purpose	Sources	Example
Influence	To influence policy conversations, discussion, and debates	Weiss (1981, 1991b, 1991c, 1999)	Now that I see the data, my thinking has changed. I might agree with you if the data support your argument. Given these data, it looks like we should move in this direction.
Inform	To inform key constituents about how the institution is performing in certain policy areas	Weiss (1981, 1991c)	Based on these data elements, the situation at our institution is as follows . . . The implications of that are as follows . . .
Monitor	To monitor and evaluate policies and practices	McCorkle (1977) Weiss (1981, 1999)	Do we actually follow our policies in practice? How do our policies and practices "stack up" against performance expectations?
Orchestrate	To promote a shared understanding and a common language on a policy issue	Weiss (1981, 1991c, 1999)	Are constituents all "on the same page" regarding a particular problem or issue?
Signal	As a signal of legitimacy in an institution As a signal of a good decision	Feldman and March (1981) Schmidtlein (1999) Stacey (1996) Weiss (1991b, 1999)	Look at all the data we gathered prior to making this decision; it must be good. Ours is an institution that collects data; therefore, we are legitimate.

Table 10.1 (*continued*)

Function	Role of data	Sources	Questions answered/statements made by the data
Socialize	As a way to embed culture in an institution	Schein (1992)	The institution's leaders are asking for, paying attention to, and measuring data about faculty employment. It must be important to our institutional culture.
Substantiate	To provide evidence to affirm or refute existing beliefs and perceptions	Feldman and March (1981) March (1994) Schmidtlein (1999) Stacey (1996) Weiss (1981, 1991c)	How does an institution test its assumptions regarding policy questions? What do the data say that support existing beliefs? Are there disconfirming data?
Symbolize	As a symbol of rational decision-making in an institution As a symbol of knowledge and alertness	Feldman and March (1981) March (1994) Schmidtlein (1999) Stacey (1996) Weiss (1981, 1991c)	What data are present for use in decision-making? Did decision-makers actually use the data? How rational could the decision have been without data? Look at all the data I have; I am knowledgeable on these issues.

Data also help institutions place the institution's policies and practices in a broader or different context and counter insularity and parochialism by allowing them to *compare* data. In this fashion, data provide a window into a world that faculty and staff might not otherwise view. Faculty, and maybe to a lesser extent administrators, tend to be rather uninformed about policy and practice elsewhere, except by anecdotes swapped among colleagues in one's discipline. Dissemination of the template data heightened the curiosity of constituents about faculty appointment practices elsewhere and comparable data from peer institutions. As one administrator noted, "I'd like to see some comparative data so I can address the question 'Are we as good as we think we are or as bad as we think we are?'" This question begs the follow-on questions: Compared to whom and to what? Based on what reference point in time?

Administrators and faculty from several institutions wanted to obtain comparative data from peer institutions to ascertain normative trends and conditions and to consider whether the institution's policies and practices were outside the norm. This is consistent with data as reorientation (Weiss 1981). As a dean observed, "We know a lot about ourselves since we are a small institution, but we don't know whether our numbers are higher, lower, or the same as those at peer institutions." Said one provost, "We don't want to be all that different from everybody else on most of these measures. If we are, who are we different from and in what ways?" Another said:

> I'm most interested in our peer/aspirant institutions. If we're 30% above or below, we should be concerned. But we also need to look at these data in the context of everything we do. How helpful would it be to know that we have two unsatisfactory faculty and another system has thirty-five? So what? We would need to know more than this to act strategically based on these data. But to know that one department here has two unsatisfactory faculty and another has sixteen, or that most have none, well, that would be another matter.

On another campus, a faculty senate leader said, "It is critical from a planning standpoint to have these data. We need comparative data because if our peers' data are very different from ours, we can use this information as a 'convincing point' with the board of trustees or the legislature."

One by-product of collecting and disseminating data was curiosity about relative standing, much as the National Research Council or the *U.S. News & World Report* rankings engender conversations. The template data provided institutions with an opportunity for informed comparison. A senior academic administrator noted, "Data such as those in the template help the institution to see itself in a new light, from a different perspective, and in comparison to other institutions." He added, "These are data we never had before; they help us to highlight important issues and concerns." While several institutions in the pilot group sought comparative data from peer institutions, they did so only on an ad hoc basis. Participants felt that having the template would help them more systematically collect these data on an ongoing basis.

At most institutions, the template data clarified, confirmed, or refuted what many campus constituents had known intuitively about faculty employment trends at the institution, thus allowing decision-makers to *substantiate* opinions, claims, and beliefs. An administrator stated, "This is so much better than the usual anecdotal stuff; it's very helpful because it provides a reality check." A data provider said, "We need these data as proof that we are doing what we say we are doing, to defend our faculty practices to external constituents like legislators and board members." A state legislator acknowledged, "We all harbor perceptions, or misperceptions, as the case may be. Data like these can provide a reality check to test these perceptions" and to create a new impression or to correct a misimpression. He provided specific examples of how lawmakers might use the template data:

There is sometimes a perception among some legislators that once faculty earn tenure their scholarship declines, their teaching loads decline, and there is no accountability or review after tenure. The template data can be used to refute this proposition. You can say, "We have post-tenure review, and here are the results." You can use the data to show that faculty members have to adhere to a standard. If there is a perception that a particular institution is too heavily loaded with tenured faculty and that this drives up compensation, you can use the template data on tenure rates, the overall profile of the tenure status of faculty, and data on salary/payroll commitments to show what is actually the case. If legislators think that the institution is not making progress regarding the hiring and retention of women and minorities, the template data can be used to inform recruitment and retention policies.

In some cases, the template data provided confirmation of conventional wisdom about faculty employment. For example, an administrator noted, "There were no surprises; we knew this was the situation at our institution, but now we have actual data to show us what is going on." A provost remarked, "What one might have suspected anecdotally about faculty resignation rates is actually the case."

The template data played a "rumor management" function at one institution, where a common perception was that few junior faculty can achieve tenure there. The template data and supplementary analyses, which distinguished between the voluntary departure of tenurable faculty and faculty counseled to leave, helped to discount rumors that most candidates for tenure were denied.

At another institution, department chairs were routinely asked by prospective faculty about tenure probability rates. For the most part, department chairs answered these questions anecdotally. One chair remarked, "Anecdotes often lead to rumors. Perhaps having the actual data will help us dispel rumors. Some department chairs say things like, 'Well, I've been here for nine years and I've only seen one person denied tenure.' Someone else might tell a very different story." A data provider at another institution termed this use of data "changing the mental image or cliché that people hold in their heads." In a number of instances, the template data did just that.

Constituents at several institutions appeared to take the insights derived from the template data quite seriously. In this sense, one could argue that data play an important role as objective evidence of the actual impact of faculty employment policies (e.g., How many and what percentage of faculty are awarded tenure? How many faculty resign prior to the tenure decision?). Hard data make it more difficult to initiate misperceptions or perpetuate myths. Data have the power to separate fact from fiction and rumor from reality. In a data vacuum, misperceptions can flourish easily. Even with data, rumors may abound; however, they are less likely to persist and prevail. When asked to talk about what the template data revealed, a faculty member at one institution noted, bemusedly, "The data show that we tenure everyone who comes up, period," a powerful and irrefutable data-based conclusion.

Stories May Outweigh Statistics

Anecdotes about faculty employment issues play a significant role on campuses and are often cited by lawmakers to support proposed legislation. Frank Schmidtlein (1977) described reliance on informal information from trusted sources, past experience, and the power of anecdote:

> Even with the advances made in modern systems of data collection and analysis, most of the information brought to bear on decisions continues to come from personal experience and knowledge obtained from sources other than formal data systems. The impact of informal information is evident in the frequent cases where recitation of a few concrete examples has more weight on a policy decision than a statistical portrait of the area. Policy makers sense the problems of data accuracy, the loss of detail in aggregations, and are suspicious of the motives of those who furnish and use data. Often the advice of a friend or associate whose judgment is valued counts for more than an analysis of data. Policy makers have a tendency to evaluate higher education in terms of their own past experiences attending a particular institution. (p. 37)

In the legislative arena, policymakers often depend more on informal sources of information and anecdotes than on systematic data and analysis about faculty employment. The power of a vivid story conveyed in a well-timed telephone call from a well-placed source cannot be understated, especially for policymakers deluged by information on a myriad of issues and problems. A state legislator tersely characterized his approach as follows: "When my phone rings, I write bills; when I write bills, I effect change; when I effect change, I get reelected." This legislator emphasized the advantage of linking legislation, whenever possible, to an actual person (e.g., the Brady bill) or event (e.g., Columbine) because such connections are so much more memorable than dry data.

A lobbyist for one institution remarked, "Anecdotes are more powerful than formal data for many policymakers." In the same vein, a longtime institutional researcher from a system that gathers extensive data on faculty employment policies and practices declared, "The legislators in my state actually say, 'I don't care about the data. I don't want it.'" Indeed, a "don't confuse me with the facts" attitude characterizes many policymakers. If one constituent had a bad experience in college, there may be sufficient political reason to act, regardless of overall data. In these cases, a sample size of one suffices to pass judgment and even legislation. In some states, compulsory post-tenure review was triggered by powerful stories about relatively few allegedly deadwood professors.

Data Use Differs by Constituent Group

Most legislators and trustees want headlines and punch lines, and data in small doses, if at all. The few with a proclivity for data want the information presented in a fashion that tells a simple story, embellished with pie charts and bar graphs. Legislators want data that prove a point. In short, legislators want ammunition. If the data are unavailable, ambiguous, or complicated, they will be replaced by anecdotes.

On matters of data usage, trustees resemble legislators. Many board members expressed greater interest in what the data simply mean than in nuances of numbers and methodology. One trustee complained that discussion of the template data focused more on "the mechanics of the data" than on their importance. He had two key questions: How can you link these data to efforts to improve the quality of education, and how can these data help the institution do a better job? He said, "If these data can help us answer these questions and questions about curriculum and faculty hiring, then they might be useful." In short, trustees—and others—want less information with more meaning.

Presidents and provosts used data to shape an agenda, to provide support for hunches, to demonstrate accountability, to make comparisons with peer institutions, to change culture, and to make a case to board members or legislators. Those presidents and provosts with an appetite for data were more likely to use the template data in a variety of venues with many constituents, although this also depended on the issue and the executive's leadership style. For example, at one institution, the provost's desire to disseminate and use the template data

explains why data on several issues (i.e., post-tenure review and resignations) will continue to be collected and monitored. The provost intends to use the data with both internal and external constituents.

Deans and department chairs valued data that apply specifically to
their discipline or profession. Many expressed reservations about the
utility of institution-wide template data, preferring instead data disaggregated by school and department so as to reflect the culture and
market in the various disciplines. One department chair observed,
"Most of my actions with faculty are individual ones. We like to think
that we're all exceptions, so at first blush, the template data are not very
helpful." Another department chair remarked, "I need help solving
problems involving individual faculty, not more data." A number of department chairs wanted data by department, gender, and race/ethnic-
ity. One chair stated, "It is important to identify those departments
where women and minorities are not faring well and encourage improvement." On a somewhat more pragmatic level, a department chair
desired data to argue for additional money for his unit. Convinced that
his unit was more productive and efficient than others, he remarked,
"We argue for positions every year; we could use the template data to
make the case for more faculty lines."

Faculty are often involved on campus committees and task forces
charged with policy review and in that capacity are sometimes asked to
draft faculty handbook language. Members of faculty welfare and promotion and tenure committees were particularly interested in faculty
employment data. Frequently faculty comprise, for example, the campus committee on the status of women or the task force on women and
minorities. Their interest in data would typically be tied to involvement with such groups or with disciplinary associations where faculty
employment issues were under review. Not unexpectedly, faculty with
leadership roles in campus governance, senates, and unions tended to
have more interest in the template data.

There Is No Single "Owner" of Faculty Data

This project revealed that institutions had data providers and data
checkers, and usually data users (although the users were not always
readily identifiable), but no data "owners." Where should these data
reside? Who "owns" these data? Who will insure that they are captured

in the future in a systematic way? Is it the responsibility of the provost's office, where many institutions place faculty personnel matters? Or should it lie with the institutional research office, where other institutional reporting lies? Does the human resources office bear responsibility for housing these data? Even beyond where the data reside lie the questions of who owns the data and who is ultimately responsible for insuring that the academic institution has viable, accurate, and ongoing faculty appointment data. In the words of a vice provost, "Regardless of the technical, structural, and organizational issues surrounding data collection and use, there still remains that issue of a data owner who speaks up and says, 'This is the kind of long-term data that I need.' Provosts and presidents are like corporate CEOs who want to know what the next quarter shows rather than what the company is going to be like in five years. In fact, the tenure of senior leadership is not long, so it is rare that you get a long-term perspective in terms of data." As noted earlier, it is sometimes difficult to find data users, let alone data owners, in many academic institutions. With so many urgent matters at hand every day, most data get lost, and data about faculty appointments, for example, can easily be placed on a back burner and forgotten entirely until an issue where it is required comes into play.

Implications for Practice

While there are a number of problems and challenges endemic to the use of data on faculty employment policies and practices, decision-makers and data providers can mitigate some of these difficulties. This section identifies several strategies and approaches, first for decision-makers and then for data providers, that should increase the likelihood that systematic data collection and analysis will inform the review and development of faculty employment policies.

Recommendations to Leaders and Decision-Makers

Be careful what data you ask for. The very fact that a leader or decision-maker asks for certain data can raise suspicion or anger. When those data concern faculty employment, the potential for trouble increases. However innocent the motives may be, demands for such data elicit questions such as "Who wants to know?" "Why?" and "What is this all about?" Faculty anxieties rise proportionate to administrative requests for employment data.

Remember that data are not neutral. C. O. McCorkle (1977) writes, "We must always bear in mind that none of the information, neither the judgmental elements nor the quantitative 'factual' information, is neutral. Although we sometimes might like to think otherwise, the information we use to analyze . . . is subjective, reflecting the opinions and biases of the individuals who gathered and analyzed the data" (pp. 4–5). Minnesota's experience in its review of the tenure code offers an instructive example. There were no neutral data elements, and the parties could hardly agree on the facts.

Clarify your data and analysis needs with data producers prior to the collection and display of data. Lack of data is rarely a problem on most campuses; however, ill-defined demands for data are common and problematic. Data providers at several institutions expressed frustration about having the data but not knowing how best to present it to those who ask for it. When the requests are vague, data providers may spend an inordinate amount of time producing reams of information that will never be used. As one data provider noted, "Decision-makers don't always know what they really want; or if they do, they aren't sure how to get it. My advice to decision-makers is to ask knowledgeable questions and know the limitations of the data you are seeking." Another said, "If decision-makers want us to track something, they should be as specific as possible about definitions and also how they intend to use the data, so that we can produce reports tailored to those needs."

Be clear about what policy questions you are trying to address and about the data you want. "Data become informative only when we have specific policy questions that need illumination and resolution. The kind of policy question that is asked dictates information requirements" (McCorkle 1977, p. 3). In other words, the answer depends in large part on the question. At several institutions, specific policy questions were not linked intentionally to the data being collected. As a result, opportunities were missed to use data to enlighten policy discussions and to meet the analytic needs of decision-makers. Questions posed by senior administrators, trustees, and faculty leaders should shape the agenda for data acquisition and analysis, not vice versa.

Model the behavior that you want others to show. Presidents, provosts, deans, and other senior administrators play a critical role in establishing institutional norms for data collection, dissemination, and use. If leaders make clear that data matter to decisions, then others are more apt to marshal data, whether to advocate positions or to monitor progress. A provost at one institution deliberately involved campus constituents in data-driven policy discussions of faculty employment issues and was careful to exemplify the point that policy discussions would be grounded in data and analysis, not anecdote and conjecture.

Recognize the symbolic functions data serve that are not directly tied to decisions. Some data will be ignored, and some will be used in ways that cannot be directly observed. Data collection provides symbolic legitimacy to decisions and by extension to organizations. When data inform decisions, those decisions may be perceived as better, sounder, or more rational than they would have if no data were used at all. As Carol Weiss (1981) put it, "Decision-makers and organizations establish legitimacy by their use of information. Decisions that are viewed as legitimate will tend to be information-intensive" (p. 178). One reason that organizations collect so much data is that the "use of information is embedded in social norms that make it highly symbolic" (p. 171). "Decision-makers," notes James March (1994), "often seem to treat the gathering and use of information as part of the pursuit of symbolic meaning rather than as part of the resolution of decision uncertainties. Gathering information and making decisions are signals and symbols of competence. The possession and exhibition of information symbolizes (and demonstrates) the ability and legitimacy of decision-makers" (p. 226). In fact, several leaders noted that participation in this research project to collect and disseminate faculty employment data conveyed a message of enlightened management at work on campus.

Recommendations to Data Providers

Understand the appetite and aptitude of decision-makers for data, and tailor analytic products to their preferences and abilities. Be aware of how decision-makers frame particular policy issues or problems and provide data accordingly. Present data in clear, preferably graphic, formats that decision-makers can understand quickly and easily. In a number of instances, data providers gave decision-makers data and analyses that the latter did not want or could not use. Part of the problem in a number of cases was that data providers appeared to neither understand nor appreciate how policymakers viewed particular policy issues and problems. The concerns and interests of policymakers were not aligned with the data and analyses that were presented.

One state legislator provided very explicit advice to data providers: "You've got to do two things. First, target the data to your audience; you need to link to their interest and affinity or their eyes will glaze over. Second, you need to present data in 'tiers,' moving from the general to the specific. Start with one-page highlights, then provide tables, charts, and subcharts as supporting material. Don't give us those one-inch thick reports—no one reads them."

"Perfect" data do not exist; so data providers should be realistic about what is possible and avoid "analysis paralysis." "The near infinite amounts of data that can be collected, and severely limited resources for collection and analysis, always constrain the practical uses of data" (Schmidtlein 1977, p. 31). If organizations and decision-makers waited until they had all the data that could be brought to bear on an issue, "or if they sought to ground all decisions in objective evidence," they would be paralyzed (Weiss 1981, p. 187). Expect repeated requests for more data or the same data arrayed slightly differently. Very often, less is more. Decision-makers are more apt to drown in too much data that makes too little sense than to die for want of a datum.

Don't just provide data; be explicit about how to use it. Data providers can play an important role in helping decision-makers use information by being explicit about which data answer what questions and whether the answers are complete or partial, certain or uncertain. Prior to data collection, institutional researchers should understand the policy issues underlying the need for the data. Data providers should ask questions to clarify the purpose of data collection and analysis. They should also explain the findings to decision-makers, being careful to explain the limitations of the data.

Making Sense

Perhaps with some naïveté, we began this study with the idea that data might make a difference—that is, that the presence of data would lead to better decisions. We assumed that the academy is grounded in scientific inquiry, that scientific inquiry requires data and analysis, and that better decisions are made when data are at hand. Yet experience in the academy could easily lead one to reach a conclusion similar to the one David Dery did: "Confronted with such common patterns as systematic gathering of information with little decision relevance, the gathering of information after the decision has been made, the non-consideration of available information, and the tendency to ask for yet more information, one is tempted to conclude that organizations are systematically stupid" (1990, p. 22). Since it is not heartening or particularly useful to conclude that colleges and universities are "systematically stupid," we have to dig deeper to answer such questions as: How are data used? Why do data play so many roles but not a definitive one? Why are we unable to establish a link between data and decisions? We first answer these questions in generic terms and then offer possible answers where the decisions to be made concern faculty work life.

Analyzing how decisions are made in universities may require a consideration of organized anarchies[5] and garbage cans. In describing how decisions are made in universities, Michael Cohen and James March (1986) discovered one "quite consistent theme: Decision opportunities are fundamentally ambiguous" (p. 81). Analyzing decision-making in universities is quite complex because often "organizational participants arrive at an interpretation of what they are doing and what they have done while doing it" (p. 81).

From this point of view, an organization is a collection of choices looking for problems, issues and feelings looking for decision situations in which they might be aired, solutions looking for issues to which they might be the answer, and decision-makers looking for work.

A key to understanding the processes within organizations is to view a choice opportunity as a garbage can into which various problems and solutions are dumped by participants. The mix of garbage in a single can depends partly on the labels attached to the alternative cans; but it also depends on what garbage is being produced at the moment, on the mix of cans available, and on the speed with which garbage is collected and removed.

Using the Cohen and March (1986) framework, we offer six possible explanations of why there are so few direct links between data and decisions.

1. A dominant assumption is that universities are engaged in a rational process when they make policy decisions. Reality

suggests, however, that data are used selectively for political and symbolic purposes that may or may not be directly tied to decisions. Further, "creative organizations operate at the edge of chaos where the links between action and long-term outcome get lost, making it impossible for their members to use rational, intentional processes." We cannot postulate "a link between a particular kind of overall decision-making process and a successful outcome, because such links get lost" (Stacey 1996, p. 251).

2. We tend to assume that all participants have all the data at the same time. In truth, various participants have different types and amounts of data at different times, so that decisions are in part a function of the availability of data.

3. The amount of data that people can or choose to consume differs; people have different appetites for data, and these appetites change over time and as a function of the issue at hand.

4. Sometimes a sample of one (e.g., a single deadwood faculty member or a Nobel Prize winner) is all people need to draw a conclusion or make a case. These "data points" become iconic and lessen the need for any additional information.

5. Data appear in different places at different times. Because participation is fluid, people carry data from one arena to another and use it in ways not originally intended. This makes it difficult for leaders in a particular "garbage can" to get the right data into play in the right venue. Data sets come and go as people come and go.

6. Data use is an ambiguous concept. In the interactive model of decision-making, information is sought from a number of sources in a nonlinear way. In this model, "the use of research [data] is only part of a complicated process that also uses experi- ence, political insight, pressure, social technologies, and judg- ment" (Weiss 1991b, p. 177). Often decision-makers are not even sure what data, if any, they are using and how they are us- ing it. People gather data but use other means to make deci- sions. Decisions are often made before seeing data, and the data are then used to justify the decision. In fact, decision-makers will rarely admit to gut-feel decisions—because they sound so irrational and anti-intellectual—so instead they pretend to use

data. "When asked why they [senior managers] were pretending to make the decision one way when they had already effectively made it in another way, they indicated that they were not aware of doing this and then said that the real reasons were so general and experience-based—gut feeling is the pejorative for this—that they could not hope to persuade [others]" (Stacey 1996, p. 270).

In sum, a link between data and decision-making has not been established in other studies of organizations and policymakers. When the spotlight turns to academic institutions and issues of faculty work life, matters are even more complicated. Why?

Faculty work is complex and not easily quantified.

Because of the high degree of faculty autonomy, there is at best only a weak internal market for performance data that "supervisors" might use to regulate behavior.

Even when faculty work is quantifiable, the data are subject to multiple interpretations. For example, does the fact that 85% of all tenure decisions are positive mean that standards are too low, the undeserving were weeded out during the probationary period, faculty development and mentorship programs succeeded, the performance criteria were so clear that faculty knew precisely what to do, or something else entirely?

In the faculty work life domain, data do not address visceral concerns. Data do not address public resentment of tenure as privilege, for example, or concern that tenure overempowers faculty. These issues are not illuminated by data. How do you place academic freedom into the realm of data? It is difficult to bring data to bear on many questions that are at the core of the current debates about faculty work life.

When the issue at hand concerns beliefs and values about academic freedom, academic tenure, the intrinsic worth of knowledge, or political correctness, data have less sway. There are few aspects of faculty work life where incontrovertible data illuminate policy issues, as might be the case with budgets or enrollments.

It is often difficult, and sometimes impossible, to find the locus for many decisions in academe. Shared governance clouds the identity of decision-makers, so data assume other functions. Even if we could establish that data lead to better decisions, or at least that data enlighten decision-makers, we do not always know who the decision-makers are or will be. In some cases, decisions seem to occur mysteriously from out of nowhere. Henry Rosovsky, former dean of the Harvard Faculty of Arts and Sciences, presents a wonderful example in his 1990–1991 Dean's Report. In a section on a "decision" to reduce faculty course loads, Rosovsky wrote: "First, the Dean has only the vaguest notion concerning what individual professors teach. Second, the changes that have occurred were never authorized at the decanal level. . . . No chairman or group of science professors ever came to the Dean to request a standard load of one half course per year. No one ever requested a ruling concerning, for example, credit for shared courses. Change occurred through the use of *fait accompli*—i.e., creating facts" (p. 10).

While we cannot assert that data on faculty work life drive policy decisions, we would argue that data matter in numerous and more ways than we first thought possible. But they also matter in unpredictable ways. It is rarely clear, and never obvious, which data on faculty employment will be used, by whom, and in what ways. In fact, as we gather data about faculty work life, productivity, and the outcomes of post-tenure review, we cannot be sure that they will be used or, if used, what the impact will be.

One thing is clear: once a person's mind is made up, it is unlikely that data will change that person's position. As the old maxim proclaims, "Everyone is entitled to my opinion." It is also clear that some issues do not lend themselves well to data collection and numerical evidence. Data about instances of teenage pregnancy, for example, or on capital punishment as a deterrent to crime will not alter the views about abortion or the death penalty of someone for whom the sanctity of life is an inviolate moral principle. If tenure is indeed "the abortion issue of the academy" (Chait 1997, p. B4), data will not matter much. In fact, where emotions are involved, people will disregard or ignore disconfirming data and perhaps even resent the very fact that data were trotted out at all. As Rosovsky (1990, p. 259) wryly observed:

Never underestimate the difficulty of changing false beliefs by facts. . . . Currently, over 90 percent of our senior faculty teach at least one undergraduate course per year. The firmly held belief that Harvard professors do not teach undergraduates is not the least bit weakened by these statistics. . . . When given the opportunity—in the absence of incontrovertible scientific proof, and sometimes even then—people believe what they wish, and empirical evidence does not lead to quick altering of cherished positions.

Notes

Thanks to Jared Bleak, who conducted the literature review, assisted in conceptualizing the uses of data, and helped with interpreting the data that we collected throughout this project. We are also grateful to William Connellan, Carol Weiss, and Dean Whitla.

1. Cathy Trower, as a subcontractor to one of the regents' consultants in Minnesota, gathered, analyzed, and provided data in this case, especially concerning policies and practices at other Big Ten institutions.

2. To obtain the glossary of terms and the data template, e-mail the Project on Faculty Appointments at *hpfa@gse.harvard.edu.*

3. The templates required institutions to gather race data by two categories only: white/Caucasian and color. Faculty of color were grouped to provide anonymity for those faculty members at especially small colleges.

4. Three months after the site visit, the president at this institution reported that they lifted their tenure cap after searching the Faculty Appointment Policy Archive CD-ROM for other institutions with a tenure quota (and finding very few), making a careful analysis of their template data, and conducting numerous conversations on campus.

5. There are three defining properties of an organized anarchy (Cohen and March 1986): (1) ambiguous and therefore problematic goals, (2) transient participants, and (3) unclear technology.

References

Besnette, Frank H. 1997. "Arizona's Tenure Dialogue: Forging a Middle Way." Association of Governing Boards Conference Presentation, April 14, San Diego, Calif.

Chait, Richard. 1997. "Thawing the Cold War over Tenure." *Chronicle of Higher Education*, February 7, pp. B4–5.

Cohen, Michael D., and James G. March. 1986. *Leadership and Ambiguity: The American College President.* 2nd ed. Boston: Harvard Business School Press.

Dery, David. 1990. *Data and Policy Change.* Boston: Kluwer Academic Publishers.

Ervin, Elizabeth. 1998. "All in a Day's Work." *Higher Education Issues: Shaping Arizona's Future,* 1 (2), August.

Farber, Daniel A. 1997. "The Miasma in Minnesota." *Trusteeship,* 5 (3): 6–10.

Feldman, M. S., and James G. March. 1981. "Information in Organizations as Signal and Symbol." *Administrative Science Quarterly*, 26: 171–186.

Keffeler, Jean B. 1997a. "A Case for the Renewal of Tenure." Remarks to the 25th Annual Conference of the National Center for Collective Bargaining in Higher Education and the Professions, April 15.

——— 1997b. "The Minnesota Tenure Debacle: An Ironic and Damaging Failed Exercise in Intellectual Inquiry." Remarks made to a class on academic governance at the Harvard Graduate School of Education, Institute for Educational Management, July 21.

March, James G. 1994. *A Primer on Decision Making: How Decisions Happen*. New York: Free Press.

McCorkle, Chester O. 1977. "Information for Institutional Decision Makers." In Carl R. Adams, ed., *Appraising Information Needs of Decision Makers*. New Directions for Teaching and Learning, no. 15. San Francisco: Jossey-Bass, pp. 1–9.

Rosovsky, Henry. 1990. *The University: An Owner's Manual*. New York: W. W. Norton & Co.

——— 1991. "Dean's Report, 1990–1991." Harvard University Faculty of Arts and Sciences.

Schein, Edgar H. 1992. *Organizational Culture and Leadership*. 2nd ed. San Francisco: Jossey-Bass.

Schmidtlein, Frank A. 1977. "Information Systems and Concepts of Higher Education Governance." In Carl R. Adams, ed., *Appraising Information Needs of Decision Makers*. New Directions for Teaching and Learning, no. 15. San Francisco: Jossey-Bass, pp. 29–42.

——— 1999. "Common Assumptions about Organizations That Mislead Institutional Researchers and Their Clients." *Research in Higher Education*, 40 (5): 571–587.

Stacey, Ralph D. 1996. *Complexity and Creativity in Organizations*. San Francisco: Berrett-Koehler Publications.

Trow, Martin A. 1964. *Social Research and Educational Policy*. Paper presented at the Invitational Conference on Educational Research, Harvard University.

Weiss, Carol H. 1981. "Use of Social Science Research in Organizations: The Constrained Repertoire Theory." In H. D. Stein, ed., *Organization and the Human Services*. Philadelphia: Temple University Press.

——— 1991a. "Knowledge Creep and Decision Accretion." In D. S. Anderson and B. J. Biddle, eds., *Knowledge for Policy: Improving Education through Research*. New York: Falmer Press.

——— 1991b. "The Many Meanings of Research Utilization." In D. S. Anderson and B. J. Biddle, eds., *Knowledge for Policy: Improving Education through Research*. New York: Falmer Press.

——— 1991c. "Policy Research: Data, Ideas, or Arguments?" In P. Wagner, C. H. Weiss, B. Wittrock, and H. Wollman, eds., *Social Sciences and Modern States*. Cambridge, U.K.: Cambridge University Press.

——— 1999. "Research-Policy Linkages: How Much Influence Does Social Science Research Have?" In A. Kazancigil and D. Makinson, eds., *World Social Science Report 1999*. Paris: UNESCO/Elsevier.

11

Gleanings

RICHARD P. CHAIT

$\mathcal{U}$NLIKE THE TEN PREVIOUS CHAPTERS, this one is not organized around a question. It is instead chiefly animated by answers to the questions that guided earlier chapters. Principally from those chapters, we can derive four important inferences.

First, *context counts*. Almost 1,300 four-year colleges and universities, from public research universities to private liberal arts colleges, and over 665 two-year colleges award faculty tenure (National Center for Education Statistics 1996, p. 21, Table 4.1). Within Carnegie classifications, and even more dramatically across institutional categories, there are monumental differences with respect to governance, mission, structure, programs, curricula, culture, wealth, admissions criteria, and student life, to name only a few variables. Knowledgeable observers of higher education unfailingly cite the unusual degree of institutional diversity that characterizes American higher education (e.g., Jencks and Riesman 1968; Birnbaum 1983; Clark 1987). Academicians do not expect to see uniformity; in fact, we tout the variety of colleges and universities. With such heterogeneity, members of the academy generally do not find the "industry" as a whole to be a particularly useful unit of analysis.

Yet many academicians, trustees, and politicians speak often about the tenure "system" as if there were just one. The research reported in prior chapters suggests that the practice of tenure across the academy varies as much as Division I revenue sports differ from Division III club sports. The centrality of tenure, as gauged by the proportion of tenured and tenure-eligible lines, diverges noticeably by institutional type and by program areas. For example, 28% of full-time faculty in the health sciences are non–tenure track versus 1.5% in agriculture. More than a quarter of full-time non–tenure track faculty work at public research universities; only 5% are at private comprehensive colleges (see Chapter 5, this volume). Likewise, 60% of community college faculty are part-time against only 19% of public research universities (National Center for Education Statistics 1998, p. 2-2). In short, the very composition of the workforce, let alone the provisions of policy, differs markedly across the spectrum of American colleges, universities, schools, and departments.[1]

True enough, the Recommended Institutional Regulations of the AAUP establish a national template for policy, and most institutions have adopted the prescribed procedures. There are, however, notable exceptions with respect to definitions of academic freedom, the length of probationary periods, and provisions for post-tenure review, financial exigency, and program discontinuation (see Chapter 2, Table 2.2). And that analysis excludes some 150 four-year colleges, 7 private doctoral universities, and more than 330 two-year colleges without tenure (National Center for Education Statistics 1996, p. 21, Table 4).

Even were we to set aside deviations from AAUP policy and acknowledge the Recommended Institutional Regulations as a national consensus, the studies presented herein indicate that identical or similar policies yield to considerably different norms and interpretations when actually implemented. In other words, to understand how tenure works on one campus is to understand how tenure works on one campus. (And even that overstates the similarities across colleges and professional schools within a single complex university.) Some research universities depend heavily on external reviews, while many liberal arts colleges seek no outside assessment. Character, collegiality, and citizenship matter enormously at some institutions and very little at others. Some institutions (e.g., Harvard University) cloak tenure reviews in great secrecy, while others (e.g., the University of Alaska) have a nearly transparent process. Some have post-tenure reviews with sanctions and penalties for substandard performance; others are toothless.

Context truly confounds the concept of a tenure "system," however, when we consider normative expectations, specifically with respect to selectivity and autonomy. Academicians repeatedly stress that tenure reviews are finely grained screens that carefully and reliably separate quality from mediocrity. Yet empirical data suggest that tenure candidates have different success rates across institutions. For example, at the colleges with tenure discussed in Chapters 2 and 9, denial of tenure was a rare occurrence. Indeed tenure at these institutions, and many others of similar stripe, was regarded as the routine culmination of the probationary process, contingent upon acceptable levels of performance and the absence of conspicuous deficiencies. By contrast, the tenure rate at Yale for assistant professors hired between 1980 and 1990 was reported to be 13% in the humanities, 19% in the social sciences, 19% in the biological sciences, and 53% in the biological sciences (Wilson 1996). The rate for faculty at Harvard achieving tenure in approximately the same period in the arts and sciences was estimated by a former dean to be "below 10%" (Rosovsky 1990, p. 196).[2] Because few, if any, institutions publicly disclose cohort probability rates—further reinforcement of the observation in Chapter 10 about the inconspicuous role of hard data on questions related to tenure—subtle analyses of selectivity cannot be made.

Tenure levels can be ascertained, however, from the AAUP annual salary survey, which includes the percentage of tenured faculty at each rank at each institution. As might be expected, nationwide most faculty at the ranks of professor and associate professor are tenured: 96.7% and 85.7% respectively (American Association of University Professors 2000, p. 32). On some campuses, however, where the tenure ratio for assistant professors approaches or surpasses the levels of senior ranks, nearly everyone has tenure. In the 2000 AAUP salary survey, for instance, more than 60% of assistant professors at twenty-six four-year colleges were tenured. The overall tenure ratio at these institutions averaged 81%; fourteen had tenure levels over 85%; and five exceeded 95% (American Association of University Professors 2000, Appendix I, pp. 38–92). While not a direct measure of selectivity, such high tenure ratios signal a lack of stringent standards and suggest that the threshold for tenure has been set at minimally acceptable, rather than superior, levels of performance.

Examples of institutions where more than 80% of the ladder rank faculty hold tenure are plentiful enough to ask why the tenure "system" produces such dissimilar selectivity rates and tenure ratios. Different criteria and different emphases are easy to comprehend in light of the institutional assortment of American higher education. But why does that lead to disparate outcomes? How can the award of tenure be the rule on some campuses and the exception on others when policies at both institutions are roughly the same? The answers bear far less on policy language and far more on whether faculty and administrators view tenure as a rightful expectation for satisfactory performance or an uncommon reward for extraordinary achievement and potential. Throughout the academy, tenure may broadly denote similar employment arrangements. In reality, though, tenure carries very different connotations from one college to the next about performance and merit. Similar definitions generate dissimilar results.

So too with respect to autonomy. The degree of professional autonomy varies more as a function of institutional prestige, culture, and ethos than is suggested by a faculty member's tenure status (Chapter 8). An untenured professor or researcher at a first-tier university that offers tenure, or a professor at a medical school without tenure (e.g., Boston University, Morehouse, Brown, Michigan State, and Tufts)[3] will usually experience more latitude and independence than a tenured colleague at a third-rate college; within the same tier, however, faculty at colleges with tenure are apt to be somewhat more independent than colleagues on campuses with term contracts (Chapter 3).

Conditions in elementary and secondary schools clearly illustrate the disconnect between tenure and autonomy. There are some 2.9 million full-time equivalent public school teachers; the majority are tenured. Yet schoolteachers usually have very limited autonomy, particularly over matters of curriculum, pedagogy, selection of peers, and allocation of time and effort. Teachers, notes Dan Lortie (1975), "do not seem to share the sentiments of university professors who believe they are exclusively equipped to control instruction" (p. 111). Ironically, teachers at independent schools, which rarely offer tenure, enjoy a far greater degree of professional autonomy than peers at public schools with tenure. In the K–12 environment, autonomy and tenure are negatively correlated.

The obvious conclusions that context matters and that we do not have a tenure "system" lead to a somewhat less evident implication: wholesale indictments or universal affirmations of tenure make little sense because the attributes, affects, and outcomes of tenure diverge so much by institutional type. Critics can correctly cite colleges where tenure generates neither quality nor productivity, and advocates can rightly counter that tenure represents "best practice" at every premier university in America. Detractors can properly label tenure an impediment to strategy, efficiency, and creativity, and proponents can credibly argue to the contrary. These are all correct assertions *when qualified by context*. The only mistaken position would be to categorically condemn or defend tenure as if there were uniform practices and results. Sadly, precisely such stances are all too commonly staked.

A second point to be gleaned from the evidence presented in the preceding chapters is that *times change*. Nearly one hundred years have elapsed since the establishment of the AAUP, and almost sixty-five years have passed since it issued its *1940 Statement* on tenure and academic freedom. Since then, the institutional ecology and professorial demography of American higher education has changed dramatically. As described in Chapter 1, the number and variety of colleges and universities have expanded rapidly, and the distribution pattern of faculty across institutional segments has profoundly altered. Also, perhaps more pertinent, the faculty looks quite different. At the turn of the twentieth century, the professoriat was 80% male; in 1997, it was 59% male (National Center for Education Statistics 1998, p. 2-11). Women earned 42% of all doctorates in 1998–99, a new peak on a thirty-year upward slope. While historical term data on faculty of color are scant, just within the past twenty-eight years, the percentage of minority faculty has increased from 3.8% in 1969 to 13.4% in 1997 (Bayer 1970, p. 12; National Center for Education Statistics 1999). Although we lack comparative data over time, the percentage of full-time faculty with a full-time spouse at home undoubtedly declined precipitously over the course of the twentieth century.

The effects of these changes were manifest in the research reported in Chapter 7 on faculty recruitment (e.g., the relatively great weight candidates placed on quality of life issues) and in Chapter 4 on the promotion and tenure process (e.g., tenure candidates self-described as "under siege" and beset by "overloaded plates"). Underneath these tangible problems lie subtler concerns. New scholars want to balance work and family, most presume a dual-career household without an extended family nearby, and many recognize (and some embrace) the likelihood of multiple appointments in various locations, and maybe even several different careers, over a lifetime.

Such attitudes prompt junior faculty to reframe old questions and ask new ones. The new generation of scholars, as well as the next generation now in graduate school, have fresh perspectives rooted in priorities and values that depart from the conventional norms of senior faculty. If these new voices were to convene a constitutional convention to design tenure policy from scratch, what proposals might be advanced? Based on the research reported herein, we would anticipate popular support for the following propositions:

> The candidate's dossier, as well as the portfolios of "comparables," should be open to review and comment by the candidate.
> Tenure review committees should reflect a commitment to diversity.
> The scholarship of discovery should not outweigh the scholarship of teaching and engagement.
> Collaborative research should be valued as much as independent research.
> Interdisciplinary research should be prized as much as disciplinary research.
> Probationary periods should either be eliminated or varied contingent upon the candidates' circumstances, preferences, and discipline.

These ideas are predicated on suppositions that challenge the "assumptive world" of orthodox tenure—namely:

> Transparency yields fairer results than secrecy.
> Merit is a socially constructed and subjective concept.
> Cooperation is better than competition.
> Research should be organized around problems, not disciplines.
> "Nurturing" activities, like teaching and advising, are as worthy as research.
> Personal priorities are as important as professional imperatives.
> Faster is not necessarily better.

While nominally about policy and practice, the new agenda implicitly, and occasionally explicitly, concerns whether traditional tenure, basically developed by white males for white males, remains appropriate to contemporary conditions and beneficial to a more heterogeneous professoriat. On or just below the surface lie issues of values and power. Two pointed questions are embedded in the new conversations about tenure: Who should makes the rules? and Who should make the decisions? The current debate should not, however, be construed as a reductionist argument about race and gender. While these are undeniably prominent elements, the research reported or cited in earlier chapters would suggest that the current turmoil reflects foremost generational differences. The times have changed. Academics disagree about whether tenure has adequately changed or even should change with the times.

Third, *there is no substitute for the status of tenure.* Colleges and universities are normative organizations (Etzioni 1961) where peer recognition tops the reward structure. Academics do not enjoy enormous salaries, lavish bonuses, stock options, sumptuous offices, corporate jets, or sales jamborees in exotic places. For faculty, tenure is the coin of the realm, and there are not many other currencies, especially at four-year colleges or comprehensive universities. Arguably, at research universities, status can also be denominated by externally funded grants, national and international disciplinary awards, leadership roles in professional associations, and offers from peer institutions. Even so, tenure, more than any other attribute, confers status, shapes a faculty member's self-image as a proficient professional, and signals quality, rightly or wrongly, to colleagues everywhere.

Not unexpectedly, therefore, three chapters, each focused on a different population, reached the same implicit conclusion: without an alternative and equivalent source of status, tenure will remain the preferred choice of most faculty. Even when hypothetically there were other prizes, senior faculty members were extremely reluctant to exchange tenure for another set of rewards (Chapter 8). The reputational risks were simply too great; without tenure, one could be mistaken for an academic ne'er-do-well. The exchange rate between tenure and alternative rewards will remain unfavorable unless and until a critical mass of prominent faculty locally and at peer institutions also relinquish tenure, or the exceptional instances of preeminent professors without tenure are disclosed either by the individuals themselves or by their employers—both highly unlikely scenarios. Similarly, first- and second-year faculty and advanced doctoral students decidedly favored the prestige and "validation" of tenure-track positions to the "stigma" of non–tenure track positions, although the nature of the work and life-style considerations influenced their choices (Chapter 7). And on campuses that moved from contracts to tenure (Chapter 9) faculty likewise were attracted to the "professional legitimacy" and external credibility tenure imparted. In fact, the trustees and administrators at these colleges believed that the introduction of tenure would enhance the prestige of the institution as well as the status of faculty.

The policy adopted by the Boston University School of Management "solved" the status issue with a plan that offered faculty a salary premium and a ten-year contract, but only *after* peers judge the individual to be tenurable. Under this policy, the non–tenure track faculty have been accorded the status associated with tenure, minus the commitment to lifetime employment and plus an enhanced salary. Thus far, about half of the junior faculty have accepted this arrangement (Chapter 8). By contrast, the University of Central Arkansas has had to date no takers for a non–tenure track option that includes a sizable salary premium but lacks the requirement that faculty be judged tenurable in order to secure a long-term contract (Rule 1999).

These are instructive examples of the importance of tenure as a status symbol of the academic profession. Proponents of the overhaul or abolition of tenure will be hard pressed to devise a comparable designation. The status of non–tenure track positions could be augmented by endowed chairs or named professorships, but few institutions can underwrite such a program on a wide-scale or even limited basis. A more financially feasible alternative might be voluntary professional certification, a standard practice in medicine under the auspices of the peer-governed American Board of Medical Specialties. There are twenty-four specialties (e.g., internal medicine, family practice), many with subspecialties (e.g., nephrology, geriatrics). Certifications, which last seven to ten years, are usually based on a written, and sometimes oral, examination. While not required to practice, board certification provides "assurance to the public that a physician specialist certified by a Member Board of the American Board of Medical Specialties (ABMS) has successfully completed an approved educational program and an evaluation process which includes an examination designed to assess the knowledge, skills, and experience required to provide quality patient care in that specialty" *(www.abms.org)*.

A parallel effort was launched in the late 1980s by the then newly created National Board for Professional Teaching Standards "to establish high and rigorous standards for what accomplished teachers should know and be able to do" *(www.nbpts.org)*. Also voluntary, the board, dominated by active classroom teachers, sets standards, which are publicly reviewed at regional and national meetings and in focus groups, for more than thirty fields. Certification, which runs for ten years, has two components: (1) a peer review of a teacher portfolio that includes classroom videotapes, lesson plans, and student work samples; and (2) a one-day written assessment. Certified teachers normally receive a financial bonus ($10,000 in California); and in certain districts, such as Boston, certified teachers are eligible to be "lead teachers" which includes a 10% to 20% salary increase.

The point here is not that professors should be required to submit to certification once a decade. Faculty will argue that student evaluations, annual performance appraisals, peer review of scholarship, and applications for grants and fellowships render certification duplicative and unnecessary. Rather, the procedures used in medicine and public schools are illustrative of one means other than tenure that academic disciplines, professions, and institutions might use to confer status and differentiate quality. Board certification could offset, or at least mitigate, the stigma attached to nontenured status, particularly for faculty primarily engaged in teaching and advising—individuals without much opportunity to establish legitimacy within a profession that is based on scholarly research, irrespective of tenure status. In the absence of any designation with equivalent stature, tenure will remain the Holy Grail for faculty and the gold standard of the academy.

And yet, *there may be a latent market for tenure reform.* The internal market for tenure reform has little strength for several reasons. Most obviously, the majority of faculty believe that traditional tenure best serves the academy, society at large, and (not incidentally) the self-interest of the professoriat. Therefore, even an incremental reform, such as post-tenure review, originates far more often with legislators and trustees than with faculty. While most academics are unconvinced of the need for change, most presidents and provosts are dissuaded by the political calculus. Tenure reform consumes too much political capital at too fast a pace with too uncertain a payoff to justify the effort. As a result, the advocates for changes to tenure policies have little power on campus. In the main and with important exceptions, full- and part-time faculty without tenure and some women and minority faculty with tenure comprise the on-campus phalanx for reform. As Olga Bain and William Cummings (2000) put it, "The procedures for advancement in academia were decided long ago when universities were the exclusive province of males. In most university settings, the males continue to hold the uppermost ranks, and it is reported that they are reluctant to modify these procedures" (p. 499).

In the course of the Project on Faculty Appointments, project researchers encountered little enthusiasm among faculty leaders, and only slightly more among provosts and presidents, to confront issues of tenure. Among eight institutions that volunteered to participate in a reexamination of faculty work life, not one produced a fundamental change in tenure policy. Even among these colleges and universities, where the leadership had some predisposition to entertain change, not much happened. There was some new embroidery—clarifications of the criteria for tenure and modest refinements to allow more individualized faculty workloads—but no new cloth. Written reports from Project sites noted that institutional partners "plowed old ground," "encountered resistance," "rejected new approaches," "learned more than changed," and did "not see any single, radical difference in our institution." At one university, the (male) faculty chairman of the Project task force appointed only full professors to the committee. In a letter to the provost, the chairman explained that "the current system [of tenure] at least has the virtue of familiarity, and any reconceptualization of the normative form of a faculty career must, in order to be persuasive, be generated by the faculty itself. . . . I have assembled a group that would command the respect of the entire faculty." A year later, the provost reported, without surprise, that the committee "confined its study of faculty appointments and rewards to the most traditional of forms."

In another Project study, Jared Bleak and Frances Shavers (2001) inspected 92 faculty union contracts at four-year colleges and universities with an eye to whether the collective bargaining process generated any particularly innovative policies regarding promotion and tenure, performance evaluation, and reasons for termination. The study revealed only a handful of significant departures from tradition, and even fewer that were actually implemented. Furthermore, some of the more unusual provisions were intended to reinforce convention, such as a mandated *minimum* proportion of tenured faculty.

The weak internal market for tenure reform (epitomized by the University of Minnesota case—see Chapters 1 and 10) suggests that champions of change may have to stimulate a latent, external market for reform. The core strategy would be to engage the issue of tenure with audiences that matter to colleges and universities and to do so on terms that matter to these constituents, thereby raising the ante for the institutions. For example, would colleges and universities be more inclined to adjust tenure policy and practice if:

U.S. News & World Report, as well as other guides, used tenure selectivity rates as a measure of academic quality, which would in turn influence a college's overall ranking?

Moody's, Standard & Poor's, and similar agencies used percentage of instructional payroll tied to tenured faculty as an indicator of program flexibility and financial liquidity, which in turn would affect a college's credit rating?

The National Association for the Advancement of Colored People (NAACP) or the National Organization for Women (NOW) used promotion and tenure rates by race and gender as one criterion among several to publicly certify (or rank) whether colleges offer a hospitable environment to minority and women students and faculty?

Candidates for faculty positions had web-based access, through a third party (e.g., the AAUP or J. D. Powers), by school or department, to tenure probability rates and to measures of work satisfaction among past and present junior faculty on or off the tenure track?

Trustees and legislators required annual reports on the percentage and distribution, by department or college, of chronically low performers in the tenured ranks and actions taken to remediate or terminate deadwood?

In testimony before the U.S. Senate, William Massy (2000, p. 3) asserted that "markets can discipline the price and quality of education

... but not with the information available today." The same principle may apply here. Thus the crucial question arises: If external stakeholders, important to the university, had access to reliable, relevant data on promotion and tenure specifically tailored to those constituents' interests, would colleges and universities be more attentive to the policies, practices, and organizational norms that shape the results? We do not know the answer to that question because the external market for tenure reform has not yet and may never be activated to a sufficient degree to test the proposition. We do know, however, that the single greatest change in faculty employment practices over the past quarter century—the explosion of part-time faculty—was propelled by outside market forces of both supply and demand.

Without any powerful external stimuli for reform, few if any colleges or universities will voluntarily initiate major tenure reforms. The dominant faculty coalition on most campuses sees neither the need nor the incentive to do so. From the professors' perspective, the system already works very well, thank you. In fact, those institutions that are the first to change would almost assuredly be at a competitive disadvantage with respect to faculty recruitment, just as a president or provost who was behind such change would be at a competitive disadvantage in the search for a new position, a task likely to be necessitated by an early and ardent support of tenure reform.

Whether the durability of academic tenure has served and will serve well professors, students, and the larger society was not one of the questions we endeavored to answer in this book because we realized that that question could only be answered in context. Rather, we intended that the answers to the questions we did pose would enable, within institutional and local contexts, more enlightened conversations and more informed conclusions among all parties on all sides of the issue. We take that to be the foremost ethical and professional responsibility of every academic, tenured or untenured, pro or con.

Notes

1. Worldwide the differences are even more pronounced, from the abolition of tenure in the United Kingdom, to the linkage of tenure to civil service in Germany, France, Italy, and Spain, to de facto tenure by cultural norms in Japan, to the absence of tenure altogether in most of Latin America. (See Chapter 6 for details.)

2. Nationwide 73.4% of all candidates considered for tenure in 1992 (the

most recent data available) succeeded (National Center for Education Statistics 1996, p. 22, Table 4.2).

3. Boston University and Morehouse offer no tenure; Brown, Tufts, and Michigan State offer tenure to basic science faculty but not to clinical science faculty (Jones and Gold, forthcoming).

References

American Association of University Professors. 2000. "The Annual Report on the Economic Status of the Profession, 1999–2000." *Academe*, 86 (2).

Bain, Olga, and William Cummings. 2000. "Academe's Glass Ceiling: Societal, Professional-Organizational, and Institutional Barriers to the Career Advancement of Academic Women." *Comparative Education Review*, 44 (4): 493–514.

Bayer, A. E. 1970. *College and University Faculty: A Statistical Description*. Washington, D.C.: American Council on Education.

Birnbaum, Robert. 1983. *Maintaining Institutional Diversity in Higher Education*. San Francisco: Jossey-Bass.

Bleak, Jared, and Frances Shavers. 2001. "Faculty Unionization for a New Generation: Innovative Provisions in Faculty Collective Bargaining Agreements." Paper presented at Faculty Roles and Rewards Conference, American Association for Higher Education, Tampa, Fla., February 2.

Clark, Burton. 1987. *The Academic Life: Small Worlds, Different Worlds*. Princeton, N.J.: Carnegie Foundation for the Advancement of Learning.

Etzioni, Amitai. 1961. *A Comparative Analysis of Complex Organizations*. New York: Free Press.

Jencks, Christopher, and David Riesman. 1968. *The Academic Revolution*. Garden City, N.Y.: Doubleday.

Jones, Robert F., and Jennifer S. Gold. Forthcoming (October 2001). "The Present and Future of Appointment, Tenure, and Compensation Policies for Medical School Clinical Faculty." *Academic Medicine*.

Lortie, Dan C. 1975. *Schoolteacher: A Sociological Study*. Chicago: University of Chicago Press.

Massy, William. 2000. "Clippings." *University Business*, 3 (10): 70.

National Center for Education Statistics. 1996. *Institutional Policies and Practices Regarding Faculty in Higher Education*. Washington, D.C.: U.S. Department of Education.

——— 1998. *Fall Staff in Postsecondary Institutions, 1995*. Washington, D.C.: U.S. Department of Education.

——— 1999. *Fall Staff in Postsecondary Institutions, 1997*. Washington, D.C.: U.S. Department of Education.

Rosovsky, Henry. 1990. *The University: An Owner's Manual*. New York: W. W. Norton and Co.

Rule, Cheryl S. 1999. *The University of Central Arkansas*. Cambridge, Mass.: Programs in Professional Education, Harvard Graduate School of Education.

Wilson, Robin. 1996. "Yale's Review of Tenure Is Unlikely to Change Tough Standards." *Chronicle of Higher Education*, December 20, pp. A11–A12.

Contributors

Philip G. Altbach is J. Donald Monan, SJ, Professor of Higher Education, and Director, Center for International Higher Education, Boston College.

Roger G. Baldwin is Professor of Higher Education, School of Education, The College of William and Mary.

Richard P. Chait is Professor of Higher Education, Harvard University Graduate School of Education.

Jay L. Chronister is Professor Emeritus, Center for the Study of Higher Education, Curry School of Education, University of Virginia.

Charles T. Clotfelter is Z. Smith Reynolds Professor of Public Policy Studies and Professor of Economics and Law, Duke University.

James P. Honan is Lecturer on Education, Harvard University Graduate School of Education.

William T. Mallon is Senior Staff Associate, The Association of Medical Colleges.

R. Eugene Rice is Scholar in Residence and Director, Forum on Faculty Roles and Rewards, American Association for Higher Education.

Mary Deane Sorcinelli is Associate Provost and Director, Center for Teaching, University of Massachusetts at Amherst.

Cathy A. Trower is Senior Researcher, Project on Faculty Appointments, Harvard University Graduate School of Education.

Index

325

Macalester College, 14
MacDermid, Shelley, 148
Machlup, Fritz, 1, 255
Macy, John W., Jr., 183
Madsen, Holly, 10
Maeroff, Gene I., 32, 115
Magrath, C. Peter, 11, 246
Mahoney, Richard, 15
Malaysia, 169, 176
Managerial concerns, about tenure, 12–16
Managerial culture, 105
March, James G., 77, 82, 88, 267, 284, 286, 288–291, 301, 303, 307n5
Marchese, Ted, 21
Maryville State University, 67n8
Massachusetts, charter colleges in, 24
Massachusetts Board of Higher Education, 9
Massachusetts Institute of Technology, 37, 61, 199
Massy, William, 319–320
Matheson, Nancy, 136
Matthews, Anne, 18
Maturity, institutional, 264–267
McCarthy, Joseph, 169
McCorkle, C. O., 282–283, 290–291, 300
McGee, Robert, 182–183
McPherson, Michael S., 14, 70, 183, 223–224, 226
Melchionno, Rick, 130
Memetrics, 219n4
Menges, R. J., 102–103
Merrill Lynch, 10
Metzger, Walter P., 26n1
Michaelson, Martin, 26n4, 156
Michigan State University, 48–49, 114, 121, 312, 321n3
Microsoft, 129
Middle Ages, 160–161
Milem, Jeffrey F., 17
Miller, John Perry, 182
Ministry of Education (France), 174
Minnesota, review of tenure policy in, 273–276, 300, 307n1
Mintzberg, Henry, 69, 82
Mission, institutional, 48–49, 63
Monitoring of progress, using data, 289
Monsanto, 15
Montana State University, 56
Mora, José-Ginés, 166
Morehouse University, 312, 321n3
Morreale, Joseph, 8, 12, 53, 67n7
Moscati, Roberto, 174

Motorola, 10
Mues, Fran, 109

National Association of State Universities and Land-Grant Colleges, 11–12, 112
National Board for Professional Teaching Standards, 317
National Center for Education Statistics, 19–20, 25, 26n5, 185, 309–310, 313, 321n2
National Center for the Study of Collective Bargaining in Higher Education, 98n4
National Research Council, 294
National Study of Postsecondary Faculty, 127–128, 131, 138
Native Americans, and tenure, 134
Nelson, Cary, 70, 78
Netherlands, 167, 173, 175, 178
Neumann, Anna, 82
New York, tenure for school principals in, 24
New York Times, 6
New York University, 21
Non–tenure track faculty, 8–9, 15, 17–22, 26, 35, 45–47, 63–65, 126–129, 132–157, 182–183, 194, 215–216, 218–219, 316
Noone, Laura Palmer, 22
Nortel, 10
North Carolina, focus groups in, 222, 226, 231–232
North Carolina State University, 35, 41, 44, 51, 56, 65, 67n8
North Dakota, academic freedom in, 35
North Dakota State University, 67n8
Northern Arizona University, 56, 67n8
Northern Kentucky University, 41, 44, 66n4
North Park College, 56
Northwest Christian College, 36
Northwestern University, 121, 199
Norway, 167, 175–176

Oakland University, 277
O'Brien, Dennis, 13, 70
Office of Educational Research and Improvement, 23
Ohio State University, 199
Ohio Wesleyan University, 44
Oklahoma State University at Oklahoma City, 113
"On Collegiality as a Criterion for Faculty Evaluation" (AAUP), 40–41
O'Neil, Robert, 18
Online universities, 21–23